Coaching in Times of Crisis and Transformation

Coaching in Times of Crisis and Transformation

How to help individuals and organizations flourish

Liz Hall

KoganPage

LONDON PHILADELPHIA NEW DELHI

First published in Great Britain and the United States in 2015 by Kogan Page Limited

2nd Floor, 45 Gee Street	1518 Walnut Street, Suite 1100	4737/23 Ansari Road
London	Philadelphia PA 19102	Daryaganj
EC1V 3RS	USA	New Delhi 110002
United Kingdom		India

© Liz Hall, 2015

The right of Liz Hall to be identified as the author of this work has been asserted by her in accordance with the Copyright, Designs and Patents Act 1988.

ISBN   978 0 7494 6830 9
E-ISBN   978 0 7494 6831 6

British Library Cataloguing-in-Publication Data

A CIP record for this book is available from the British Library.

Library of Congress Cataloging Number

2015032590

Typeset by Graphicraft Limited, Hong Kong
Print production managed by Jellyfish
Printed and bound by CPI Group (UK) Ltd, Croydon CR0 4YY

CONTENTS

DEDICATION

I dedicate this book to the three amazing women in our original family unit of five. To my very-much-missed beloved mother Joan and sister Dilys, on the tenth anniversary of your deaths; your liveliness, sense of fun, resilience and ability to laugh through adversity – and you both experienced plenty of it – have been truly inspiring. And to my 'big' sister Denise – your love, generosity, creativity and capacity to see the best in people and situations have buoyed me up for as long as I can remember. Through thick and thin, all my life, your support and love have been unwavering. I don't want to do it without you. With love and gratitude.

ACKNOWLEDGEMENTS

I am deeply grateful to many people for their help and support in writing this book. To Lucy and Katy at Kogan Page for your patience and support. Thanks too to those of you who have looked through the manuscript or part of it and made helpful suggestions: Ray Freeman, Rachel Ellison and Aboodi Shabi. Thanks to those of you who have given up your time to be interviewed including John Blakey, Louise Buckle, Margaret Chapman-Clarke, Erik de Haan, Anthony Eldridge-Rogers, Bridget Farrands, Kathyrn Jackson, Peter Hawkins, Ann Lewis, Anton Obholzer, Kate Pearlman-Shaw, Keri Phillips, Angela Ryrie, Ernesto Spinelli, Caroline Talbott, Alison Whybrow and Lindsay Wittenberg. Thanks to all my teachers including Thay, my family, my friends and my clients.

FOREWORD

In the era of positive psychology and orientation for higher performance and competitive edge, a volume on coaching in crisis may seem controversial if not risky. Some coaching communities could consider a focus of this nature as dangerously close to the therapeutic. I cannot however support any more strongly the intention of this book to extend the application of coaching to real needs of individuals that often include dealing with crisis and difficult transitions.

The main reason for this support is not that being Russian I am more of a 'negative psychologist' who associates the development of the soul mainly with suffering. There might be some truth in this, but there are more important reasons for endorsing this book. One of these is the need for coaching to deal with a whole person and not turn away from the shadow sides or 'negative' emotions. Negative emotions are an intelligent response of the whole organism to difficult situations when our usual ways to fix them do not work or our own interests and intentions are in conflict. It would be a shame if coaching were used only for manipulating clients' emotions because of particular cultural or organizational expectations – or worse still, the inability of a coach to stay with them. In crisis all emotions are a useful indicator of the process and in coaching we should learn from them rather than tame them.

Another reason for siding with the intention of this book is an acknowledgement that coaching does not need to avoid difficult issues people face, but address them as part of the challenges that life brings. Existentialists say that crisis is inevitable and expecting life to be of the same shade all the time is naive. Therefore, helping clients to live with and to learn from crisis would be a reasonable intention of a coach. It is also important to remember that crisis can be triggered by external changes, as well indicated in this book, but can also come as a reaction to internal shifts and clashes of values. This can make learning both meaningful and painful. Moreover, the internal crisis can sometimes create an amazing opportunity for development and even for transformation – an outcome that is seen as the greatest ambition of coaches.

This book rises to the challenge of addressing the role of coaching at the time when the shades of life become darker for our clients. To convey a flavour of this collection I will comment only on a selection of chapters to show how the themes of coaching in crisis and transition are discussed and what is offered for coaches to try under these circumstances. To start with, the introduction sets the expectation illustrating how timely this topic is. The need for coaching in crisis and transition in the context of recent events in the world becomes transparent from the very first pages.

In the first four chapters Liz Hall sets the scene with excellent definitions, an overview of useful models, extracts of her interviews with coaches and examples from coaching practice. This makes the book grounded in practice and in reality of coaching experiences. The voices of real people (some of them you may recognize), with examples from their life crises and transitions make the reading live and help to connect the reader to the authors.

In Chapter 7 Anthony Grant and Sean O'Connor address the role of executive coaching in turbulent times of organizational change. The reader can learn not only about the complexity of the situations organizations encounter, but also about the complexity of coaching that functions as a complex adaptive system. The chapter also describes an actual case of a coaching programme in an organization and the learning that took place as a result.

In Chapter 8 Erik de Haan and Anthony Kasozi explore the darker side of leadership that comes to the fore at times of crisis and transition. They classify different types of shadows in leaders and discuss how a coach can help them to face their shadows and to rise to the challenges presented by their teams and organizations.

On the whole, the book represents a collection of different voices engaged in different types of practice and looking at coaching through different lenses. This is a welcome diversity as it reflects the reality of our multidisciplinary field that benefits from multiple associations. It means at the same time that some voices in this book will resonate with you more than others. There is however an important common thread that connects us all. All voices are concerned with helping clients to meet their challenges at the time of crisis and transition and not to turn away from the harsh reality they face. What helps this connection is the overall tone of the book, the tone of courage and compassion, both of which are important if we want to be there for our clients when they need us most.

Dr Tatiana Bachkirova
Reader in Coaching Psychology
Co-Director of the International Centre for Coaching
and Mentoring Studies
Faculty of Business
Oxford Brookes University

ABOUT THE CONTRIBUTORS

The editor

Liz Hall is the Editor of *Coaching at Work* magazine and a Senior Practitioner coach, specializing in work–life balance, crisis/transitions, stress management/resilience, and happiness. She is also a mindfulness teacher, running programmes for coaches, the general public, and businesses. She is the author of *Mindful Coaching* (Kogan Page, 2013) and has contributed chapters on mindfulness to *Mastery in Coaching* (Association for Coaching/Kogan Page, 2014); *Mindfulness in Organizations*: *Foundations, research and applications* (Cambridge University Press, in press), and *Developing Mental Toughness in Young People* (Karnac, 2014). As well as winning the Association for Coaching's Award for Impacting (Leadership/External Focus) in 2010–11, she's an award-winning journalist, with almost 30 years' experience, writing for publications including the *Guardian*, the *Observer*, the *Financial Times*, and *People Management*. She divides her time between the United Kingdom and southern Spain, where she lives with her husband, son, two daughters (she refuses to accept they've left home even though they're away at university), and three rescue dogs.

The chapter contributors

Dr Paul Brown is Faculty Professor, Organizational Neuroscience, Monarch Business School, Switzerland; Honorary Chairman of the Vietnam Consulting Group, Saigon and International Director of SIRTailors, Saigon. A clinical and organizational psychologist and executive coach, his main fascination is in creating a General Theory of the individual and the organization based upon mapping how energy flows or gets blocked in the pursuit of profit or other outcomes within the organizational system. He has recently co-authored *Neuropsychology for Coaches: Understanding the basics* (2012); *River Dragon* (a novel, 2014); *Neuroscience for Leadership: Harnessing the brain gain advantage* (2015); and *The Fear-Free Organization* (2015).

Tony Buon is a workplace psychologist, speaker, mediator, executive coach and author. He is presently the Managing Partner of Buon Consultancy based in London. He has previously been a Lecturer at Robert Gordon University in Aberdeen, Scotland and a Senior Lecturer at Macquarie University, Australia. His areas of expertise include workplace psychology, leadership coaching, workplace mediation, and cross-cultural communication. He is the author of *Communication Genius: 40 Insights from the Science of Communicating* (2015), *The Leadership Coach* (2014) and over 100 book chapters, academic papers and journal articles.

Margaret Chapman-Clarke is a Chartered and Registered Psychologist, Gestalt practitioner and Mindfulness Facilitator and Researcher. She's co-founder of the British Psychological Society Special Group in Coaching Psychology, she designed the United Kingdom's first Psychology of Coaching programme for the Chartered Institute of Personnel and Development, co-developed the first Business School Coach Referral Service at Manchester University as a Senior Fellow in Leadership, and was the only British presenter at the first Australian conference on evidence-based coaching. She is author of *The Emotional Intelligence Pocketbook* and the forthcoming *Mindfulness at Work Pocketbook* and *Organizational Applications of Mindfulness* (published by Kogan Page). Margaret serves on the editorial boards for *Coaching at Work; Coaching: An international journal of theory, research and practice* and the *International Journal of Evidence-Based Coaching and Mentoring*. Margaret is passionate about advancing the use of qualitative methods in coaching research and her own doctoral work employs an autoethnographic approach to explore advanced coaching practitioners' experiences of mindfulness training using poetic inquiry.

Rachel Ellison MBE trained as an internal coach at the BBC, where she was a news reporter and international project director. She was awarded an MBE for her human rights and self-empowerment work with women in Afghanistan. Her team won BBC Team of the Year. Rachel launched her own coaching business in 2006, working with commercial and public sector clients in banking, retail, electronics, international diplomacy and health. Specializing in complex multinational organizations and coaching across multiple different cultures, Rachel is becoming a thought leader on cognitive diversity, self-coaching in crisis and how to lead ethically for higher profit.

Dr Anthony M Grant PhD is widely recognized as a pioneer of Coaching Psychology and evidence-based approaches to coaching, with more than 100 publications in this area. Leaving school at 15 with no qualifications he trained as a carpenter and ran his own contracting business, beginning tertiary studies in 1993 as a mature age student and commencing a third career as a coaching psychologist. In January 2000 he established the world's first Coaching Psychology Unit at the School of Psychology at Sydney University, where he is the Director and an Associate Professor. He is a Visiting Professor at the International Centre for Coaching and Leadership Development, Oxford Brookes University, UK, a Senior Fellow at the Melbourne School of Business, Melbourne University, Australia, and an Associate Fellow at the Säid School of Business, Oxford University. In 2007 he was awarded the British Psychological Society Award for outstanding professional and scientific contribution to Coaching Psychology, and in 2009 the Vision of Excellence Award from Harvard University for pioneering work in developing a scientific foundation to coaching. He is the 2014 scientist in residence for the ABC – the Australian national broadcaster. He also enjoys playing loud (but unfortunately not very good) blues guitar.

Professor Erik de Haan is Director of the Ashridge Centre for Coaching and Professor of Organization Development and Coaching at the VU University in Amsterdam. He has an MSc in Theoretical Physics, a PhD in Psychophysics, and an MA in psychodynamic psychotherapy. He has published some 140 professional and research articles, and ten books, covering his main fields of expertise as a leadership and organizational consultant, facilitator and coach. He focuses on organization-development consulting, supervision, action learning, politics and power, leadership hubris, and emotional aspects of working in teams and organizations.

Dr Anthony Kasozi is Director of Quilibra Consulting (UK) and an Associate with Ashridge Consulting (UK). He is an experienced executive coach, and an organization development and management consultant, who has coached senior executives and leaders from across different work sectors in Europe, the United States, Africa, Russia and Asia. A social scientist with degrees in financial economics, institutional economics and international relations, Anthony has a keen and active interest in the roles organizations and leaders in science and public service play in shaping responses to developmental, health and change issues relating to Sub-Saharan Africa. Anthony is married with close family in Europe and Africa.

Andrew Kinder is a British Psychological Society Registered Coach and a Chartered Counselling and Occupational Psychologist. He was recognized by the British Association for Counselling and Psychotherapy with a Fellowship for his contribution to workplace counselling. He has published widely, particularly in the areas of work-related stress, trauma and stress management, and is currently clinical director of a large Employee Assistance Programme (**www.helpeap.com**). He is active as a coaching practitioner with his own caseload of clients. Further information is available from his website, **www.andrewkinder.co.uk**.

Helen Leeder Barker is an Organizational Psychologist and Coach with 15 years' experience. Formerly based in the United Kingdom and Australia, she now lives and works in Singapore. She's the Director and owner of Leeder Consulting, providing coaching and leadership development to individuals/organizations in the Asia-Pacific Region. Her background includes consultancy, banking and fast-moving consumer goods. She's fascinated by how our background and story makes each of us unique and feels very lucky to be working at a time when we're on the cusp of a huge leap in understanding how our brain enables us to create the changes that we seek. As such she is a strong advocate for the movement that is bringing applied neuroscience into the heart of coaching. She also has a strong interest in mindfulness, and she encourages each of her clients to learn to meditate. Her own ability to be mindful is challenged daily through her gorgeous children and when she isn't coaching she's usually playing with them.

Dr Sean O'Connor is a practitioner, researcher, and academic within the fields of coaching, organizational development and positive psychology. Sean's PhD explored the influence leadership coaching has on the wellbeing of others within organizational networks. His coaching specializes in applying complex adaptive systems and relational dynamics to intervention. He has worked across a broad spectrum of industry leadership. Sean is a lecturer and researcher at the Coaching Psychology Unit, University of Sydney in Australia.

Neil Scotton and **Dr Alister Scott** are co-founders of The One Leadership Project. They support those taking on big, systemic change. Clients include forward-thinking businesses, educational bodies and charities. Their work, with the Project's growing team, blends coaching, consultancy, training, event design, convening collaborations, building communities, working with partners and writing. The goal is 1 billion positive impacts by 2020. Both based in South-East England, they love their families, the natural world, and people taking on enormous, well-intentioned challenges. Neil has received the ICF President's Award for 'evolutionary leadership' and 'contribution to the global profession'. Alister was instrumental in Antarctica receiving World Park status for 50 years. Together they received the Best Thought Leadership article award 2013 from *Coaching at Work* magazine, with the editorial board saying 'Neil Scotton and Alister Scott provoke us to higher thinking... Their commitment to bringing leadership to life and making the world a better place is evident in their writing and their work.'

Introduction

The seed for this book was sown in 2008–9, when the reality of the extent of the financial crisis began to strike home. Many coaches reported feeling ill-equipped to work with those clients most impacted by the crisis, who perhaps were losing their jobs, their homes, their security, certain relationships, even their mental wellbeing, particularly where there were parallels in the coaches' own lives. One high-profile coach shared later how she'd gone through a four-year-long financial crisis from 2009, feeling as if her life 'had imploded' and 'everything I'd worked for in my whole life was slipping through my fingers – very scary'. Unsurprisingly, she found it very hard to keep her coaching practice on track. Career coaches shared how it felt irresponsible and unrealistic, cruel even, to encourage clients to create their dream job at a time of job scarcity and insecurity.

As well as serving to highlight that in highly challenging times there needs to be more depth and breadth in our coaching approaches, I was reminded by these shared experiences and my own crises that there can be diamonds to be mined from the muck, even though they may take time to appear. The coach who struggled financially says she has 'no regrets' and has 'learnt far more than I would have done otherwise'. She's 'more contented and more resilient', more able to 'let go, to hold the not-knowing space, quietness, letting the emotions come through'. For her, 'that's where the juicy bit of coaching is'.

I've wondered how widespread this growth post-crisis is, whether we might even need crisis to spark true transformation, and what implications there might be for coaching. Does it enhance our coaching if we've been through our own crises? How can coaching support individuals, organizations and even the wider system to emerge from crisis transformed? This book explores these and other questions.

The Global Financial Crisis (GFC) highlighted the recklessness of over-promising as coaches and burst the bubble that many inhabited, one of more, more, more. Some remain in that bubble, of course, with the number of billionaires doubling by 2014 (Oxfam, 2014), and the world's richest

1 per cent set to own more than the other 99 per cent combined by 2016 (Hardoon, 2015). And whilst the landscape has shifted since 2008–9, we continue to face challenging times; individually, organizationally, societally, environmentally. As I write this in April 2015, another natural disaster has occurred – an earthquake in Nepal causing more than 5,500 deaths. Meanwhile, in business circles, the term VUCA (Volatility, Uncertainty, Complexity, Ambiguity) is ubiquitous. Originally coined by the US military, it's become a 'trendy managerial acronym... and a catchall for "Hey, it's crazy out there!"' (Bennett and Lemoine, 2014). Coaches and coaching sponsors I interviewed for this book report seeing more clients having difficulties. Louise Buckle, Lead Coach, KPMG UK Advisory Practice, reports: 'we do have individuals struggling more as a result of the VUCA world that we live in and increasingly high performance expectations... my personal view is that we're seeing deeper psychological issues starting to show up more at work', while Grant and O'Connor (Chapter 7 of this book) argue that 'organizational change and the resultant turbulence have become part of the everyday experience in organizations in the contemporary commercial world'.

Whether it's actually 'crazier' than before out there perhaps doesn't matter. The fact is that it seems and feels tougher to many of us. And just as we remind our clients that they can choose how they respond, so too can we as coaches choose how we respond to this seemingly crazier climate. Exploring what even more depth and breadth look like. Becoming better able to get to the 'juicy bit' of coaching, whilst respecting boundaries.

This book doesn't claim to be able to equip coaches to charge in to save the world in its hour of need, although they may want to play their part in tackling bigger issues, and Chapters 10 and 12, for example, offer some pointers for doing so. But it does seek to support coaches generally to have a clearer idea of the terrain of crisis and transformation, including potential obstacles. It explores potential treasure to be found in this territory, and offers ideas for how coaches might help clients be better 'mapmakers' and 'map readers'. It highlights the value of being more courageous and 'turning towards' difficult territory such as vulnerability, 'negative' emotions, and our 'shadow' sides, rather than charging off in the other direction. It argues that it behoves us as coaches to get more in touch with our own humanity and vulnerability, so we are better able to bring more of ourselves into our coaching, which in turn opens up the potential for more transformative coaching.

With these aims in mind, this collection first maps out some of the territory, with chapters written by myself (Liz Hall) on definitions of crisis, transition and transformation; on some of the territory commonly shared across humanity, including natural life transitions; on frameworks and models for understanding and interpreting crisis and transition; and on the potential for post-crisis growth. It also features chapters which set out useful compasses and approaches for VUCA times. These include Ellison's chapter on self-coaching, which argues that coaches should explicitly set out to develop clients' self-coaching capability; Brown and Leeder Barker's chapter on neuroscience, which highlights the importance of understanding how the brain operates, and of working with all emotions in facilitating change; de Haan and Kasozi's chapter on working with leaders' shadow sides; mine (Liz Hall) on Mindful Compassionate Coaching, which argues that drawing on mindfulness, compassion, and the body's wisdom helps us turn towards, safely be with, and transform difficulty; and Chapman's on compassionate resilience, reflecting the rising acceptance of autoethnography, a form of self-reflection that explores personal experience and connects autobiographical story to wider cultural, political, and social meanings and understandings.

The book features original research, case studies and stories, with some from coaches including chapter contributors, reflecting these trends of turning towards difficulties, and exploring our own experiences in relation to our practice and bringing more of ourselves into our practice. Working with turbulence does of course carry a mental health warning, and Kinder and Buon's chapter looks at this from the organizational perspective. Grant and O'Connor argue that in times of organizational turbulence and change, executive coaching is a vital support and developmental mechanism. And we end on a note of inspiration, speaking as does Ellison to the theme of sustainability, with Scott and Scotton's chapter on their legacy thinking approach.

Essentially, this book seeks to help us be much more than solely 'fair-weather' coaches who struggle when the outlook is highly stormy – our own or others'. It aims to play a role in helping us support clients in all sorts of climates, whether that be their own micro-climate or not. And to remind us that struggling individuals are often like pit canaries, highlighting with their own difficulties problems in the wider system, as Dr Anton Obholzer pointed out in an interview for this book.

Beat poet Anne Waldman (1996, p xxi) says that the beat writers empowered themselves through their writing at a time when the rest of the culture was under a 'collective hallucinatory yoke'. It sometimes feels to me that we are still under that yoke, and that the answer to waking up lies in part in being prepared as coaches, as human beings, to turn towards all that lies within. As the mystic poet Rumi reminds us: 'Keep your gaze on the bandaged place; that is where the light enters you.'

References

Bennett, N G and Lemoine, J (2014) What VUCA really means for you, *Harvard Business Review*, January

Hardoon, D (Oxfam International) (2015) Wealth: Having it all and wanting more, *Oxfam* [online] www.oxfam.org [accessed 14 June 2015]

Oxfam (2014) Even it Up: Time to End Extreme Inequality, *Oxfam* [online] www.oxfam.org [accessed 14 June 2015]

Waldman, A (1996) *The Beat Book: Writings from the Beat Generation*, Shambala, Boston

Definitions

01

LIZ HALL

> *The beginning of wisdom is to call things by their right name*
> **CHINESE PROVERB**

Words have power. I was reminded of this during the research for this book. Words trigger such varying responses and reactions in people; they can destroy, and also inspire, acting as catalysts for transformation, as portals into new realities.

Take the word 'crisis', which has peppered so many conversations in recent years, often in relation to the Global Financial Crisis. It's not a word that some individuals, and most organizations, want to be associated with, at least not publicly. 'Change management', 'transition' and 'transformation', absolutely. But not crisis. For individuals too it can be a heavy, difficult, or emotive word. Sports and CEO coach John Blakey says:

> I typically work with senior business leaders who are confident and robust, and I don't think the word crisis is one they'd use. But they might talk about 'difficult times'. I worked with one client who didn't use the word crisis but they wanted to talk to me at short notice, and I would have described what had happened as a crisis.

Who we are as the observer, and our choice of label, impacts how we relate to something. Bridget Farrands, a coach and organization consultant specializing in transition and identity, agrees:

> How we name something is how we relate to it, so if we're not encouraged to think of something as a crisis, it's not necessarily a crisis; the name gives us a cultural reference point. For example, to leaders in Mali, rain coming after months of drought is 'earth food', for me, when it's a holiday, it's a 'crisis'.

Interestingly, the idea that we're all increasingly required to operate in VUCA (volatile, uncertain, complex, and ambiguous) times is widely accepted. VUCA in some ways has become shorthand for everything that might be interpreted as challenging and crazy (Bennett and Lemoine, 2014). However, there's usually a sense that the VUCA climate isn't our doing, it's 'out there'. Scotton and Scott pick up further on this theme in Chapter 12.

Although some of the coaches I interviewed at first struggled to bring to mind clients in crisis, once they'd had a chance to reflect, they usually had many examples. Transitions coach and author of *Essential Career Transition Coaching Skills*, Caroline Talbott, says, 'My first thought was that I've not coached anyone in crisis. [My clients] are always OK and then I thought about it and I couldn't think of anyone not in crisis.'

Clearly as coaches we need to be prepared for our clients being in crisis, however they describe it. Denial of being in crisis may mean us and our clients missing out on all sorts of riches, as we explore in Chapter 4. First, let's explore what we actually mean by crisis, and two other terms which can come with the territory – transition and transformation.

Crisis

Oxford Dictionaries Online defines the noun crisis as:

A time of intense difficulty or danger.

A time when a difficult or important decision must be made.

The turning point of a disease when an important change takes place, indicating either recovery or death.

James and Gilliland (2001) describe crisis as a perceived or experienced event or situation as an intolerable difficulty exceeding the person's current resources and coping mechanisms. Caplan (1961) describes it as a state when people face an obstacle to important life goals, one which is for a time insurmountable by using customary methods of problem solving. This failure of one's traditional problem-solving approach results in disorganization, hopelessness, sadness, confusion, and panic (Lillibridge and Klukken, 1978). It threatens the high-priority goals of the decision-making unit, restricts the amount of time available before the decision is transformed, and surprises the members of the decision-making unit by its occurrence (Hermann, 1972). The element of threat is highlighted by Lerbinger (2012), who says a common denominator for most organizational crises is that an organization's reputation is endangered. He lists the following elements common to definitions of organizational crisis:

- the event is sudden, unexpected and unwanted;
- decisions must be made swiftly;

- it's a low-probability, high-impact event;
- it has ambiguity of cause, effect and means of resolution;
- it interrupts the normal operations of an organization;
- it hinders high-priority goals and threatens an enterprise's profitability, growth, and survival;
- it may cause irreparableness and degeneration of a situation if no action is taken;
- it creates significant psychological stress.

Coaches

Themes which emerged from my research among coaches, and my own reflections/experience, included the following:

- a breaking down of what was before;
- feeling not good enough/being wrongly equipped/insufficiently resourceful/insufficiently knowledgeable/ill-informed to respond;
- sense of stuck-ness;
- uncertainty and sense of being lost;
- clash between exterior/interior world;
- element of surprise;
- things not going to plan and not going to sort themselves out;
- dependent on context.

Below, some of this book's contributors and other coaches share how they see crisis:

Rachel Ellison, chapter contributor:

As a grandchild of refugee holocaust survivors and one of three children born to their only son, I've had significant exposure to people with heightened and sometimes inappropriate levels of fear, anxiety, pessimism and even paranoia. This is sometimes diagnosed as 'annihilation anxiety'. It's a familiar way of life and can be experienced as if passed on somehow, by subsequent generations in a family, even if they haven't actually been through a trauma such as a war or an earthquake. So for me, crisis translates as fear; running, hyper-vigilance, taking of risk or conversely, risk aversion; the normal can be misinterpreted as something enormous and overwhelming. Another person might just stay optimistic. My definition of crisis is informed by this underpinning existential part of my inheritance, upbringing and exposure to human beings who have suffered colossal loss. Crisis means a collapsing or a crumpling; a potential tsunami of destruction – be it emotional, psychological, physical, environmental, organizational or systemic. But arguably, it is unidimensional to assume crisis can only impact negatively. In my view, crisis can also present positive impacts such as the opportunity for renewal, innovation, reinvention of self and circumstances, heightened personal resilience, depth of character, wisdom and self-resource.

Margaret Chapman-Clarke, chapter contributor:

> It's where there is an absolute overload of demands on us or the client, perceived as not having the resources to deal with this multitude of demands, almost as if a number of things come together that challenge the sense of who you are. A good metaphor to describe it is a mirror that shatters in thousands of pieces.

Bridget Farrands describes crisis as 'a period of uncertain turbulence where your familiar/personal compass offers very few bearings to help you know what to do and where to go', while Professor Ernesto Spinelli describes crisis from an existential stance as comprising any or all of three focal points:

- Sense of continuity: 'being confronted with death would be an extreme version; someone could no longer have a job, or it could be how an organization recognizes its own sense of continuity, such as being taken over by a rival'.

- Around dispositions (meanings, values, beliefs, biases that the person/ organization holds): 'so it's a crisis in that they thought they had those values etc but the reality is that they don't, or there is a conflict of values. Organizationally speaking, there might be a conflict between different levels in terms of what the organization stands for.'

- Identity: 'this is quite often expressed as, I don't know who I am any more or I've lost all sense of myself'.

As recovery coach and coach trainer Anthony Eldridge-Rogers points out, crisis is a relative term:

> Cultural reference, context and the way people deal with things are so different in Soweto, Johannesburg (where I was running a recovery and wellbeing coach training programme) to the West. It can be very humbling and quite shocking because of all the things we take for granted [in the West] and when we run into other people's experiential paradigms... It was a very warm community and we'd all become quite connected, and at the end when we were all wishing each other well, one coach trainee said, 'You're so lucky, you can leave, you

have choices.' Suddenly I got it; none of them can leave, all they can do is walk home, they have nothing with which to leave. Elsewhere, someone shared in a [recovery] group how her crisis was when her dad sold her favourite racing horse. She had a terrible heroin problem and used to hide her syringes in a saddle bag on her horse, and finally knew things had to change when she lost the horse. [Her story] triggered others in the group, [some of whom] had been in prison. Her crisis wasn't deemed worthy but her spiritual suffering had been very acute and that was difficult for people to understand.

Transition

It isn't the changes that do you in, it's the transitions. (Bridges, 2009, p 3)

Oxford Dictionaries Online defines transition as follows:

The process or a period of changing from one state or condition to another.

Sometimes, when we talk about crisis, we actually mean transition, although transition is not easy. According to Bridges (2009), many people use the words change and transition interchangeably too; however, change is situational (such as the move to a new site) while transition is psychological and trickier.

Linley, Biswas-Diener and Trenier (2012) define transition as a period of change from one stage to another, stressing too that transitions are notoriously difficult.

Coaches

Themes that emerged from interviews with coaches included:

- transition and crisis are linked – crisis sparks transition;
- transitions can be planned, unlike crisis;
- you can't go back but you don't yet know how to go forward;
- transition implies movement, a journey, a shift;
- it can take time;
- it can bring choices;
- transitions are an ongoing part of life;
- they're not easy... but can be times of growth;
- they're the threshold between old and new.

Deborah Price, leadership and 'menopause' coach, says:

> Transition is accompanied by a sense that you can't get back; you know you can't go back to your old ways but you haven't yet got new strategies in place. You have a sense of being all at sea, a sense of 'whatever I do doesn't make a difference', of not being able to go backwards, which can be quite disturbing and quite scary.

Transformation

Oxford Dictionaries Online defines transformation as follows:

> A marked change in form, nature, or appearance.
>
> A sudden dramatic change of scenery on stage.
>
> A metamorphosis during the life cycle of an animal.

Coaches

Themes that emerged from my research and reflections in relation to transformation included:

- marked change in form, nature, or appearance;
- metamorphosis;
- there really is no going back;
- transformation and transition go together;
- you have to be ready.

With transformation there is more of a sense of something or someone becoming something or someone different, of a deeper more marked change, perhaps one that is irreversible even. As executive coach and psychologist Dr Alison Whybrow says:

> Transition is a systemic opportunity for transformation to take place...
> With some clients I've coached who were in a bit of a crisis, there has been an absolutely huge shift from one phase to the next; they can't go back as they've grown so much. There is a threshold that people step over and see the world in a different way as a result.

Now we have started to describe the territory, let's start to map it out.

References

Bennett, N G and Lemoine, J (2014) What VUCA really means for you, *Harvard Business Review*, January

Bridges, W (2009) *Managing Transitions: Making the most of change*, 3rd edn, Nicholas Brealey Publishing, London

Caplan, G (1961) *Prevention of Mental Disorders in Children*, Basic Books, New York

Hermann, C F (1972) Some issues in the study of international crisis, in C F Hermann (ed) *International Crises: Insights from behavioral research*, pp 3–17, Free Press, New York

James, K J and Gilliland, B E (2001) *Crisis Intervention Strategies*, Brook/Cole, Pacific Grove, PA

Lerbinger (2012) *The Crisis Manager: Facing disasters, conflicts, and failures* (2nd edn), Routledge, Abingdon, Oxon

Lillibridge, E M and Klukken, P G (1978) *Crisis Intervention Training*, Affective House, Tulsa, OK

Linley, P A, Biswas-Diener, R and Trenier, E (2012) Positive psychology and strengths coaching through transition, in Palmer, S and Panchal, S (eds) *Developmental Coaching: Life transitions and generational perspectives*, Routledge, Hove

Shared territory

02

LIZ HALL

> *We don't just need a map; we need ways to change the mapmaker*
>
> **KEN WILBER (2001, p 55)**

By their mid-thirties, most adults can list more than 30 or 40 transitions or significant life events that they've experienced to date (Hopson, 1981). Many coaches use a lifeline exercise (eg Sugarman, 2001), inviting clients to draw a line representing peaks and troughs. Sometimes there's laughter, but often there are tears.

When we think about humankind's struggles and growing pains, recurring themes, patterns, stories and archetypes emerge from cultures all over the world. It can be helpful to explore these recurring universal themes to shed light for client and coach on the journey. In challenging times, as we explored in the last chapter, people can feel lost, and sometimes they lack a compass and a 'road map' for the territory. Elsner and Farrands (2012), for example, bemoan the lack of a road map for leaders in transition, which they seek to address in their book.

This chapter offers some maps and frameworks for exploring the territory of crisis and transformation. But it's important of course to remember that everyone's unique.

Uniqueness

As Wilber (2001) points out, even if we all had a map that was 'all-inclusive and unerringly holistic, that map itself would not transform people'. Everyone's voyage through life is, of course, unique, and we do our best work as coaches when we appreciate and draw from our own and each client's uniqueness. It's important to avoid stereotypes; we can be more prone to fall prey to these when we enter new stages in life (Linley, Biswas-Diener and

Trenier, 2012). We do of course, as Wilber says, need to find ways t
the mapmaker, and this book explores some of those ways. And the
shining a spotlight onto what might be shared territory.

Shared territory

Sharing stories, highlighting and exploring universal themes and patterns
with the client can help to build self-awareness and to normalize their experience. Coaching can offer a space in which to mourn or celebrate rites of
passage, or common themes can simply be held in the background by the
coach, offering pointers for potential lines of enquiry.

In this chapter, we look at the following: 'natural' life stages and typical
work transitions.

Natural life transitions

Rites of passage

For those of us fortunate enough to live to a ripe old age, we will go through
a number of different life stages or transitions, and many of us will do so
alone, with potential negative impact.

Van Gennep (1960) highlights the significance of rituals that mark the
transitional stages in our lives, what he called rites of passage. He describes
many rituals to mark birth, puberty, marriage and death, for example, which
are universal in function, although they may differ in detail. He identified
three major phases in rites of passage:

- separation;
- transition; and
- incorporation.

Van Gennep comments upon the disturbances that changes in status
produce in individuals. He sees rites of passage as devices which serve to
incorporate an individual into a new status within a group (Kimball, in
Van Gennep, 1960).

Arrien (1999) describes ritual as 'the conscious act of recognizing a life
change, and doing something to honour and support the change through
the presence of such elements as witnesses, gift-giving, ceremony and
sacred intention'. Although many cultures still value rituals and ceremonies
to mark important transitions, there is a marked decline, particularly in

the West, partly because of increased secularization (Kimball, 1960). This decline means many individuals don't get the opportunity to celebrate or normalize what's going on for them, and potentially even negatively impacts their mental wellbeing. It's a decline that leaves an opening into which coaches can step, helping to 'ritualize' important transitions. Anthropologist Solon Kimball goes as far as to suggest that mental illness may ensue if we are left struggling with important transitions on our own:

> The critical problems of becoming male and female, of relations within the family, and of passing into old age are directly related to the devices which the society offers the individual to help him achieve the new adjustment. It seems likely that one dimension of mental illness may arise because an increasing number of individuals are forced to accomplish their transitions alone and with private symbols.
>
> (Kimball, in Van Gennep, 1960, pp xvii–xviii)

Liminality

This term describes the psychological process of transitioning across boundaries and borders. The term limen comes from the Latin for threshold; literally the threshold separating one space from another. In Celtic mythology, there is the concept of 'thin places' where the barrier between this world and the other is thinner, allowing greater connection between the two. The contemporary usage of liminality comes from Van Gennep, who noticed that many, if not all, of the rituals across cultures have the function of moving a person from one status or social circumstance to another. The threshold is the neutral zone in Bridges' Transition Curve that we look at in the next chapter (Bridges, 2009).

In all spiritual traditions, there is the concept of suffering, often in the form of a crisis, offering a gateway to awakening – the dark night of the soul in medieval mysticism, the biblical story of Job, the transformative power of understanding the nature of suffering in Buddhism, and so on.

Jungian analyst Murray Stein describes midlife transitions as periods of liminality, times when we stand between two phases or worlds. However, we can view all major transitions, if not all transitions, through this perspective. Another Jungian analyst, Bolen (1994) says that in times such as midlife crises, we are 'often thin-skinned and vulnerable, which accompanies being psychologically receptive and open to new growth'. At such times, 'we resemble a snake, the ancient symbol of transformation, which must shed its old skin in order to grow, and while moulting and growing a new skin is vulnerable, irritable, and, for a time, temporarily blind'.

Lifespan

The lifespan approach emphasizes that development does not stop when we cease to be adolescents but continues throughout adulthood and into old age.

Erikson

Erikson, in his Eight Stages of Man (1950), sets out the following stages in human development: infant (0–18 months); toddler (18 months–3 years); pre-school (3–5 years); school years (6–11); adolescence (12–18 years); young adulthood (19–40 years); middle age (40–65 years); and maturity (65–death).

Most coaches will be concerned with coaching clients in the last four stages. Erikson highlights specific conflicts associated with each that serve as turning points for development, offering the chance at each stage to build on skills learned previously (in Palmer and Panchal, 2011). These are:

Adolescence: Identity versus role diffusion
Task: Explore the world and develop a sense of self. Those who are less successful can feel confused about who they are and how they fit into the world.

Young adulthood: Intimacy versus isolation
Task: Develop intimate relationships and the ability to develop secure, committed relationships. Failure to commit can lead to feeling alone.

Middle age: Generativity versus self-absorption and stagnation
Task: Contribute to future generations. Failure to do so can lead to experiencing life as unsatisfying and unproductive.

Maturity: Ego integrity versus despair
Task: Look back over one's life. People can see meaning and feel satisfied with what they have achieved or feel bitter and regretful.

Sugarman

Sugarman (2001) suggests that we can construe the life course in the following ways, as:

- a series of age-related stages;
- a cumulative sequence;
- developmental tasks;
- key life events and transitions;
- a narrative construction which creates a sense of dynamic continuity.

Palmer and Panchal (2011) point out that while theories such as Erikson's highlight the similarities and universalities within the life cycle, 'they have been criticized for ignoring the complexity and individuality of adult development'. Sugarman (2011) agrees that these days life stages identified by shared tasks and transitions are largely fictitious. However, she says, age and life stage have not disappeared as key dimensions along which we order life experiences. Whilst advocating the need for caution in identifying and describing life stages based on chronological age, Sugarman acknowledges that we live in an 'age-graded' society. But unlike Erikson, she sets out two stages in late adulthood, saying that it is inappropriate to have just one category for late adulthood because of the 'increasing health, wealth and vigour of many older people' (Sugarman, 2001). Instead she offers up the following framework, identifying a number of challenges for each. Here I only include those for early adulthood and above, with apologies to those coaching younger people:

Early adulthood (18–40)

Socially and personally, early adulthood can be more stressful and more difficult than any other phase of adulthood (Bee, 1994). Successful management of the challenges of this period can lead to increased self-confidence and independence (Sugarman, 2001).

Challenges include:

- Achieving intimacy, making career choices and attaining vocational success (Rice, 1995).
- Making decisions with long-term or possibly lifelong implications (Sugarman, 2001).
- Potentially forging an alternative identity to that of adult worker where that may be unachievable or unrealistic (Sugarman, 2001).

Middle adulthood (40–60)

Challenges include:

- Potential deterioration on tasks highly dependent on speed of response or the use of unexercised skills and memory.
- Increase in physical signs of ageing – people whose identity is closely tied in with how they look may have problems adjusting.
- Menopause for women (and male equivalent).
- Career expectations may need to be revised.

- Parents may need to renegotiate their relationships with children and each other.
- Potential for mid-life crisis 'triggered by personal, work and family pressures: for example, the need to come to terms with the reality of ageing (with its implication of mortality), the realization that the next generation – both at home and at work – is snapping at one's heels, and possibly the need to care for ageing parents and come to terms with their death' (Sugarman, 2001).

Early late-adulthood (60–75)

Challenges include:

- 'Smaller, slower, weaker, lesser, fewer' in relation to age-related physical changes (Bee and Mitchell, 1994, cited in Sugarman, 2001) – physical decline can become more marked.
- More renegotiation in relationships – retirement, becoming a grandparent.
- Possibly dependency on others.
- Coming to terms with loss: 'an important element of the crisis of integrity versus despair (Erikson, 1959, 1980) revolves around the acceptance of one's life for what it has been and for what it will not now be' (Sugarman, 2001).

Late late-adulthood (75 years and above)

Challenges include:

- Adjustment to further physical and mental decline.
- Adjustment to more restricted social and personal circumstances.
- Reviewing and reinterpreting personal life experience.

More on identity crisis

The term identity crisis was coined by Erikson to describe the failure to achieve ego identity during adolescence. Successful resolution of the crisis depends on the individual's progress through previous developmental stages, centring on issues such as trust, autonomy, and initiative. However, it is nowadays used much more widely, as we saw in some of the definitions of crisis and transition. As Linley, Biswas-Diener and Trenier (2012) point out, a 'person's identity is central to how they function, relate to those around them and perceive themselves, their capabilities and outlook for the future. Many life transitions are particularly difficult psychologically because they involve integrating new elements into one's identity while shedding outdated self-concepts.'

Mid-life crisis

As I researched and wrote this book, I was aware of changes to two aspects of my own identity – motherhood and womanhood, both of which sparked a minor crisis. Two of our children went off to university and the youngest became a teenager. Feelings of grief manifested, mingling with pride and satisfaction, as we waved goodbye to Emma and Molly; the house felt empty at times. Then, our son Dylan started to swing between being sweetly affectionate, protective of me, and still wanting to snuggle up with me and sometimes furry cuddly animals, and pushing me away, protesting that I'm 'nagging', or being 'annoying'. I've felt a shrivelling of my role as mother at times, feeling no longer so obviously needed.

Apart from feeling unpleasant and painful, I became aware that this little identity crisis was having an impact on my confidence. I felt as if I had less worth than before. I was concerned that this might play out somehow in my coaching so I explored it with a somatics coach and coach supervisor, which has helped me be much more grounded in my dealings with my son, as well as surface any impact on coaching clients. I also worked on it through a constellation at a Coaching at Work master class on Systemic Coaching and Constellations with John Whittington. What emerged from this was that my son didn't want me to tell him what to do – no surprises there – but he didn't want me standing behind him, as I thought, but alongside him, albeit it on his own terms. I've felt more confident around him and for now, at least, he seems to respect me and listen to me. And my mindfulness practice has helped me turn towards difficult feelings – the grief at the girls leaving home and our son no longer being a little boy.

During the writing of this book, too, I turned 50 and hurtled towards the menopause. The menopause remains a taboo subject in many circles but is starting to get more recognition as a potential problem for many individuals and those around them, including employers (eg Price and Taylor, 2014). Specific physical and mental symptoms can have a negative impact, such as having 'hot flushes' during important meetings or presentations or not feeling mentally alert, sometimes due to insomnia, while there are issues around identity – transitioning from fertile female to wise crone, or however we choose to perceive it. In many ways, I didn't care that I'd entered my fifties – I knew I was lucky. I had a loving husband and three beautiful children; despite some financial struggles due to the recession, we were coming out the other side; I enjoyed much of the work that I did; I had lots of friends, including some longstanding deep friendships; I was still alive – one of my sisters had suddenly died at 54, my husband's father had died at 52, and I'd lost a number of friends and other family members. And 50 is only a number. But 50, seriously?!? I began to explore different perceptions and archetypes and labels for ageing women. I embraced the word 'crone', I read many books including Bolen (1994). And I gathered with five other women for a rite of passage we called a Crones' Gathering. We bemoaned our ageing, turning towards what was difficult about it, supported by one another. And we explored the positive, such as being supposedly wiser, less selfish, moving towards a time when children needed less of our time so we could be more creative, perhaps.

I reflected how transformative it was to normalize what I was going through, having a greater sense of the 'road map'. And also to take joy and feel compassion as I heard from others as they were going through similar yet different experiences. I reflected how all major transitions, while having the potential to tip into crisis, are highly charged with potential energy for transformation; it's partly a matter of channelling this energy. In the excellent book, *How to Age*, Karpf (2014) writes: 'Our lives, from their very beginning, are a constant interplay between continuity and transformation... One of the greatest challenges of ageing, perhaps, is to recognize what endures and what changes.'

During this period, I've been reminded often of a coaching session with a client, 'Rowena' (see below) which threw me face-to-face with my own prejudices about ageing, and illuminated some of the territory I now find myself in, and which lies ahead.

CASE STUDY   Rowena and her silk dressing gown

Rowena, a 60-year-old learning and development director, was having a crisis about the impact of growing older, including having less energy, and feeling that she was now less attractive and therefore had fewer career opportunities. In previous sessions, I had worked with the FEEL model (Chapter 10) with her.

Below are extracts from a transcript of one of the coaching sessions:

R: 'This thing about being older... it hurts. I really don't like it. I look in the mirror and see my mother. I don't like her and don't want to be her.'

Coach: 'What do you not like about her?'

R: 'She couldn't accept that she wasn't young and pretty and a femme fatale any more. I label myself as older, therefore less attractive and therefore less effective. I don't want to be treated as older but I need to respect that I don't have the energy I used to. I want to carry on being as attractive as I can be without doing the thing my mum did, flirting with people when you're not attractive. There is an energy of my youth I want to maintain. I think it's something about not really valuing who I was and my attractiveness when I was younger.'

C: 'What is it about your youth that you wish you'd valued more?'

R: 'I'm mentoring someone, she has just got a job in a consultancy and I have to be so careful not to be envious.'

C: 'If you were allowing yourself to be envious, what would you be envious of exactly?'

R: 'I'm wishing I could have my time again, professional and personally. I didn't come into my own until I was 35. (silence) I underplayed myself. (silence) I've always seen myself as an attractive woman and as effective professionally, but there's always been that lack of confidence that I've not quite accepted either of those things, or the talent, all that stuff I could do, that huge gamut of things I could do. The only thing I really valued was this sort of attractive girl. I have got the other stuff.'

C: 'Other stuff?'

R: 'Professional, creative, all of that, but it is almost as if that doesn't matter because I'm not pretty any more and I'm turning into my mother, and how on earth do you do something about the menopause, about not having that fertility any more, it's like I'm doing everything for no reason, that nothing matters any more.'

C: 'I'm feeling grief.'

R: 'It is grief. I can work until I am blue in the face... there is something I'm missing...'

C: 'So what is missing?'

R: 'Something about whatever fertility means, a new-ness, growth, spring thing, to be brutally honest, there are fewer springs now than they were. I have a more limited span of time and it's how do I want to be for this bit when I've no longer got what as a girl I was brought up to believe was important, the attractiveness. It was like my mother shrivelled, not intellectually or in terms of friendships, but her true core self shrivelled right up.'

C: 'What does this make you feel towards her?'

R: 'How come she let herself shrivel up? And then post-menopause myself, I think very easily, because the body doesn't do it any more.'

(The coach then invites R to explore mindfully what's going on for her emotions-wise and where she's feeling these.) Then:

C: 'Is there anything you want to tell her?'

R: 'You wasted your life. Why did you bother carrying on?'

(C invites R to address her mother represented by a chair. Later, R shares how she finds it hard to be compassionate towards herself.)

C: 'What does it feel like to bring to mind a loved one, someone you feel really compassionate towards, giving them space to have needs, and then turning that feeling inward?'

R: 'I'm not really good at that, I am hopeless when people are ill, with X, I can get competitive.'

(C invites R again to turn towards and explore.)

C: 'That sense of not feeling you deserve compassion, where are you feeling that in your body?... Can you breathe into your heart?... What is happening for you? Does it hurt? Tell me about the hurt.' (R responded to some of these questions.)

R: (silence) 'I feel safe enough to say I feel broken-hearted.'

C: 'What do you need?

R: 'Not love actually, I don't know, I still have a light touch with that – "You're loved, you have all your critters."'

C: 'I feel love, there is lots of love around you... can you let that in?'

R: 'It's really hard to do that.' (sounding tearful)

C: (silence)... 'What is going on somatically?'

R: 'Layers and layers of not putting myself in the way of accepting the love that's there because I've done something not to deserve it, that I have rendered myself unlovable, that I allowed myself to get ugly. A little bit of me wants to say so what? I've survived so far.'

C: 'A bit of attitude.'

R: 'Real attitude... why can't I survive another 30 years? It's like I can't say any more because I don't have this magical pretty ability, like I used my attractiveness to shore myself up against my age.'

C: 'And what does the bit of attitude Rowena want to do and be?'

R: 'Wear spiky clothes.' (sounding more uplifted)

C: 'What would funky spiky Rowena wear?

R: 'I don't know, I want to turn round and say, who do you think you are? No... really sticky out hair, Vivienne Westwood clothes, lots of black.'

C: 'How would you walk?'

R: 'She'd be able to wear high heels as well. Mega spiky. Bright red fingernails.'

C: 'And her attitude towards getting older?'

R: 'I don't think she likes it either actually; she would like to be French, Juliette Greco getting older and getting away with it, gay guys throwing flowers to her, sexy at 75.'

C: 'So you can be sexy at 75?...

R: (silence)

C: Where have you gone?

R: 'I'm trying to find a place where it is OK to be sexy at 75? Hilary Clinton? There aren't enough of them.'

C: 'The ones you're thinking of, they don't seem like very simpering women, they seem to have attitude. Are there any qualities that stand out for you?'

R: 'They believe in themselves and believe in their power. They're standing in their power. Juliette Greco knows what she does is good.'

C: 'She doesn't seem spent?'

R: 'No, and not minding being feisty. Not hiding that? Believing in themselves?'

C: 'What makes them sexy, what else do you admire in them?'

R: 'Talent. At home with their ability.'

C: 'It seems a lot less about having kept their looks, having looked after themselves but having all these other qualities? Doesn't seem to be about getting away with it, not looking like you did when you were younger?'

R: 'Hmm, yes, it's like I'm not growing into it.'

C: 'If you didn't fight it and just sat with it, and allowed it to be, is there anything different about it?'

(Silence)

R: 'I think there is there is something in there about breaking rules, and not having to play by young girls' rules, the pretty girls' rules, which maybe women who aren't attractive broke early on. Instead of trying to be a pretty younger woman which I am not, there is something about enjoying, not the pat trite stuff about growing old gracefully/disgracefully... there is something more real, more traction.'

C: 'Tell me more about this traction, what's going on there?'

R: 'My rules are I shouldn't let myself go, nobody will take any notice of me if I let myself go, usually means getting a tummy and going grey, stopping growing...'

C: 'Which rules do you want to break'?'

R: 'It's really hard, this, as each rule is a double-edged sword. I could say I don't want to do any more work or yoga or meditating. Let my hair go grey, wear old ladies' clothes... I may just have to sit with the tension, if I want to maintain health. I think I might need to shift that script to "not doing bad for 60". What does a normal 60-year-old look like? I don't know! I look at people on the train all the time.'

C: 'All of those qualities you were highlighting before were all things that weren't dependent on looks.'

R: 'I guess what I've done, running into society's expectations of what women should look like'...

(R and C explore further what this 'new R' would look like and wear)... a silk dressing gown.

(C leads R through a somatic centering practice, to access from an empowered place a 'mantra' going forward.)

R: 'Beautiful in my own skin.'

Reflections: two years later

C: It was tough coaching R on this topic, particularly as a peri-menopausal (now much further along that path) woman. I was conscious in the session of the strength of my desire to get R to a place of it being OK to grow older, and that this desire was in part my own for myself. I wanted to give R the space to really 'let it hang out' without feeling judged, and felt honoured that she felt safe enough to share her 'negative' feelings about her mother, and about the importance of attractiveness in women in general, which I imagine we were both aware were not in line with our wider feminist views. Such a tension exists in many women, myself included. Exploring this tension safely without judgement felt important, allowing R to identify what she was mourning, and openly mourn it.

Karpf (2014), writes:

> *If ageing is embraced, then we inevitably recognize that some things are no longer possible and we mourn them. So, for example, an older woman*

might find her creeping invisibility hard to bear, especially if she's invested a lot in her appearance... Although it might seem paradoxical, mourning is an essential part of ageing with gusto, because it helps you say goodbye to some features of life, freeing you to welcome in new ones... Being able to tolerate some sadness and grief about necessary losses is a vital human resource to help us age – at any age.

It was tough emotionally to hear some of the harshness R directed towards herself, I was highly aware of wanting to rescue and comfort and reassure, yet this wasn't the territory. It felt important to bring in compassion explicitly, though.

R: Reading this, I actively disliked myself at the beginning, but towards the end, I started to make sense of myself. I guess this mirrors the coaching process exactly, that you took me from dislike of self to compassion for self which was pretty skillful. Since then, I'm not exactly channelling Juliette Greco but there's some of that going on... Two years on, I'm still working with this... I'm beginning to get the truly post-menopausal thing, whereas back then I was only just getting glimpses. It is very different and the attractiveness is different, more solid somehow. I still have conflicts about it but the image of the silk dressing gown has really stayed with me. The way I relate to my memory of my mother is qualitatively different now; I do recall calling her negative things in that session but it was my growing old self I hated more. I'm getting to know her now. Attractiveness when older is less to do with being fanciable, and more to do with being loved and loving yourself (the prerequisite)... so this session was a station on the way, and very helpful at the time. Reading it back now has reminded me just how far I've come, but that the issues don't, and probably won't, ever go away.

Typical transitions and crises at work

In addition to transitions associated with life stages, many clients will experience work-related transitions. Talbott (2013) suggests the following key transition points in a career where coaches can support a client: education to first job, career change, promotion to higher level, redundancy/redeployment, self-employment and portfolio life, return from career break, and retirement. Such times can be immensely exciting but also very tough, particularly where the role is high profile, there is inadequate support for the person, or there are other stressors, for example.

Elsner and Farrands (2012) researched what really happens for individuals and organizations when a new leader joins. They say (p 2) that although little is known, and even less said, about this period, 'for many leaders it is a time of struggle, chaos and search for mastery and personal coherence'. They continue, 'if well-handled, transitions are opportunities for step changes in self-understanding and transformation, but only after grappling with personal demons and the fearless confronting of their own and others' outdated limitations'.

Farrands interviewed almost 50 leaders from a range of industries about their experience of transitioning into a new role. Three key themes stood out:

- Perceived importance of keeping the leaders' experiences secret from those around the leader to protect the leader's image of invincibility. Yet this secret-keeping was an obstacle to the success of the transition.

- 'Undiscussability' of the experience, as if discussing low self-confidence or the need for personal change would incapacitate the leader further.

- Unpreparedness of leaders for the work of the transition. Most couldn't see the possibility of using the experience to promote personal change although several described how tougher past experiences had shaped their present experience as leaders.

Identity and burnout

Over-identifying with work can be problematic, potentially leading to burnout. Casserley and Megginson (2008) say that burnout is fundamentally an issue of individual identity, meaning and purpose. They found that high-flyers who derived their identity primarily from work and career success, whose sense of purpose was rooted in the need for fame and recognition, for example, were vulnerable to burnout. For most, this derailed their careers and froze the development of identity.

Other 'maps' for navigating transition and crisis include The Hero's Journey, which we look at briefly below, and models of change, which we will look at in the next chapter.

The Hero's Journey and archetypes

Campbell (2008) maps out a number of stages and challenges in The Hero's Journey, drawing on Jungian psychology and his own mythological studies. The journey can be seen as follows (Vogler, 2011):

- Hero is introduced to the Ordinary World;
- Hero receives Call to Adventure;
- Hero is reluctant or refuses the Call but is...
- encouraged by a Mentor (we might also think of a coach here) to...
- cross the Threshold and enter the Special World where they...
- encounter Tests, Allies, and Enemies;
- they approach the Inmost Cave, traversing a second threshold...
- where they endure the Ordeal;
- take possession of their Reward;
- are pursued on the Road Back to the Ordinary World;
- cross the third threshold, experience a Resurrection, and are Transformed by this experience;
- they return with the Elixir or treasure of benefit in the Ordinary World.

Figural within the journey are archetypes, which we touch on very briefly below.

Archetypes

The following archetypes are seen as aspects of the hero's personality: Mentor, Higher Self, Shapeshifter, Threshold Guardian, Trickster, Shadow, Herald and Allies. Meanwhile, Arrien's (1999) research shows that almost all shamanic traditions draw on the power of four archetypes so as to live in harmony and balance with our environment and our inner nature. These archetypes and their tasks (pp 7–8) are:

- Warrior: show up and be present;
- Healer: pay attention to what has heart and meaning;
- Visionary: tell the truth without blame or judgement;
- Teacher: be open to outcome, not attached to outcome;

Arrien says we need to learn to live with these archetypes within to 'begin to heal ourselves and our fragmented world', highlighting how indigenous peoples consider it vitally important to be balanced in leading, healing, visioning and teaching, yet few people are. And sometimes we express the shadow of these archetypes. Arrien (1999) describes the Trickster as 'the quintessential master of boundaries and transitions. It is by this mastery that he surprises mundane reality with the unexpected and the miraculous.' The primary purpose of the Trickster archetype is to teach us about detachment, about caring deeply from an objective place, about letting go, about maintaining a sense of humour, she says, so 'we can accept the experience as it is and then be creative with it, rather than be resigned or fatalistic about it' (p 112).

There are many other ways to interpret the aforementioned archetypes, and there are other archetypes too, including the Queen/King, and the Magician. And of course, clients might have their own versions.

In the next chapter, we look at some frameworks for mapping out the process of change and transition.

References

Arrien, A (1999) *The Four-fold Way: Walking the paths of the warrior, teacher, healer and visionary*, Wisdom Circles

Bee, H (1994) *Lifespan Development*, HarperCollins, New York

Bee, H L and Mitchell, S K (1984) *The Developing Person: A life-span approach* (2nd edn), Harper and Row, San Francisco, CA

Bolen, J S (1994) *Crossing to Avalon: A woman's midlife*, HarperCollins, New York

Bridges, W (2009) *Managing Transitions: Making the most of change* (3rd edn), Nicholas Brealey Publishing, London

Campbell, J (2008) *The Hero With a Thousand Faces*, 3rd edn, New World Library, CA

Casserley, T and Megginson, D (2008) Feel the burn, *Coaching at Work*, **3** (4)

Elsner and Farrands (2012) *Leadership Transitions: How business leaders take charge in their new roles*, Kogan Page, London

Erikson, E (1950) *Childhood and Society*, Norton, New York

Erikson, E H (1959) Identity and the Life Cycle, *Psychological Issues*, **1** (1), pp 1–171

Erikson, E H (1980) *Identity and the Life Cycle: A reissue*, Norton, New York

Hopson, B (1981) Response to the papers by Schlossberg, Brammer and Abrego, *Counselling Psychologist*, **9**, pp 36–39, in Sugarman (2001)

Karpf, Ann (2014) *How to Age*, Macmillan

Kimball, S (1960) in Van Gennep, A (1960) *The Rites of Passage*, The University of Chicago Press, Chicago (pp xvi–xviii)

Linley, P A, Biswas-Diener, R and Trenier E (2012) Positive psychology and strengths coaching through transition, in Palmer, S and Panchal, S (eds) *Developmental Coaching: Life transitions and generational perspectives*, Routledge, Hove

Palmer, S and Panchal, S (eds) *Developmental Coaching: Life transitions and generational perspectives*, Routledge, Hove

Price, D and Taylor, T (2014) Time of your life, *Coaching at Work*, 9 (1), pp 32–36

Rice, F P (1995) *Human Development: A life-span approach* (2nd edn), Prentice Hall, Englewood Cliffs, NJ

Sugarman, L (2011) In the foreword to Palmer and Panchal (eds) *Developmental Coaching: Life transitions and generational perspectives*, Routledge: Hove

Sugarman, L (2001) *Life-span Development: Frameworks, accounts, and strategies*, Psychology Press, Hove

Talbott, C (2013) *Essential Career Transition Coaching Skills*, Routledge, Hove

Wilber, K (2001) *A Theory of Everything: An integral vision for business, politics, science and spirituality*, Shambhala Publications

Vogler, C (2007) *The Writer's Journey*, Michael Wiese Productions, CA

Models and frameworks for exploring change and transition

03

LIZ HALL

In this chapter, we focus on some models and frameworks commonly used in coaching to understand and work with change, crisis and transition.

Specifically, we look at Bridges' Transition Curve, the Kübler-Ross Change Curve, Prochaska and DiClemente's Transtheoretical Stages of Change, and Dilts' Logical Levels, as well as suggesting additional ones to look at. Although the aforementioned models have evolved from people trying to make sense of specific situations, they've been adapted and extended to work with change in general, and have in common that there are a number of stages which will be experienced, some of which can be very challenging (Talbott, 2013). Keeping in mind that these are merely maps, albeit very useful ones, and that it's important to consider differences in individual mapmakers and map readers, let's look at these models, starting with the Transition Curve.

Bridges' Transition Curve

Bridges' Transition Curve (eg Bridges, 2009) sets out three phases or processes. These may go on at the same time and there may be more than one transition happening at once:

1 **The ending.** Letting go of the old ways and the old identity, where clients can need help to deal with their losses. Losses typically fall into six categories – loss of:

- attachments;
- turf;
- structure;
- future;
- meaning; and/or
- control.

2 **The neutral zone.** Going through an in-between time when the old has gone but the new isn't fully operational. This is when critical psychological realignments and repatternings take place.

3 **New beginning.** Coming out of the transition and making a new beginning: when people develop the new identity, experience the new energy, and discover the new sense of purpose that make the change begin to work. According to Bridges (2009), with a change, we naturally focus on the outcome whereas with transition, the starting point is instead the ending needed to leave the old situation behind. Letting go is key to success.

Working with the model

Talbot (2013) suggests it's best to work with this model when you sense the transition is starting to have a psychological impact on the client. This could be when someone has just been made redundant, or perhaps is getting frustrated when job applications are not paying off. She argues that if you mention it too early, the client won't appreciate how or why it is relevant to them; if left too late, they will already be struggling. Phase 3 is pretty straightforward; the first two phases more challenging to work with. Below are some pointers for coaching in Phases 1 and 2.

Phase 1

Help the client to recognize what has ended, whatever this may be, including beliefs and assumptions. Helping them to grieve for what they've lost will help to avert a crisis, and help them move on. Any coaching will need to surface what's being let go of. Sometimes organizations – and individuals – seek to sweep all of this under the carpet, focusing only on wonderful outcomes, but this is an important phase. Organizations failing to deal with

losses and endings properly can face hordes of employees resistir
and transitions. For things to really transform in an organizati
some employees will have to let go of something, such as cert:
working or chances of promotion in the new organization.

Phase 2

> The neutral zone is thus both a dangerous and an opportune place, and it is the
> very core of the transition process... It is the winter in which the roots begin
> to prepare themselves for spring's renewal. It is the night during which we are
> disengaged from yesterday's concerns and preparing for tomorrow's. It is the
> chaos into which the old form dissolves and from which the new form emerges.
> William Bridges (2009)

This phase or process can be experienced as an 'emotional wilderness' or
'no-man's land' (Bridges, 2009), a time when we don't know who we are or
what is real, when we shed the old and take on the new. This is the liminal
point I talked about earlier, and can be highly challenging. People can feel
very frightened in the 'neutral zone' and try to escape. As Talbott (2013)
explains, this is when the psychological adjustments take place and why it's
so important to support your client in preparing for their new life, job or
career so that they don't slip back into their old being and give up on their
ambitions. Clients may of course act on their desire to escape. There's often
a higher level of staff turnover during organizational changes, and even more
so when an organization is in crisis and coming to the end of a life cycle.
Yet difficult though this phase is, it offers the best chance for opportunity,
creativity, and renewal.

Talbott (2013) emphasizes the importance of really understanding this
model to work with it. One danger here, for example, is that clients may
start to think about giving up. The neutral zone sounds benign but it's not,
and it's confusing. Also, we may mistake thoughts and behaviour clients
exhibit here as 'typical' of them or symptomatic of their personality type,
rather than characteristic of the neutral zone or the bottom of the Kübler-
Ross change curve, she warns.

Kate Pearlman-Shaw, clinical psychologist, leadership coach and lead
consultant at ORConsulting, stresses the importance of empathy:

> People will vary in how receptive they are to different kinds of messages as
> they move along transition curves. With someone who is experiencing anxiety,
> anger or loss, these emotions will have an impact on their cognitive functions,
> meaning that your information is unlikely to be effective, no matter how
> reasoned it is. A more empathic approach is needed here, for example.

If clients aren't given or don't give themselves the chance to move properly through the different stages, they can become blocked, with negative outcomes, as the case study below highlights. 'Denise' was a member of a senior leadership team that embarked on a two-year transformational coaching programme which included team and individual coaching. UK-based leadership and 'menopause' coach Deborah Price coached Denise.

CASE STUDY   Giving Denise permission to grieve:
working with the Transition Curve

Denise (D): 'I didn't know I needed it or that I would benefit from coaching. I don't know now how I would have got through that period without it. It was a well-timed connection. We hit it off straight away. I'm now aware that I could work through personal issues but then I'd never experienced coaching before in my life. I felt that it helped me to look at myself as a whole person. I talked to others in our team and discovered that they, too, had gone through a similar process and were discussing personal issues. I found it holistic and very, very therapeutic. I didn't often talk about myself so intently and, certainly, not for so long. It was a strange time in my career – I'd got to a certain level in the organization but I was stuck in a rut. The coaching really helped me to move myself on personally – I gained a lot of confidence. It wasn't instantaneous – it was definitely a journey. It was a very difficult time in my life. I was just coming to the end of implementing a very big and stressful project which involved many of my team being made redundant and me setting up a new team 180 miles away. I was on the road every week and away from home several nights a week. My Dad had died ten months earlier and I hadn't given myself time to work through that. I was back to work and on the road within weeks. I remember sobbing my heart out in my sessions with you. You recommended me to read Bridges book *The Way of Transitions* – he (WB) thought that he was as tough as old boots but he couldn't cope when his wife died. My life had changed shape. The model really helped me to let go and to acknowledge and make sense of the neutral zone. I started to understand what it was and that it takes as long as it takes to get through it. Everyone feels differently – I pass this on to other people and let them know that it's a normal feeling and that we just need to go with it and not fight it. Your reassurance that it was normal that I couldn't make decisions or move forward was the most powerful part. It was what I needed... to have that permission/understanding of the process. You protected me from what I was feeling – I stopped beating myself up.'

Deborah (C): 'What was the impact of the coaching?'

D: 'It helped me to really gain confidence in my ability to sort out my own problems. Towards the end of our coaching I would answer my own questions. You would ask me such clear questions that it made me realize that I was capable of so much more and that I didn't need to worry about what other people thought about me. I was really quite shy and self-promotion wasn't my thing.'

C: 'Was the change sustainable?

D: 'I was able to keep going. Even now (two years after the end of the coaching) I am self-sufficient and I reflect on that still. The last few weeks have been really weird – life-changing things have happened. I've bought a new house and I've been on my first date in four years. Coaching helped me to grow. My new job is helping me to grow further, too. I would never have gone for my current role without the coaching experience. I've never been so busy or under so much pressure... and I can deal with it! It keeps on happening (my realization that I am resourceful and can cope). I am looking forward to whatever's coming next. Dating is a big step for me. I couldn't cope with the highs and lows that came from dating – it was unsettling and made me feel off balance. It was easier on my own and it allowed me to maintain control... I've got coping mechanisms for life and I've changed beyond all recognition in the last few years. I've let go of all my hang-ups. I feel like a far more authentic leader without my shadow – what you see is what you get. I'm not trying to be anyone else. It was, without a doubt, a very significant period in my life and I am really grateful to have had the experience of coaching to get me through it. It has changed me forever. I now acknowledge myself and know that I am inspiring.'

C adds:

D had been an employee of the sponsor organization for 15 years and was part of the senior management team and on the executive committee. She didn't feel that people really saw her as senior and felt that she was feeling/playing 'small'. She hadn't grieved her father's death and was being strong to carry out her work commitments and to support her mother and sister. She lived out of a suitcase for most of the week, ate unhealthily due to her schedule and being on the road so much. Her home life was interrupted by her frequent absences and she was unhappy with her health and fitness. As the project she was working on came to an end she found it difficult to focus on what she wanted to do next and was frustrated by her inability to make plans for the future. She'd lost her motivation and was in survival mode. She often cried in the early sessions.

As her coach I initially simply held the space for her to feel safe enough to cry, to reassure that her that it was OK to bring her personal issues to executive coaching and that she was experiencing was normal. She was grieving and needed to let it out. She was also burnt out. We spent many sessions just talking about and normalizing her experiences – she was unused to not having goals and having the motivation to achieve objectives. We explicitly related what was happening to her to the phases she'd read about in Bridges' *Way of Transition*. She was able to validate her letting go phase and having a process she could relate to seemed to enable her to accept that what was happening would, eventually, pass, making way for a new way of being. A time in the future when she could, again, make plans and find her enthusiasm for life and her work.

As the coaching progressed and she became more comfortable with the notion of being in transition; she started to be kinder to herself and to take more care of herself and her life outside work. She was able to share her coaching experiences with colleagues and her employer was very supportive of her needs.

Over a period of a year she started to focus on new personal beginnings – she worked with a personal trainer and lost 28 lbs. She ran a half marathon (never having run before) and could then start to think about new work beginnings – she took on a newly created role in change management with her employer. She had no team in her new role which she found odd, though a relief, as she didn't have to worry about other people. The new role offered her a blank sheet of paper and after the first few months of feeling guilty that she wasn't 'working flat out' she settled into creating the role in the way she felt the organization needed. She was well supported by her employer and felt that she was being given breathing space to grow and recover. After two years in that role she applied for and got a role in an area of the business that she'd never worked in before and, on paper, was unqualified for. She is thriving in it and, despite the substantial pressures, rises to the challenges. Her peers clearly respect her and spontaneously offer positive feedback about her presence and successes in her new role. She appears to me to be comfortable in her own skin and fully alive again!

Prochaska and DiClemente's Transtheoretical Stages of Change

This model (Prochaska and DiClemente, 1994), originally designed to promote healthier behaviours around smoking and overeating, describes how people modify or change a problematic behaviour, or acquire and create new patterns of behaviour. It describes five stages of readiness for change:

1 Pre-contemplation (not ready to change): Avoidance – failing to see a problem behaviour or to consider change.

2 Contemplation (still not ready to change): Acknowledging there's a problem but struggling with ambivalence. Weighing pros and cons, and benefits to, and barriers to, change.

3 Preparation/Determination: Taking steps and getting ready to change.

4 Action/Willpower: Making the change and living the new behaviours, which is an all-consuming activity.

5 Maintenance: Maintaining the behaviour change that is now integrated into the person's life.

Again, these stages are not necessarily linear. Clients may revert to an earlier phase or abandon change efforts completely.

Working with the model

The model can be used to explore how clients understand change, and shed light on their worldviews. Do they see change as an opportunity? Or do they feel they are victims of external change rather than having choices? With clients in crisis, the steps taken will often be small. They may only be concerned with the most basic of needs such as shelter, work, or survival. However, in this place people are often potentially and actually at their most creative and flexible when it comes to change.

The coaching can be used to explore and challenge their assumptions, but of course they may not be ready for change. It's important to also consider the key factors of 'importance' – determined by what value a person places on making the change – and 'self-efficacy' – the belief or confidence in one's ability to achieve change. The client may struggle to make choices that conflict with their values – or may not know what their values are. People high on importance but low on confidence need encouragement that change is possible and help in working out how to make it happen.

Anthony Eldridge-Rogers is a coach who runs recovery and wellness programmes.

Key models (and frameworks) I draw on (personally and in the training we offer) include Prochaska and DiClemente's Stages of Change, Jungian archetypes, narrative psychology (the latter two fit really well together), NLP, some Positive Psychology, the Coactive Coaching model, a little bit of Motivational Interviewing, and a little bit of CBT. One of the things that is key in my work and our recovery and wellness coach training is explicit and implicit priming – the way we're triggered, the fact that we're primed to be triggered, and noticing how and when we're triggered. This means that the use of language is key. Every word that falls from our mouths is like a ripple in a lake. We have no idea though how those ripples will be interpreted. We have to step back and realize that just because we think we understand a word, not everyone else understands it in the same way. This is vital for conscious coaching and is part of the self-management focus.

The Stages of Change model helps people learn how to coach appropriately because they can do some damage (if they aren't familiar with the stages), (for example) you can increase the risk of relapse with an inappropriate intervention within the stages of change. I'm always quite surprised at how few coach training programmes tackle this. If you pile into something in a certain way, you're going to collapse the whole thing.

The Kübler-Ross Change Curve, or the Five Stages of Grief

Elizabeth Kübler-Ross originally described five stages of grief in her book *On Death and Dying* (1969):

1 Denial;

2 Anger;

3 Bargaining;

4 Depression;

5 Acceptance.

She later added the stage of Adaptive Behaviour. The model was originally intended to map out typical responses, or defence or coping mechanisms, to

FIGURE 3.1 Change curve – after Elisabeth Kübler-Ross

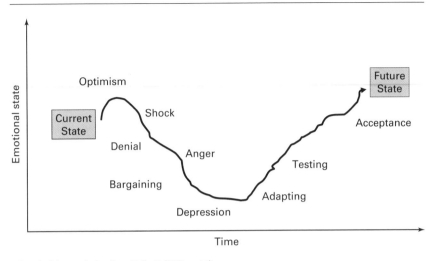

Printed with permission from Talbott (2013, p 44)

tragic news such as their own terminal illness or the death of a loved one. However, it's been adapted and is used widely to help people in all settings explore the normal range of feelings associated with dealing with any significant change or upheaval. It's widely recognized that it applies to unwelcome and enforced changes but less so for those that have been eagerly sought and anticipated (Talbott, 2013). Most organizational change consultants agree that people react to organizational change in ways similar to Kübler-Ross's. There are lots of versions of the Change Curve – see Figure 3.1 for one of these. Nowadays, there is usually a grouping into three phases: Shock or Denial; Anger and Depression, and Acceptance and Integration.

Working with the model

The stages can last for different periods of time, can replace one another or exist side by side. So it's not a case of working through the stages in a neat and linear way. Plus people can get stuck in one stage. I saw my father, who was devastated by the death of my mother, 'neatly' go through the different stages until he became stuck in Stage 4. He never reached Acceptance. In fact, he was very vocal about not wanting to accept her death as this would have meant for him to deny her somehow, to deny his love for her. However, in coaching, the hope is to support clients to reach Stage 5 even if they tip back and forth and around the other stages from time to time. Let's look at the phases in more detail.

Phase 1: Denial and shock: 'It can't be happening to me!'

Shock

When people first hear difficult news, they can feel shocked at first, perhaps due to lack of information and fear of the unknown, then move into denial. Usually a temporary defence, this gives them time to absorb news of change before moving on to other stages.

Potential impact here includes:

- loss of productivity;
- inability to make clear decisions or meet deadlines;
- need for more support, guidance and reassurance from others.

Denial

When people move into denial, they tend to be focused on the past, feeling that everything was OK before; why did it have to change? They may feel threatened, and afraid of failure. Clients who have not ever experienced major change can be particularly affected by this first stage.

Potential impact: performance may go back to previous levels but people may deny having been told about changes, and/or make excuses to avoid forward planning.

Clients need to be listened to and have their emotions acknowledged as legitimate. Showing empathy is important. And as with other models, it's helpful to support the client to identify significant things they're losing so they can mourn, and what significant things they'll be glad to lose. Nothing is perfect! Helping them to reframe, such as 'I was in the wrong place at the wrong time' can be helpful.

Phase 2: Anger and depression

Anger: 'It's not fair!' 'I can't believe I did that, I am such an idiot!'

Once we realize that the change is real, denial can turn to anger, and we look to blame something or someone – the boss, ourselves, God, the bankers, the Government...

Clients may look for scapegoats, thus prolonging the denial in some way by shifting the focus of fears and anxieties. Common feelings include suspicion, scepticism and frustration.

Depression: 'What's the point of trying, nothing is going to change how I feel?'

When people really take on board the extent and reality of the change, and the associated losses, they can become depressed. This is the lowest point of the curve, when the anger wears off.

Potential impact:

- low morale;
- high levels of self-doubt and anxiety;
- difficulty expressing emotion;
- apathy;
- a sense of isolation and remoteness.

It can be hard to express feelings easily here. In the workplace, people facing upheaval or crisis can feel demotivated and uncertain, or even suicidal. I recall one coach telling me how about a year after the Global Financial Crisis (2008), a public sector client who was being made redundant came into their session sharing how he was having suicidal thoughts, even though he didn't honestly feel he was going to act upon them. Obviously here, there would be a judgement call to make on whether to continue coaching. She did, although she did suggest he saw a therapist.

When clients are going through this stage, it can be helpful to realize that others experience the same feelings.

Bargaining: 'I'll accept a pay cut if you keep me on'

At this point, people can try to bargain their way out of the change or transition, to avoid it being real.

Phase 3: Acceptance and integration

Acceptance: 'I can cope with this, it's OK'

This stage may not be marked by happiness at first, rather resignation to the fact that the change is here to stay. But it becomes possible to explore options and next steps, paving the way to future happiness. This can be a creative space, and requires courage. Robust clients may find themselves at this stage quickly whereas less resilient clients will require more support to work through the other phases. And rushing to acceptance too early is another form of denial. It's important to acknowledge what's going on in the other phases.

After the darker emotions of the second stage, clients can start feeling more optimistic and enthusiastic, accepting that change is inevitable, becoming more open to opportunities, experiencing relief that they have survived the crisis or change, and even feeling impatient for change to be complete.

Integration

The final steps involve integration. Here, the focus is firmly on the future, the changed situation has become the new reality. The primary feelings now include acceptance, hope and trust.

Impact includes:

- at first, energy and productivity remain low but start to pick up;
- there can be lots of questions and curiosity;
- there can a return to an earlier stage if the level of support suddenly drops.

CASE STUDY   Bravery and a blend of coaching and consultancy

Caroline Talbott, transitions coach

In 2012, I helped the chief executive and leadership team work out what their role was in leading the change at a non-UK technology organization. They wanted to carry out an employee engagement survey which was very brave because they had done one before and hadn't done anything with the results. I helped them by holding up the mirror to tell them the ghastly truth. It was interesting because to begin with, I didn't have access to the chief executive and I realized the person I was working with didn't have the influence needed. I got an appointment to see the chief exec and started pulling all this absolutely awful stuff out of the survey. I thought, 'How do I hide this and soften the blow?' But I thought, 'I'll be brave.' [This meeting] prompted an action so I ran a leadership for change day workshop for him and his top team. I used the Kübler-Ross curve, getting them to map out what they were seeing and hearing at different stages of the curve, and to think about what they should be doing to help their team. They had done some talent assessment which they hadn't come out very well on so they were in the depths of despair about their own future. I realized they needed to manage that first. I'd set it out to create an environment where they could share things authentically so I kept it playful, informal and offsite. I asked them how they were feeling and where they were on the change curve (in relation to the talent assessment) and there were tears in some people's eyes. I said the first thing was for them to look after themselves and each other. [The day] reinforced the bond between them. They wanted to engage more with staff and wanted to get the monthly management meeting to be a proper engagement tool so I got them to use the engagement survey results as a mechanism to start more authentic conversations. I designed the session for them, and said one of them needed to run it. The chosen person backed out a few days before so I coached someone else to do it. There was lots of embarrassed laughter at the results but the guy suddenly said 'I don't know what you're laughing at, this is about *us.*' He became authentic. And you could have heard hear a pin drop. [He talked about what people] needed to be the best managers they could be and what they needed from the top team.

Dilts' (Neuro)logical Levels of Change

This model was developed by Robert Dilts (Dilts, accessed June 2015), who was inspired by the work of Gregory Bateson (1972), an anthropologist and philosopher involved in the early development of Neuro-Linguistic Programming. Logical Levels offers a framework to help clients explore problems and opportunities, and to identify obstacles to change and where – at which level – change can take place. The levels are called logical because each level has to be congruent before change can occur and be sustained. Figure 3.2 shows the model (Talbott, 2013).

The six levels are:

1 Environment (where, when and with whom?)

2 Behaviour (actions – what?)

3 Capabilities (how?)

4 Beliefs and Values (why?)

5 Identity (who?)

6 Mission (spirituality: what am I here for? The transpersonal.)

Working with the model

This framework can be used to identify what an individual needs to do differently to work through a crisis or transition, and to achieve their goals. This might mean changing their environment or what they do; advancing

FIGURE 3.2   Logical Levels – based on Robert Dilts' model

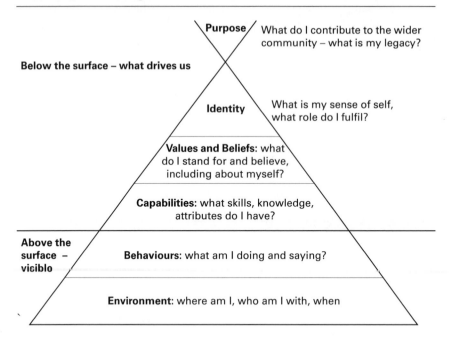

their knowledge; re-evaluating what they hold to be true; changing how they think of themselves; or reflecting on their purpose in life. It can be used to break down what might be an overwhelming experience into 'bite-sized' pieces, identifying potential problems or areas of possible resistance or blocks to change, clarifying how they perceive a situation, and highlighting at what level work has to be done to achieve change.

It can be used with individuals or in organizational situations to help facilitate change, such as project management to prioritize tasks and who does what, problem solving, and improving relationships and teamwork.

Talbott (2013) suggests asking the client to find a place in the room to physically walk through the levels, walking 'beside them so that they sense that you are with them rather than just taking notes and perhaps judging them'. She suggests that this approach can work especially well for clients who are 'Activists' (ie who like to learn and take in information in an active and practical way) or kinesthetic (who process things through their senses rather than visually or auditorily). Walking through the levels works particularly well when clients are feeling overwhelmed, as it can shift their energy and helps them become unstuck.

Below is a case study illustrating how to use the model.

CASE STUDY Lost and found

Jane Worthington is a self-employed leadership and management consultant and trainer, personal and professional coach and a 'Mind Calm Coach'. She was a team leader at Loughborough College of Further Education in the United Kingdom at the time of coaching. As a result of the insights gained from the coaching, she transitioned into independent practice, coaching, designing and teaching on executive programmes internationally. The coach was Margaret Chapman-Clarke. She comments: 'Dilts is deceptively simple to use, yet powerful in its impact. Through appreciative inquiry with gentle questions Jane was able to develop her emotional intelligence and recognize the style of leader she wanted to be, to learn to "flex her style" with different teams and individuals and yet at the core, to remain and be authentic.' Jane says, 'I was telling Margaret that I'd "lost" myself and was wondering how to make sense of events at work. As she explained the model to me it began to occur to me that this was answering my unconscious and conscious questions of confusion about where and who I am. I felt an overwhelming deep sense of emotion as I began to develop greater levels of my personal and professional selves. The questions helped me begin to make sense of my situation; Dilts helped me embark on a journey of self-discovery which led to me exploring my desire to be an authentic leader.'

Below, Jane's reflections at each level are captured.

Neurological Level Six: Mission (questions: *Who? And what else?*)
Reflections:

A need for a sense of belonging, friendship, to be successful and the best in field. My metaphor for this is a 'circle of friendship'. Applying this metaphor allows me to think about the teams in a different way and the relationship I want with them. Through understanding the team's needs and being true to my own values, the team should go on to become more successful.

Level Five: Identity (*Who?*)
Reflections:

I'm at my best when I'm in the 'thick' of it. I'm passionate, lively, funny, have self-belief, am self-directed and motivated and focus totally on being successful. I also have leadership qualities, I'm a team player, and enjoy problem solving and being creative. And yet, 'who do I think I must be' is at odds with the above, because of the culture and the peer group that I work in. My first thoughts are that I should be 'sensible, fit in with management thinking, be political, game player, conformer and communicator'. This is how I view my world at work, rather than what's necessarily the case. It's with these thoughts in mind that I wish to explore leadership models that focus on the authentic leader and having a sense of presence to help me identify who I am at work.

Level Four: Beliefs and Values (*Why do you believe you are effective? What is important to you about that? What for you are the most important values, which allow you to be effective? List at least three or four and place in priority order.*)
Reflections:

- Committed and loyal to my organization.

- Get things done through hard work which also means I meet deadlines –
  I have a sense of outputs not inputs which means I go that extra mile.

- I receive very good and positive feedback from my teaching practice and leadership role and also from 360-degree feedback.

- See achievement in others through my teaching and leadership roles.

- Problem solver and decision maker – through listening to others' point of view – at times I do adopt a 'paternalistic' leadership role based on gathering feedback from staff and using this feedback to make decisions.

These things are important to me because they demonstrate to me that I'm valuable to my organization and part of its overall success along with the need to know that I'm doing a good job and am recognized for it.

1 people first;

2 lead the way and empower people;

3 achievement;

4 recognized for being one of the best in field (team and personal level).

Level Three: Capabilities (*How? What skills do you have to make you effective? List skills and qualities. What do you need to acquire? How will you do this?*)

- self-motivated and driven;

- understand people;

- intuitive;

- lifelong learner;

- listener;

- value others' contributions;

- better emotional intelligence skills;

- confidence and self-belief;

- believe that failure *can* be an option (not either/or, but both/and);

- be aware of the impact I have on others;

- to make better use of language;

- explore leadership theories and models;

- attend CPD activities that relate to EQ and Coaching;

- self-reflection ;

- discover my sense of 'self'.

Level Two: Behaviours (*What? – What do you do to be at your best? What is it that you do to be a success?*)

- learn (read, attend seminars and training, reflect and evaluate my performance);

- network with peers;

- where possible have 'professional' discussions about teaching and learning and leadership;

- socialize.

Level One: Environment (*Where? And When? Reflect on your current circumstances at work. Where and when are you at your best? Where and when are you most dissatisfied with your current performance?*)
Dissatisfied:

- period of change – new manager and two new teams to lead;

- different values and beliefs regarding leadership which has led to a rupture in the working relationship with my line manager;

- teams are different by culture and vocation;

- I feel there are differences in the ways in which we relate;

- when I'm not delivering the goods;

- when I don't feel trusted;

- don't meet deadlines;

- fail or get things wrong;
- lack of knowledge and understanding in the team I feel ambivalent about my role as a new leader.

And satisfied? When:

- I'm with like-minded people who have a shared understanding;
- I'm clear about what is required of a task;
- I know what I'm doing – confident;
- I'm happy;
- I'm trusted.

So what did I learn? Dilts is only effective if you are willing to explore the 'inner' you for the purposes of EQ development. Once the ladder was complete, I was able to do a few things: a) re-affirm with myself who I knew myself to be, b) identify what my core values and beliefs were and c) begin to explore my own leadership style and undertake further research and study.

I was able to re-align myself and identify my sense of purpose – which I knew was there, but had lost for a while. I now realize that my core beliefs and values are mine and that it is not about another person trying to change the way you think or feel. I've been able to identify my mission and purpose. Through this I have recognized the importance of Authentic Leadership and I'm working on my personal presence in my coaching.

Through Dilts I've regained my sense of 'self', my motivation, drive and a clear direction in wanting to be the 'best I can be' and to recognize that 'losing' myself for a short time, the coaching generally and Dilts' specifically, has enabled me to find and enter a new and exciting period in my career.

A short version of this case study appeared in Coaching at Work *(2010)*

Below are some other models for working with change, which can be useful in times of crisis and transition.

Beckhard (1969) Three conditions must be present: dissatisfaction with the present, a vision of the future and the first steps to achieving it must be clear and achievable.

Fisher (revised 2012) The Transition Curve model of personal change: 13 stages based on Personal Construct Psychology (PCP) or Personal

Construct Theory (PCT). This proposes that we must understand how the other person sees their world and the meaning they attribute to things if we are to communicate and connect well with them.

Kegan and Lahey (2009) The Immunity to Change Process model seeks to help us understand that it's difficult to make changes in our lives, not because of lack of skill or even commitment, but due to hidden competing commitments, and big assumptions.

Kotter (1996) An eight-step process for leading change. Kotter and Cohen (2002) stress the power of heart over head in organizational change (*The Heart of Change*, 2002), outlining the 'see–feel–change method' in which (1) people are helped to see a compelling vision/situation needing to be addressed; (2) that compelling vision/situation hits the emotions and evokes a gut-level response; and (3) the emotionally charged response to the situation leads to changed behaviours and actions.

Lewin (1947) Three-stage model of unfreeze, change and (re)freeze.

Nicholson (1984) Theory of Work Role Transitions – examines work role transitions and relationships between personal and organizational outcomes. He proposes how outcomes are influenced by the characteristics of the person, the role, and the organization and the implications for changing patterns of adjustment over a lifetime.

Marshak (eg 2006) Outlined six overt and covert dimensions which are always involved in organizational change: Reasons (rational and analytic logics); Politics (individual and group interests); Inspirations (values-based and visionary aspirations); Emotions (affective and reactive feelings); Mindsets (guiding beliefs and assumptions); and Psychodynamics (anxiety-based and unconscious defences). Reason always gets the overt emphasis, while the other five dimensions are frequently covert, despite their influence on achieving desired results.

SCARF (status, certainty, autonomy, relatedness, fairness) (Rock, 2008) is widely used to help to promote healthy relationships and organizational cohesion, which can be sorely tested in times of crisis (eg Martin-Kniep, 2010).

Schein's (1999) Process Consultation model emphasizes shared understanding of the emotions and behaviours involved in the change process, highlighting ten principles including that everything you do is an intervention; it's the client who owns the problem and the solution, and everything is a source of data.

In terms of approaches, we explore some elsewhere in this book, including Mindful Compassionate Coaching. Other frameworks and approaches coaches I interviewed said they found useful when working with clients in crisis/transition include:

- Positive psychology and strengths-based coaching: identifying and building clients' strengths which may be taking a back seat in difficult times.

- Existential coaching: exploring meaning and purpose.

- Cognitive Behavioural Coaching: identifying self-limiting beliefs.

- Transactional Analysis: exploring dynamics and patterns of behaviour which may be the cause of or magnified in challenging times.

- Clean Language: working with the unconscious through metaphor to deal with difficult emotions.

In the next chapter, we look at how crisis can be a catalyst for growth.

References

Bateson, G (1972) *Steps to an Ecology of Mind: Collected essays in anthropology, psychiatry, evolution, and epistemology*, University of Chicago Press, Chicago

Beckhard, R (1969) *Organization Development: Strategies and models*, Addison-Wesley, Reading, MA

Dilts, R (2014) A brief history of logical levels, *NLP University* [online] http://www.nlpu.com/Articles/LevelsSummary.htm [accessed June 2015]

Fisher, J M (Revised 2012) Fisher's process of personal change, *Businessballs.com* [Online] http://www.businessballs.com/personalchangeprocess.htm [accessed 13 July 2012]

Kegan, R and Lahey, L L (2009) Immunity to change: How to overcome it and unlock potential in yourself and your organization, Harvard Business School Press, Boston, MA

Kotter, J P (1996) *Leading Change*, Harvard Business School Press, Boston, MA

Kotter, J P and Cohen, D S (2002) *The Heart of Change: Real-life stories about how people change their organizations*, Harvard Business Review Press, Boston, MA

Kübler-Ross, E (1969) *On Death and Dying*, Routledge, Oxford

Level Playing Field (2010) *Coaching at Work*, 5 (5)

Lewin, K (1947) Frontiers in Group Dynamics: Concept, method and reality in social science; social equilibria and social change, *Human Relations*, June 1947, 1, pp 5–41

Marshak, R J (2006) *Covert Processes at Work: Managing the five hidden dimensions of organizational change*, Berrett-Koehler Publishers

Martin-Kniep, G O (2010) Neuroscience of engagement and SCARF: Why they matter in schools, *NeuroLeadership Journal*, **3**, pp 87–96

Nicholson, N A (1984) Theory of work role transitions, *Administrative Science Quarterly*, **29** (2), pp 172–91

Rock, D (2008) SCARF: A brain-based model for collaborating with and influencing others, *NeuroLeadership Journal*, **1** (1), pp 44–52

Schein, E H (1999) *Process Consultation Revisited: Building the helping relationship*, Addison-Wesley, Reading, MA

Talbott, C (2013) *Essential Career Transition Coaching Skills*, Routledge, Hove

No mud, no lotus? Crisis as a catalyst for transformation

04

LIZ HALL

Without the mud, the lotus flower can't exist – the mud provides nourishment for the lotus plant to grow and bloom. This has long struck me as the perfect metaphor for the power we have as humans to transcend and transform difficulty, but also for the power of crisis itself to bring about transformation. Yet I was aware when setting out to research this book that it might all too often be wishful thinking, a case of retrospectively trying to put a positive spin on a difficult experience. Fine in itself, of course, but I wondered just how often crisis sparks growth and transformation, and more than that, whether we actually *need* crisis to truly transform? I wondered too how going through crisis, and coaching clients in crisis, impacts coaches and their coaching practice. How as coaches we can offer the best chance to clients to grow and transform through crisis. And how coaching can support organizations in crisis. This chapter explores these questions.

Crisis sparks transformation

There are many inspiring examples in the literature, both fictional and academic, of people transforming after going through crisis. Scholars such as Frankl (1963) and Yalom (1980) highlight the possibility for positive outcomes from crises. There is a growing body of research on Post-Traumatic Growth (PTG), which Calhoun and Tedeschi (1998) describe as 'the experience of positive change that the individual experiences as a result of the struggle with a traumatic event'. Calhoun and Tedeschi (2006) report that depending on the criteria, between 30 and 90 per cent of people dealing with major difficulties report at least some growth.

In many cultures and traditions, crisis is viewed as crucial to transformation. In shamanic circles, an individual crisis can represent the calling to become a shaman and one which leads to a reconstructed psyche, identity, and consciousness which are less conflicted, less symptomatic, less bound to the past and more healthy, integrated, and whole (Walsh, 1994). In the mystical Christian tradition, the descent into the difficult territory of doubt and desperation is called the dark night of the soul and often results in high levels of creativity, and significant shift and reorientation at the very core of our being (Gilbert and Choden, 2013). In psychotherapy, it's sometimes described as entering the shadow, the primitive parts of the mind we'd rather avoid, and again can result in growth and transformation. In the Hero's Journey mapped out by Campbell (2008), drawing on Jungian psychology and Campbell's own mythic studies, crisis is crucial to growth. As in the journey of the shaman, the Hero's Journey begins with a 'Call to Adventure'. Vogler (2007), who explores the Hero's Journey in relation to storytelling, describes the journey as more of an observation of the set of principles governing the conduct of life than an invention. And the inner and the outer problems facing the hero, what they lack or have lost, their tragic flaw(s), their pain which echoes universal pain, the obstacles they encounter are all essential components of the quest. In order to be transformed, it is imperative that they enter the 'inmost cave' and face the crisis, which Campbell calls the Ordeal.

So the idea, and indeed the experience, that crisis can lead to growth, and is sometimes an essential component, is widespread. Let's now look further at potential positive outcomes.

Positive outcomes

Drawing on their and others' research (eg Brunet *et al*, 2010), Calhoun and Tedeschi (2013) suggest there a number of elements commonly reported in growth experiences. These relate to five factors:

- personal strength;
- relating to others;
- new possibilities in life;
- appreciation of life;
- spirituality.

These factors fall into three conceptual categories, with changes in:

- sense of oneself;
- sense of relationship with others;
- philosophy.

Major life crisis can represent a metaphorical 'thin place' too where people become more aware of existential and/or spiritual issues, whether this be within a religious framework or not (Calhoun and Tedeschi, 2013).

Often post-crisis growth is in all of these areas, which has been my experience. When my mother and one of my sisters died within three months of one another, I was devastated. I truly no longer knew who I was and my confidence plummeted. Somewhere in the darkness, I was aware there was no going back, that if I could somehow work with all of this, I might emerge transformed. And after much reflection, licking of wounds, support from loved ones, and some very good coaching, my sense of self shifted. I came to savour and appreciate the preciousness of each day and to appreciate how strong I can be if I let myself be 'weak' first. I 'grew up' and became much closer to my surviving sister, who is 15 years older than me. I remember suggesting she no longer needed to mother me, that I could be there for her too, adult to adult, and our relationship is much more tender and honest, as a result of our shared losses.

Accelerated maturity was one of the benefits highlighted by Casserley and Megginson (2008). They discovered that for some leaders, burnout reveals its transformational learning potential, leading not only to increased maturity but also systemic growth; greater humility, causing individuals to confront their fallibilities and limitations; the development of wisdom; a greater sense of perspective; more grounded business decision making; and a sense of service to others, all of which benefits their organization.

The coaches I interviewed for this book all saw crisis as having the potential to transform 'for the better', with many reporting positive outcomes fitting into the three conceptual categories outlined above, attributing all sorts of positive outcomes for themselves and for their practice to having gone through crisis. These include:

- heightened emotional intelligence including wider emotional range, and increased self-awareness and self-compassion;
- becoming better at self-care, and improving energy management;
- becoming more focused on doing work aligned to personal values;

- normalizing experiences, helping coaching be non-judgemental, and at the same time appreciating the complexity of humankind more deeply.

Coaches' perspectives

Helen Leeder Barker, chapter contributor:

The most fundamental transitions are often accompanied or precipitated by a period of crisis. For example, Cook-Greuter (adult development expert) describes how during the shift from one state to another we often enter a period of crisis – an unraveling of some nature in our own lives – which allows our worldview to open up and shift to the next level (Cook-Greuter, 2013). It can feel very uncomfortable to let go of old 'scripts' and as such the growth process often creates a crisis in our own functioning.

Shortly after I had given birth to my second son, my older boy (then two years old) was involved in an accident at his nursery and broke his femur badly. He was placed in a full body cast for six weeks, totally immobilizing him. We were then living in Australia, far from family. Fairly soon after his cast was removed and he had learnt to walk again we moved to Singapore, where my husband started a new role necessitating him to be away from us five days a week. I needed to 'start again' to build my coaching practice in Asia. The transition to becoming a mother of two, followed by the crisis of the accident, followed by the move, represented a protracted transitional period in my life. Although at the time it felt 'copable with', in retrospect I see that I was far more impacted than I realized. What this has taught me is the importance of allowing clients time and space to be with their feelings and to process them fully in sessions.

Going through personal crisis and transition have provided opportunities to grow my self awareness, process my own story and have taken me to new levels of understanding. This in turn has deepened my ability to connect with my coachees and to work with them through the change process.

Prof. Ernesto Spinelli, existential psychotherapist and executive coach:

With existential thought, there's that sense of what we can call crisis always providing breakdown and breakthrough; it's the combination of both and the way the person holds that tension that's crucial. Quite often you look back at a crisis and you see what it destroyed and took away, and what it provided also. It's not unusual for people to say, well, actually, as awful as it was, there was something necessary, some value or possibilities that opened up.

For **Neil Scotton and Alister Scott,** also chapter contributors, crisis played a part in prompting them to develop the Legacy Thinking approach they set out in this book. Early in life, for example, Alister witnessed the extinction of a bird called the corncrake around his home in his native Northern Ireland. And in 1986 his plane was diverted because of the Chernobyl explosion, triggering deep reflection. Later, he played a key part in helping achieve a global 50-year agreement to protect Antarctica, giving him the experience of making a real difference on a complex challenge by aiming for something inspiring and by focusing the available resources in a mindful, effective way.

In 2002 Neil had a significant physical illness, a 'near death' type experience, then a 'mental meltdown that led to a deep evaluation of what to do with this precious thing called life'. He continues:

> Wanting to help people who were looking to profoundly change the way they work, exploring how work can make a meaningful contribution to life and the world, and answering the question, 'What are we going to tell the grandchildren?' were key drivers.

These and other experiences led them to a conversation in 2009 about 'What would we do if we weren't scared?' which generated the idea of supporting those leading big change on the most complex challenges that organizations face. This gave birth to their One Leadership Project and its aspiration to have one billion positive impacts by 2020. 'Not as a selfish goal, but in the spirit of "we can't solve the world's problems on our own but we can support the leadership of those who are trying to do something",' says Neil.

Executive coach **Kathryn Jackson** survived the massive earthquake in New Zealand in 2011. Writing in *Coaching at Work* (Jackson, 2013), she shared:

> I cannot pinpoint when we both realized this aftershock was going to be more severe than anything we had experienced before. Nor can I remember when I forgot my client was there and dived under the only desk in my office.
> I do remember being under that desk for what seemed like an eternity; clawing the carpet for stability as the floor rolled, bucked and flipped. All I could hear was crashing, cracking and a strange roaring sound. All I could feel were bits of roof falling onto the parts of me that weren't quite under the desk. All I could think was how cross I was to be in such a perilous situation – there was so much more I wanted to do with my life and this wasn't one of my plans.

She offered pro-bono coaching to help people rebuild their lives, and four years on, she reflects on her learning including the importance of self-care for the coach.

I was meeting with a couple of colleagues to review some training we'd designed to support a fairly significant outplacement programme. As we were talking, a very large aftershock shuddered through the café, knocking over drinks and frazzling nerves – after that I found it really hard to focus on what we were talking about even though the meeting continued for another hour or so. I decided right then that I needed to take some time to make sure I was OK before focusing on helping others. I think it's very important that as coaches we 'walk our talk' – and I mean really, truly. Although mine's a fairly extreme example, I don't really see it as being remarkably different from outplacement consultants dealing with multiple redundancies in a crisis industry, say. I worked with a local company laying off a significant number in an industry that was largely moving offshore to China. It was heartbreaking to work with so many people who'd spent their entire careers with one employer and who perceived themselves as 'discarded' with no place else to go. It was important for me at this time to work with my own coach so I could work through my own reflections and stay as objective as possible for my clients. Having said that, we're human too so it's impossible to stay completely objective, and I was often really tired and drained by the close of each day. Having an outlet was really important to me – for me I am lucky enough to have my own horse, who gives me the space and the quiet I need to reflect, refocus and recharge after assignments like this.

I've realized what's important in life – not to know whether the people you love are alive brings an incredible clarity to being. I've found myself no longer setting myself coaching targets, or maintaining the classic cycle of delivering work/seeking work/designing work. I've found myself more relaxed about opportunities and interestingly the work has never slowed. I've become much more conscious about the work I accept – ensuring that it's totally aligned with my own motivators – and I've focused even more on how I relax outside my work so that I can be even more present when I coach.

Paul Brown, chapter contributor, believes that going through crisis 'deepens one's own sense of the complexities of people's lives and the certainty that only love wins out in the end', and helps us 'acquire more capacity to cope – and especially to help us learn to remember that the sun also rises the next day'. He continues:

In 2001 I was expecting to marry someone who, one Saturday afternoon, ten days after 9/11, went off to a family event and was killed in a car smash on her way back. I learnt that the hospital/police/emergency services are so bounded by protocols of who they can and cannot speak to that they cannot react as human beings to a human situation: and it strengthened my own emerging sense at the time that the only way of behaving is from the heart and that the heart needs constant tuning in the practice of doing what is right, not what is ordered.

Margaret Chapman-Clarke, chapter contributor:

> Going through crisis increases your emotional range, it widens your capacity, it's like moving from novice to master. I think if you haven't got the range, it's hard to work with clients in crisis.

Professor Peter Hawkins, Professor of Leadership at Henley Business School, and Honorary President of the Association of Professional Executive Coaching and Supervision:

> I'm sure my own crises have deepened my ability to be empathic. I don't think we need to have had a heart attack to be able to empathize with someone who is coming to work with a heart condition... you can be too close or too distant (to something) to help someone. But if you've never had any crises, you've never been to that emotional edge of feeling, 'I'm not coping', and it does make it hard to fully empathize with being at the edge. That said, you can be too close to an event, you can over-project your own experience onto it and over-see the way you dealt with it as the way, slightly proselytizing.

Louise Buckle, Lead Coach, KPMG UK Advisory Practice, believes it can make a huge positive difference to coaching if coaches have been through crisis themselves. Helping to normalize experiences across humankind is one aspect:

> Absolutely, it's essential. I'm aware of how much richness I draw on from my own and my friends' and colleagues' experiences. It helps to be able to normalize things when people are sitting with really difficult emotional positions. It's all part of accepting our strengths and weaknesses and our humanity as flawed human beings. We are none of us perfect.

Chapter contributor Rachel Ellison's first child was born at just 26 weeks into the pregnancy, a crisis she feels delivered learning for her, and improved her coaching.

> Waves of pain during the night, then with 16 minutes' notice, a little boy was born; three pushes and a 1.5 minute labour. Two families were thrown into shock. And a third was created that day. The next three months were spent in intensive care, in three different hospitals, and many follow-up appointments and tests over the months and years that followed. In the end, we have a 'success' – a child who loves steam trains, who can sing nursery rhymes in four languages, who is appropriately attached and affectionate, creative, verbally communicative and generally treated as 'normal'.
>
> But ending up in neonatal intensive care was certainly a crisis for me. It was an intense marathon of vulnerability, uncertainty, complexity, ambiguity and fear of death. I needed resilience. I didn't have courage. The situation was happening to me, however much I wanted to stop it.

In professional terms, I was relatively new to coaching, self-employed and running a business. I'd graduated with a master's degree the week before, and won some significant work contracts through my reputation for high-challenge and deep-delve coaching. I might be about to lose a baby. I didn't want to lose my small, but meaningful business as well. My supervisor told me to carry on working; that surprised me. I thought I might not be safe to work – not present enough, too emotional, possibly setting a poor example of self-care or not honouring my supposed values. Throw in a double-dip economic crisis as well, and what you have is not the transition into motherhood that I had envisaged.

This is what I noticed:

- I used my coaching skills with the doctors and nurses on the ward. I wanted rapport and buy-in, for survival – I needed them to want to look after my baby during the night when I couldn't be there. It was all about establishing relationship and connection. Which, paradoxically, is what the medical teams wanted me to do with my child, with a child I could not hold for his first 11 days. A child who couldn't breathe for himself nor suckle.

- I self-coached. I had a choice of attitude about everything going on, although I didn't always make courageous choices. There were things I could control and things I could not.

- I learned a lot, including that I love learning. I learned more about my own resilience, which had been tested before – when I worked in a war zone. I sucked up medical information and in practical terms, nursed a baby in an incubator, arranged wires and monitors and electrode pads; I breastfed into a machine and syringed the milk down a nasogastric tube. I changed nappies the size of your palm. The baby weighed 1lb/835g.

- The result of that learning and the successful outcome of that journey includes a contribution to UNICEF's training of trauma nurses, a trustee position with child health charity Best Beginnings, and being invited by the hospital staff to be a parent visitor to current parents of children on the neonatal intensive care unit.

How working with clients in crisis and transition impacts the coach

There's a lack of research into how working with clients in crisis impacts coaches. However, there's arguably much we might learn from the literature on effects on therapists of working in challenging arenas, such as trauma.

'Negative' impact

Even therapists working specifically with clients who have gone through potentially highly severe trauma are not necessarily 'negatively' affected. Craig and Sprang (2010) report that fewer than 15 per cent of trauma therapists report significant compassion fatigue or burnout. Clinicians who are themselves trauma survivors may be at greater risk for negative work-related psychological reactions, particularly where there are unresolved issues that are raised by the client's experiences (Baird and Kracen, 2006). It seems that therapists early on in their career might be more at risk of negative reactions (eg Devilly, Wright and Varker, 2009). The severity, duration and intensity of traumatic experiences seem to increase the probability that a helping professional will develop negative psychological reactions from their work (Brady et al, 1999). Whilst it is unlikely that a coach will be exposed to the same frequency, severity and intensity of difficult experiences as a trauma therapist, these findings do offer food for thought for when to refer clients on to therapy (not only in the best interests of the client, but the coach's too), and when to step up supervision and any other supportive interventions such as self-coaching and therapy.

Positive impact

Again, research among clinicians on the potential positive side of supporting clients in crisis arguably has implications for coaching. Potential positive impact includes compassion satisfaction, which seems to be more prevalent than negative reactions to clinical work (Sprang, Clark and Whitt-Woosley, 2007), and vicarious posttraumatic growth (Arnold et al, 2005). The latter can take many forms, some of which we explore below:

- *Clouds and silver linings:* As helping professionals, we can come to appreciate the inevitable reality that life offers the possibility of great challenge and loss, but also that there are strengths that are discovered and developed in the struggle with those traumatic events (Calhoun and Tedeschi, 2013).

- *Appreciating each day more:* Those surviving crisis can come to appreciate each day more, as many of us will have experienced, and we can learn this lesson second-hand (Calhoun and Tedeschi, 2013).

- *Shaking one's beliefs:* The foundations of our own worldviews can be shaken without directly paying the high price in suffering (Calhoun and Tedeschi, 2013).

- *Stronger connection to others* and *compassion to self and others* (Calhoun and Tedeschi, 2013).

- *Inspiration:* They can be inspired by listening to clients' stories of their heroic struggles and survival (Calhoun and Tedeschi, 2013) and by the courage they display (Pearlman and Saakvitne, 1995).

John Blakey, a CEO executive coach and elite sports coach, takes inspiration from some of his clients, and sportspeople in general:

> Sportspeople put themselves on the line every day, risking crisis in every moment. An injury in a moment could end their career. I sometimes think, 'How do they do it?' I see acts of resilience that stun me compared to what I see in business. I wouldn't have the degree of resilience in the face of crisis I see in people like Team GB single sculler Alan Campbell, who I coached with lead coach Bill Barry. It's changed my mindset. It comes back to the point of never projecting yourself onto other people, never associating your benchmarks with theirs. [As coaches] we need to have an open mind about how people look at things and not jump to our own conclusions. It reinforces the need for the non-judgemental stance, and reinforces my optimism. I've seen surprising things and that influences my coaching. We should be ready to be surprised. What I've seen has helped me resist the temptation to cap other people's potential.

Sally-Anne Airey, an executive and life coach with an active practice developing mindfulness and compassion, was similarly inspired by one of her clients, John (see Case Study below). She came to appreciate the transformative power of embracing vulnerability, which, thanks to the work of social researcher Brené Brown, whose 2010 TEDxHouston talk on The Power of Vulnerability has attracted nearing 20 million views at the time of writing, is beginning to be seen more widely as a strength.

CASE STUDY   Embracing vulnerability

I first met John in 2010, as his coach on a HeartMath programme. His story intrigued me. A former Royal Air Force (RAF) fighter pilot, John's fast jet had been shot down during the First Gulf War in 1991; he'd been held captive and severely beaten by his captors, and a photo of his swollen, bruised face had been front-page news. In the years that followed his release from captivity, John didn't suffer the disabling effects of Post Traumatic Stress Disorder that can affect people who've faced a traumatic experience or sustained stress. On the contrary, he developed a highly successful leadership consultancy and global public speaking business. He set out to share his Prisoner of War (PoW) experience and his personal learning from it. When I met him, he was working on his own leadership model and writing a book on leadership.

During our four one-hour coaching sessions within the HeartMath programme, we focused on the present: what was happening in John's life right then, his goals and his barriers to achieving them. John's life seemed to have everything people might wish for: the memory of a happy, supportive childhood; a loving wife and successful son and daughter; a beautiful home, lots of friends, and a prosperous career. And yet what emerged from our coaching sessions was John's sense of personal failure, of not reaching his potential.

After the HeartMath programme, John engaged me as his coach and over the following three years we met periodically, either face-to-face or by phone. While I was naturally curious about his PoW experience, and his sense of personal failure, our conversations rarely broached these directly. John had already been the subject of considerable media and public thirst for him to put his experience into words. In the coaching, he wanted me to be his sounding board: to be able to bounce ideas, share his thinking, be heard and be challenged. By listening for clues and reflecting back what I heard, I hoped to support John to understand himself better and to feel happier and more fulfilled.

I learned that John's sense of failure came from the time when he inhabited a world in which people are paid to win, where failure isn't an option and being shot down is defined as failure. As John put it: 'a fighter pilot is not meant to be shot down! Period. It's in the job description. Could I have done more, been sharper, been a better pilot, to avoid it? Does being shot down prove that I wasn't sharp enough?' The speech that John has developed and delivered successfully to thousands of people around the world is actually about his sense of failure.

I also learned of the esteem in which John's fellow PoWs held him during captivity. One, a US Air Force colonel and considerably senior and more experienced than John, said to him after the war: 'You led us through the war. Your tone of voice and how you talked – as if you were talking over the garden fence – led us through.' John attributed this to an incident that occurred on the day that the shelling of their prison was so intense that the whole building collapsed. There was a strong smell of petrol and burning. John recalls thinking that he didn't want to die burning alive in a concrete box with a metal door. Two hours later the Iraqi guards were rampaging through the prison, smashing open the metal doors of the single occupancy cells, beating people, dragging them along the floor. Crouching at the back of his cell, waiting for the inevitable, John heard them approach his door, then stop, turn around and leave. The whole place suddenly went quiet and John sensed that they were expecting another raid.

John could hear the voice of another RAF pilot, the youngest PoW among them. He was petrified, screaming, shouting, and covered in excrement because the bombing had caused the sewage pipe to disgorge its contents into his cell. Listening to him, John felt lucky; he had at least done something in his life – married and had children – whereas the young pilot had joined the RAF straight from school. John felt that it was wrong that this young man should die. Kneeling low into the small gap at the bottom of the cell door, John talked and listened to him all night. With the help of the US colonel, John tried to help him believe that they would survive this experience.

It wasn't that John didn't feel fear – far from it. His emotional memory of captivity is dominated by a feeling of trepidation. But, from day one in his cell, John made a decision to manage his own mental and emotional wellbeing. He knew he couldn't remove his fear, but he could decide who he wanted to be at the end – whether that be in dying or in regaining his freedom. John remembers monitoring himself; jumping from thoughts to feelings, consciously using the power of his thinking to keep his feelings under control. In the disorientating environment of his very cold, concrete cell, with its small window and solid metal door, he tried to keep a sense of routine. He monitored his good and bad days and found that most of his days were 'OK'. He got to understand how he felt, how to control it and how to align his life with his circumstances, to create a sense of normality that felt OK to him.

My conversations with John have revealed to me the power of embracing our own vulnerability. My feeling is that John's success as a leader, consultant, coach and speaker flows from his courage to embrace his vulnerability. I believe that this enables him to forge his connection with others and that there's much for us to learn from this as coaches.

Crisis and transition in organizations

One organization that has faced its share of challenges is the Co-operative Banking Group. At the time of writing, the Group was going through a major transition, emerging from a crisis that saw it report losses of £2.5 billion in 2013, the worst results its 150-year history. By September 2014, it had returned to profit in the first half of the year, reporting half-year profits of £12 million, and had set in motion a three-year turnaround plan. Restorative actions included relaunching its ethical policy in January 2015 to restore confidence, for example pledging to cease trading with organizations involved in irresponsible gambling and payday loans.

So what was it like coaching within a transforming organization? At the end of 2014, Angela Ryrie left her role as Coaching and Management Development Manager (Organizational Effectiveness team) after more than 11 years at the organization. We spoke just before she left to set up learning and development consultancy Angela Ryrie Consulting. Her experience of coaching confirms that in times of crisis and transformation, 'coaching can support and galvanize people' but that coaches need to be more agile, adaptable and flexible than in other times: 'I noticed as a coach, I needed to flex around the edges even more than normal. It's been more important to be flexible. I've been having more frequent shorter conversations rather than in-depth conversations because people are finding it more difficult to free up time.'

She noticed that she was doing more work in the wellbeing space, drawing on mindfulness to get clients 'into a space where they are sharp and alert to go back into the storm. On the positive side, it gets you in the zone in the coaching so you're genuinely present.'

She had to pay more attention to managing her own energy and to freeing up more time before and after sessions, in addition to using more supervision:

> I'm having to pay closer attention to the discipline of what I'm having to do to manage myself, knowing the pressure (my clients) are under. I've changed my approach and my diary to allow myself to get into 'the zone' beforehand and looking at what I do afterwards. I know all good coaches do this anyway but it's accentuated (in this environment). I'm using my supervision more and my own reflective practice more, noticing what I'm noticing and taking that to supervision; I think that's important otherwise you can't do good work. There are marked differences (between how I used to coach and now) – I am definitely using mindfulness more, and drawing on NLP to help people think through their beliefs and helping to build resourcefulness. It's almost as if I am having to do the work to get them to a place of balance so we can then do the work on the issue, enabling leaders more. Coaching needs to step up and be really clean and slick, and almost model that for clients.

Although it has been challenging, it has been worthwhile: 'I genuinely think if I hadn't experienced coaching during this time, I wouldn't have picked up such rich learning.'

Many organizations turn to coaching in challenging times, including to help them shift their culture and to support internal clients who are struggling. In the former News International, now known as News UK, coaching is helping to transform its culture after the telephone hacking and police bribery scandals that rocked the organization.

CASE STUDY   Resurrection after crisis at News UK

'Coaching is part of the resurrection of the company,' said Jon Moorhead, night editor on News UK's *Sun* newspaper in 2014, about the impact of an internal coaching initiative launched by head of talent and development, James Hutton, in October 2012.

The internal coaching scheme is one of a string of initiatives shifting the culture towards one that is more transparent, and more supportive of learning and reflection. By 2014, the scheme was already delivering a host of benefits: supporting the organization's business strategy and culture change; helping to break down silos; supporting employees to take more time to think things through and to think more long-term; and helping the bottom line too.

James worked with i-coach academy to design and implement the internal coaching scheme. The organization is also training internal coach supervisors, and has a small preferred supplier pool of external coaches.

One major breakthrough was getting editorial staff on board, including the likes of Moorhead, an internal coach and one of the organization's chief coaching champions.

On the potential business impact of coaching, Moorhead says: 'I think increasing awareness of all aspects of yourself has got to help the business, it has to. [Journalists typically] come in and do a hard day's work and go and socialize and don't really think about it. It's looked down upon to be introspective, but I think times have changed. I'm determined to start spreading the word.

'There's a big battle persuading staff that the culture has changed. There are the old fears and doubts, and the expectations about the "Evil Empire". Certainly, under the previous administration, this type of stuff [coaching] would have been dismissed, but now it's really encouraged. If you say you're training to be a coach, the boss doesn't say, "That's no good, you need to be producing papers," he says "Brilliant."

'We're becoming a much more modern organization. Many vestiges of the old company already no longer exist, but now they're expunged certainly... What happened here was absolutely devastating and there are still a lot of scars... but this sort of area will help.'

Feedback gathered from coaches and coach-mentors (supervisors) has suggested that the coaching offers a 'grounding/reflection space to think clearly and deal with situations better'; aids culture change; helps to build self-coaching; offers a 'cathartic space for fast-paced difficult environment'; creates 'a culture of thinking things through'; and offers an 'outlet to those trying to build their career and confidence in talking about how to deal with work situations that may be getting them down and that they cannot talk about to their line manager'. Other comments included that coaching provides 'a safe environment to download and digest. We work in a manic and high-pressured environment, which doesn't lend itself to taking time out to think about what you're doing. It also encouraged me to look at alternative ways of approaching situations and having the confidence to believe in myself.'

(A version of this case study appeared in Hall, 2014)

Victim of the crisis

In another example, in a struggling financial organization, the wider challenges rocking the business were taking their toll on the long-established coaching culture too.

The HR director I spoke to, a trained coach, was still coaching clients internally but was saddened by the demise of the once-flourishing coaching culture. This leader says:

> It's been an interesting journey, tinged with sadness that coaching's not being used as much now as it could be. It's gone from having quite a big focus – internal coaches from HR have been trained up as coaches, and lots of focus on external coaches and line managers playing a big part in coaching. It's a bit of a pity. The foot on the gas has lessened in terms of the focus on coaching, which seems like a bit of a missed opportunity at a time when the coaching could be helping more people.

He describes how his internal clients were often extremely stressed, only having time for very short sessions, and that it was easy to get caught in the idea that this was the only way to do the coaching. 'Sometimes, it's important for me to point out that the client is talking really fast and has rushed into the session.'

The senior management team was unsurprisingly focused on short-term survival and on strategies that might turn the business around, but this leader hoped that in the longer term, a coaching culture might flourish once again.

Canaries

Sometimes individuals can be referred or present with challenges deemed to be their own. Yet, they may be showing up what's going on elsewhere. Dr Anton Obholzer, a psychiatrist and executive coach whose special interests are leadership and the management of change at times of stress and turbulence, likens them to the canaries that signalled the presence of toxic gases in the mining pits. He explains that the canary is the team member with the greatest valency – Bion's (2013) valency theory included the idea that someone becomes a scapegoat for a group so its members can direct aggression to that person to shield them from the truth about what is going on in the group. Dr Obholzer advises coaches to feed back issues as high up the chain as possible, helping the client to not become a pit canary, and also to 'read the subtitles'. He says:

> My way of looking at things is to listen to what the reality of the client brings is, treat it with respect but also look at what else is going on. It's a bit like going to see a movie but also reading the subtitles. So the other question is, what is the client *not* telling you about? If the coach doesn't acknowledge there are subtitles, they'll never read them. [Watch out for] slips of the tongue and so on.

In addition to watching out for canaries, what else can we do to help us as coaches, and our clients, be more resourceful in times of crisis? Below are some pointers.

What helps the coach to remain resourceful, to resource the client and to foster posttraumatic growth (PTG)?

- 'Have a broad and deep knowledge' of clients' 'assumptive worlds', including their personal worldviews and the values and assumptions of the religious, spiritual and philosophical traditions they come from (Calhoun and Tedeschi, 2013). The more we know about how clients would answer existential questions about mortality and the meaning of life, the more effective we will be in enhancing the possibility of PTG.

- Think about when and why crisis might serve people, 'listen seriously, professionally and respectfully to the client's picture of the crisis, but also in your mind, say, "Ho, hum, what else is going on?"' (Dr Anton Obholzer)

- Ensure you have time and space to reflect, refocus and recharge, paying even more attention to self-care than usual. (Kathryn Jackson)

- Keep an open mind, and be comfortable with ambiguity and uncertainty. 'You need to go in as (psychoanalyst Wilfred) Bion says, free of memory and desire, with as much of an open state of mind is possible.' (Dr Anton Obholzer)

- Consider that 'when things fall apart, primitive dynamics come in' and park your judgement. (Dr Anton Obholzer)

- Read the subtitles and watch out for the canaries. (Dr Anton Obholzer)

- Realize what is important in life.

- Get a good supervisor.

- Self-coach.

- Remember it's not just the coach's 'job' but a joint job and don't feel you need to offer an answer. 'Coaching is not about coming up with an answer but a widening of the choices that are open, because people can be astute but get tunnel vision... An astute colleague of mine says the moment you think you have the answers, stop; you're in a cul-de-sac and the more people you tell the answers to, the more people join you in a cul-de-sac, rather than learning to learn.' (Dr Anton Obholzer)

- Be careful you're not in the no man's land between therapy and coaching (and refer on where necessary). (Dr Anton Obholzer)

- Ensure you do 'really good processing' (Bridget Farrands) and consciously hold boundaries around your own 'stuff.' (Rachel Ellison)

- 'Don't enter into the territory.' Hear the statements of crisis without entering into the territory. How? One critical condition is to remind myself, 'I don't know what the crisis is'. If I can hold onto that curiosity and openness about what is being presented, still being attentive and sympathetic, I suspect it will serve the client better because I won't be overwhelmed by the need to resolve it or get out of the critical state that feels really disturbing.' (Prof Ernesto Spinelli)

- Monitor whether it's about what you or the client needs – 'I've noticed that at times I've been almost disappointed at not being able to play that role of being there for someone; that can be how we get our kicks. It's learning to catch yourself and keep challenging yourself – is it about what *you* need?' (John Blakey)

- Have interests outside work – friends, hobbies, exercise, deep conversations and variety of clients. (Rachel Ellison)

- Stay fully present. (Rachel Ellison; Calhoun and Tedeschi, 2013)

- Draw on strategies such as mindfulness.

- Be open to learning: 'Maybe you're sent the client you needed to enable you to do the work on yourself you need to do?' (Rachel Ellison)

Conclusion

In highlighting the potential for growth within challenging times, I by no means wish to belittle potential risks and difficulties, nor imply that as coaches we should put a positive spin on everything. In her excellent book, *Smile or Die*, Ehrenreich (2010) quite rightly balked at how others also diagnosed with cancer and health professionals saw her anger about having the disease as unhealthy and dangerous. Some people – my father, for example, who after the deaths of my mother and sister slid into a crisis from which he failed to emerge, attempting suicide and dying on a psychiatric ward – don't make it out the other side – in this life, at least. Research such as that on PTG acknowledges that risks associated with exposure to highly stressful events include psychological problems, possibly post-traumatic stress disorder (eg Calhoun and Tedeschi, 2013) and physical illness (eg Spitzer *et al*, 2009). Yet, say Calhoun and Tedeschi, the emergence of psychiatric disorders appears to be the exception, rather than the rule. This doesn't mean as coaches we shouldn't be wary, and mindful of boundaries, referring on where appropriate. Kinder and Buon's chapter (Chapter 9) explores boundaries in mental health in the workplace. However, it can be highly fruitful for both client and coach to be open to crisis as a potential, and perhaps even necessary, spark for transformation, and for the coach to have techniques at hand to help clients face into their ordeals, helping them become heroes in their own journeys, whatever heroism means for them (including not being traditionally heroic). In the following chapters, we explore more techniques and approaches for doing this.

References

Arnold, D et al (2005) Vicarious posttraumatic growth in psychotherapy, *Journal of Humanistic Psychology*, **45** (2), pp 239–63

Baird, K and Kracen, A C (2006) Vicarious traumatisation and secondary traumatic stress: A research synthesis, *Counselling Psychology Quarterly*, **19**, pp 181–88

Bion, W R (2013) *Experiences in Groups and Other Papers*, Routledge, London

Brady, J L et al (1999) Vicarious traumatization, spirituality, and the treatment of sexual abuse survivors: A national survey of women psychotherapists, *Professional Psychology: Research and Practice*, **30** (4), p 386

Brunet, J et al (2010) The Posttraumatic Growth Inventory: An examination of the factor structure and invariance among breast cancer survivors, *Psycho-Oncology*, **19**, pp 830–38

Calhoun, L G and Tedeschi, R G (1998) *Facilitating post traumatic growth: A clinician's guide*, Lawrence Erlbaum Associates, Mahwah, NJ

Calhoun, L G and Tedeschi, R G (2006) (eds) *Handbook of Posttraumatic Growth: Research and practice*, Lawrence Erlbaum Associates: Mahwah, NJ

Campbell, J (2008) *The Hero with a Thousand Faces* (3rd edn), New World Library, CA

Casserley, T and Megginson, D (2008) Feel the burn, *Coaching at work*, **3** (4)

Cook-Greuter, S (2013) *Nine Levels of Increasing Embrace in Ego Development: A full-spectrum theory of vertical growth and meaning making* [online] http://www.cook-greuter.com/Cook-Greuter%209%20levels%20paper%20new%20 1.1%2714%2097p%5b1%5d.pdf [accessed 24 June 2015]

Craig, C D and Sprang, G (2010) Compassion satisfaction, compassion fatigue, and burnout in a national sample of trauma treatment therapists, *Anxiety, Stress, & Coping*, **23** (3), pp 319–39

Devilly, G J, Wright, R and Varker, T (2009) Vicarious trauma, secondary traumatic stress or simply burnout? Effect of trauma therapy on mental health professionals, *Australasian Psychiatry*, **43** (4), pp 373–85

Ehrenreich, B (2010) *Smile or Die: How positive thinking fooled America and the world*, Granta books, London

Frankl, V E (1959) *Man's Search for Meaning*, Beacon Press, Boston

Gilbert, P and Choden (2013) *Mindful Compassion: Using the power of mindfulness and compassion to transform our lives*, Hachette UK, London

Hall, L (2014) Good news, *Coaching at Work*, **9** (2)

Jackson, K (2013) Shock tactics, *Coaching at Work*, **9** (1)

Pearlman, L A and Saakvitne, K W (1995) *Trauma and the Therapist: Countertransference and vicarious traumatization in psychotherapy with incest survivors*, WW Norton & Co, New York

Spitzer, *et al* (2009) Trauma, posttraumatic stress disorder and physical illness: Findings from the general population, *Psychosomatic Medicine*, **71**, 1012–17 *(3.5)*

Sprang, G, Clark, J J and Whitt-Woosley, A (2007) Compassion fatigue, compassion satisfaction, and burnout: Factors impacting a professional's quality of life, *Journal of Loss and Trauma*, **12** (3), pp 259–80

Tedeschi, R G and Calhoun, L G (2004) *Helping Bereaved Parents: A clinician's guide*, Brunner-Routledge, New York

Vogler, C (2007) *The Writer's journey*, Michael Wiese Productions, CA

Walsh (1994) The making of a shaman: Calling, training, and culmination, *Journal of Humanistic Psychology*, 3 (34), pp 7–30

Yalom, I (1980) *Existential Psychotherapy*, Basic Books, New York

Coaching for compassionate resilience through creative methods:
the case for a 'turn to autoethnography'

MARGARET CHAPMAN-CLARKE

05

> *My poetry is...*
> *The power to engage*
> *In a process of connecting and maybe believing*
> *What could be possible*
> *Or not...?*
> *Maybe a journey*
> *Of knowing*
> *Of engaging*
> *Of breathing*
> *To find... what?*
> *For me.*
> *And it started*
> *With a sound*
> *In my throat*

('FIONA', ADVANCED COACHING PRACTITIONER,
IN CHAPMAN-CLARKE, FORTHCOMING)

By beginning with a poem I alert you to the different approach that I take in this chapter on coaching in times of crisis and transition, introducing the concept of compassionate resilience and illustrating the power of creative methods. As a coaching psychologist, I want to acknowledge and 'speak' to your need, which resonates with my own, for tools to help you to help your clients survive and thrive in a VUCA (volatile, uncertain, complex and ambiguous) world. Indeed this was probably your motivation for picking up this book. However, at the same time I also want to 'speak' to the scientific or evidence-based aspect of coaching practice and inspire in you new ways of thinking about our work. In doing this I'm eager to highlight a subtle yet important shift that's taking place in coaching research. That shift is the coming together of the methods from within arts research with those of the social sciences; the domain where coaching research and practice naturally find a home (Leavy, 2009; Pitsis, 2014). So often in the coaching field we talk of our work as being both an art and a science, yet the 'tools' that we often are presented with to master our craft are focused on outputs. The focus is on the tools themselves rather than on the processes by which the tools are chosen, created and used by the practitioner, perpetuating the split between theory and practice. This chapter reflects a desire to move beyond this split and beyond mastery of techniques.

This chapter signals a 'turn to autoethnography' (AE), which calls for an inclusion of the self and our personal experiences in practising and writing about coaching. It's an approach which, whilst absent in our field, is one that is nonetheless gaining in momentum, and in sports coaching is widely embraced (for a review see Sparkes and Smith, 2014).

The idea of a 'split' is one explored in this book by peers de Haan and Kasozi (Chapter 8) who talk of how leaders' experiences are essentially about separation rather than integration; an internal 'split'. In terms of coaching to build a client's compassionate resilience, I've found that my job as a coach is in providing a conversational space in which to help them heal this split. To identify and focus on their strengths and their uniqueness as individuals; to discover that what they 'do' is not their whole 'being in the world' and to speak 'their truth' in creative ways. In order to transition from crisis through to transformation, helping clients heal deep existential ruptures is figural in my coaching 'work'; helping them to find a new meaning and purpose and to 're-story' their lives by creating a new truth, integrating this into what Joseph (2012) calls an ongoing narrative.

By making explicit the philosophy that underpins my worldview and practice as a coach, I would be inauthentic if I didn't honour this same desire for integration in the approach and tone that I adopt in this chapter. It is inspired by autoethnographic writing, or self-narrative (Sparkes and Smith, 2014). Liz invited contributors to bring themselves into this state-of-the-art book, to speak to the current zeitgeist.

This call to include our own experiences resonates with my research exploring through poetic inquiry the experience of mindfulness training on advanced coaching practitioners. Here, through mindfulness practices and creative writing, advanced coaching practitioners find a way of connecting their 'doing' as coaches, with their 'way of being'. This speaks to the notion of healing the split, which my findings suggest is integration between cognitive and embodied ways of 'knowing' (Chapman-Clarke, forthcoming). AE writing is about healing a split as it connects the personal with the cultural; the internal and external. So it's in this spirit that I've approached this endeavour, not only responding to Liz's request to write mindfully, but taking joy in the opportunity to revisit trends that I predicted would impact on our practice as 'EQ coaches' set out in *The Emotional Intelligence Pocketbook* (Chapman, 2011). These three trends are:

- neuroscience, *which is the evidence base*;

- mindfulness practice, *which is the application of neuroscience*; and

- resilience, *which is the outcome*, that is, mindful, emotionally intelligent and self-compassionate practitioners.

What is autoethnography and why is it important in coaching?

Writing that speaks to the call for an 'autoethnographic (AE) turn in coaching' (Chapman-Clarke, forthcoming; Gearity, 2014; Harrington, 2012) requires the coach to make explicit their voice. In this context, that means to be explicitly self-reflexive and to acknowledge that their authorial voice and practice are shaped by their own autobiography and experience, and to make that transparent; to put the 'I' into the story. This represents a radical stance in coaching research and practice. And in terms of training coaches it challenges one of the 'sacred tenets' of being a coach, such as that expressed (for example) in Paice (2012) who asserts that in coaching, 'it is not about the coach'. As a gestalt-informed coaching practitioner and researcher, I challenge this assertion. For me the coach is very much a part of the co-created narrative; we do bring ourselves, our experiences, our insights and all that we have experienced in our lives (including crises and transitions) into the process. As two eminent observers in our field who have inspired my work, Sir John Whitmore and Peter Bluckert, have asserted, self-awareness is the bedrock of all coaching practice. For me the 'turn to AE' in coaching practice and research takes the development of our awareness as coaches to a whole new level, one with the potential to take our research and practice, our art and science, forward and beyond mastery.

So what am I talking about when I refer to AE? Put simply it's an emerging research genre, methodology and method that is making its presence felt in the field of research in organizational psychology generally (Boyle and Parry, 2007) and in coaching specifically (Chapman, 2014; Chapman-Clarke, forthcoming; Gearity, 2014; Harrington, 2012; Kempster and Stewart, 2010). It's beyond the scope of this chapter to delve deep into the history and background of AE and the criticisms levelled at an emerging approach (for a review see Chapman-Clarke, forthcoming). However it is relevant to note here that it has a set of underlying ethics and values, a philosophy that 'speaks' to a practice that puts at its heart dialogue and relationship. Radical as it might be, AE offers the potential for a new form of coaching as is suggested by Kempster and Iszatt-White (2012) arising from their work coaching leaders.

Our role in supporting clients in crisis and through transitions succeeds in and through relationship and dialogue. AE centres on dialogue and the notions of story and truth; through a co-constructed narrative we help clients to 're-story' their lives (Kempster and Iszatt-White, 2012). As Joan Didion observes, 'we tell stories in order to live' (cited in Adams *et al*, 2014). As coaches we are subject to the same human 'givens' as those of our clients. Here is an example of how the loss of a coaching psychologist's father is captured in his most recent book:

> The writing journey was punctuated with the loss of my father, who passed away in Hong Kong on 9 May 2012... I was particularly touched by the support I received... I feel blessed. There is a Chinese saying that it is easy to add icing on the cake, but it is difficult to give support to someone in destitution.

He continues:

> My father's middle and first names are Kai Sin; they mean 'showing' and 'kindness'. These words resonate with the spirit of coaching... I shall hold onto this spirit, keep it dearly in my heart and attempt to manifest unconditional kindness in everything I do.
>
> (Dr Ho Law, 2013)

It is hard not to be impacted by the power of these words and be touched by the experience behind the authorial voice. Ho is one of the founders of coaching psychology in the United Kingdom and here I'm impacted by his expression of his emotion and I get a very real sense of how his loss influences and shapes his narrative, his way of being as a coach. I also get a glimpse of the transitional journey he's on and the sense he's making of his loss. And from there, the way in which his biography offers potential insights that feed into his writing and practice. What I feel Ho does is to make explicit the universality of pain and suffering that affects us all, coaches as well as clients. It connects us at a deeper level.

As a coaching psychologist practising over some 15 years, for me, writing ourselves into the work about which we talk represents an approach that is authentic, honest and centred on relational values and ethics. Because of these values AE has the potential, as Kempster and Iszatt-White (2012) argue, to be a form of coaching itself. In summary then, AE is comprised of three elements:

Auto – 'Self': In our discourse me as coach and all that I bring, my own biography.

ethno – 'Culture and human interaction': The context in which I practise and in relationships.

graphy – The process and product of doing some activity, here a coaching conversation to build compassionate resilience.

AE then is an approach to coaching research and is beginning to shape practice that puts at the heart the coach in relationship, in the context of which they are a part. As I noted earlier, the coach's biography is not separate from, but shapes, their narrative and their practice, so coaching is a co-created experience, which is both/and the coach and the client.

With all this in mind, my intentions in calling for a turn to AE in the context of this chapter are to:

- write autoethnographically, sharing ideas and ways of working that have shaped my work with clients;

- reflect theoretically about the concept of resilience and, from a vast literature, highlight what 'speaks' to me;

- discuss contemporary approaches to understanding crises as opportunities for transformation and growth – and to introduce the notion of compassionate resilience (CR) – and offer you 10 steps to build your CR as a coach;

- share stories about how creative approaches can reveal strengths, which are the bedrock in coaching, to build resilience – at the centre of which is enabling self-compassion;

- be authentic to the 'AE' turn; and in so doing:
- embrace a theme in the current coaching zeitgeist which is healing the split – an integration between cognitive and embodied 'ways of knowing' (our doing and being).

The inspiration behind the 'call for an AE turn' in coaching

> It is our capacity for reflexivity, the awareness of being aware, that allows us to represent and re-present the products of our imagination in a variety of ways. I would even go as far as to say we have a destiny to be creative. Unfortunately we have a tendency to label our creative endeavours as hobbies and struggle to keep the serious world of work... in an objective style.
>
> (Muncey, 2010)

The insights I share here are derived from my practice as a coaching psychologist working with medical students, junior doctors and specialist registrars employed by the United Kingdom's National Health Service (NHS) and referred to colloquially as 'doctors in difficulty'. The training that they undergo is long and intense. Trainees have to successfully graduate from medical school, qualify as doctors, study and practise and be assessed for a further two years and then, if they choose to specialize, to become consultants. Many also continue to research and even complete further master's and doctoral-level qualifications. They're continuously assessed, reassessed and have to pass annual competence reviews, in total anything from a further seven to ten years. It's a challenging and, for some, an arduous journey. This involves a constant 'merry-go-round' of transitions and placements in different settings, some nourishing and some depleting. Understandably these constant changes and transitions may at some point along the trajectory result in crises.

The stories that have been shared in the conversational space have been both inspiring and harrowing. The clients with whom I've worked are often exposed to the unfairness and fragility of life, and finality of death. The universals of pain and suffering, ever present, moment to moment. The media and television documentaries have thoroughly explored the toll this takes on practitioners. They operate in an intensively VUCA environment, a rapidly changing landscape in which there's increasing scarcity of resources and which is subject to the prevailing winds of government ideology. I've discovered just how immense the pressures are upon these trainees. I hear how these early careerists, usually in their late 20s/early 30s, balance the demands of living and working in a culture that's always responding to ever-increasing calls to raise levels of patient safety and quality of care – and to deliver all of this in a compassionate way. Danny's story brings all this to life.

CASE STUDY 'Danny'

I recall poignantly how 'Danny,' an Emergency Care Registrar, felt guilty for simply wanting to use the coaching space to explore his experiences of three deaths in a single nightshift. The guilt arose because his need was to use the conversational space to reflect upon the impact of what he'd experienced. Although not explicitly expressed, what he needed was an existential coaching conversation to explore his beliefs around loss. This is what I offered. Through our exploration it was revealed how witnessing the deaths had touched upon his mortality and bought into his awareness his attitudes towards death. The losses evoked questions about his competence and sense of responsibility, and concern that he might have been able to do something different. It was, after all, his metier, his purpose, to save lives.

Even now as I bring him to mind, I experience his warmth, his deep empathy and his passionate desire to work as doctor in emergency medicine. He discovered through our conversation what his particular strengths were, which included a love of learning, dancing, his humour and above all, compassion.

My job here was to offer him a space to meet as one human being to another and so enable him to become in touch with what was clearly his vocation; to bring into awareness the qualities and strengths that he didn't know he possessed and to extend the compassion he so evidently held for others to himself – to develop compassionate resilience. Not for him to do anything different, not to correct perceived deficiencies, but to find his voice and incorporate his experiences into an ongoing self-narrative, a new way of being with his experience and work as a trainee emergency care specialist.

Research suggests that extending the kind of compassion that 'Danny' gave to his patients, to oneself, in the form of CR, is a challenge. However, as Gustin and Wagner (2012) assert, compassionate care begins with compassion for the practitioner's self. And self-compassion is, as many commentators assert, central to achieving happiness and psychological wellbeing and facilitates resilience (Neff and Costigan, 2014) (see also Liz's Chapter 10 in this book).

Such an approach to coaching for resilience is non-directive and non-goal-oriented, and demands the capacity to 'stay with' the client and to enable them to express potentially uncomfortable emotions. It goes beyond the simple mastery of coaching techniques.

Beyond mastery: creative methods in coaching for resilience

Discovering poetry is one way that I've found for expressing difficult emotions in times of crisis, particularly when I've not been feeling heard. The pain of not having my voice is one that I've experienced at a number of critical junctures in my life. The first time was in failing the 11-plus examination in 1972; the second in defending my PhD viva in 2004; and the third, in 2008, is captured in the following poem which I wrote during a five-day conference in Esalen, California (the 'home' of gestalt), where although we had a shared language, I hardly uttered a word in the five days – and no one noticed:

The Silent Voice

It is easy to overlook the silent
voice and deny its existence...

Perhaps through
resistance, discomfort... or fear

Yet... the silence is itself a voice and needs to be
honoured ...

And to be supported if it is to
find expression
... and for the truth to be told...

(Gestalt Study Conference, Esalen, San Francisco, California,
24 October 2008, from Chapman, 2014 and Chapman-Clarke, 2015)

The poem is not designed to emulate the great poets, and what poetry is is hotly contested (for a discussion see Chapman-Clarke, forthcoming). However, the experience of not being heard, captured through poetic representation, is one that's indicative of AE writing and is fast gaining acceptance in coaching research (Chapman-Clarke, 2015; Pitsis, 2014; Sparkes and Smith, 2014). It's my own embodied 'knowing', my 'felt sense' of not being heard, that's so profoundly captured in *The Silent Voice*. As I reread this now I realize, like Ho's expression of the loss of his father, it's integral to my ongoing journey as a coach.

As a gestalt psychologist I work with clients phenomenologically, 'bracketing off' (setting aside) the issues (labels) for which clients are referred or self-refer – in 'Danny's' case, low self-esteem; suffering stress and anxiety resulting in perceived poor performance. I aim simply to be present; to hear his story, accept who he is and enable him to integrate her experience into a re-storied narrative. Finding his truth was achieved through a combination of an existential coaching conversation and, in between our sessions, his carrying out a series of collaboratively agreed activities. These included a Positive Personal Qualities (PPQ) Survey (see Figure 5.1) in which he asked people he trusted to write down three words that they saw as his qualities that they admired. He also visited Martin Seligman's 'authentic happiness' website (see useful resources at the end of this chapter) and completed the 'VIA Survey of Character Strengths'. Together in session we drew on the outputs from these activities and worked on creating a unique resilience 'toolkit'. This included ways of being kinder to himself, extending the compassion he had for others to himself.

FIGURE 5.1 Positive personal qualities survey

Ask people who are significant in your life (eg family members, friends, workplace colleagues etc to describe you positively in three words, for example, Catherine: 'funny, caring, loyal'			
Who (name...) Says about me	Three words		

This template can be useful for working with your client to build a strengths-based resilience toolkit. Simply help them to identify three people whom they feel comfortable to approach. Having done that for them to ask each person to describe them in just three words.

Healing the split: art and science

The work with clinical trainees and specialist registrars, as in the case of 'Danny', is time and again centred on helping them to overcome intense feelings of guilt at indulging in what they see as, and as the words of Muncey suggest, activities that aren't seen as serious or legitimate in an environment characterized by life and death. In 'Danny's' case his love of dancing was nourishing him physically and socially yet might be seen as frivolous. Medicine is a serious business, yet often facilitating compassionate resilience in this client population is about helping them rebalance and integrate all aspects of themselves. It's about coming to acceptance of the science-based practitioner ('doing self') with their creativity as a human ('being self') to heal the split (de Haan and Kosozi, Chapter 8). As one paediatric registrar, 'Jo', said about the outcomes from the coaching, this was about being 'OK about having "me" time'. So often it is about self-compassion, which as Neff and Costigan (2014) observe, builds resilience by loosening the grip of negative emotions and reduces self-criticism, predictors of anxiety and depression.

To summarize so far in this chapter, I've drawn on my experience as a coach and of experiencing crises, times in my life when I have not been heard and felt powerless. I've suggested that coaching for CR is a process of discovery and space for creativity. The case of 'Danny' illustrates how to go beyond mastery of techniques, to trust a process centred on a co-created dialogue, one which is holistic and enables individuals to access aspects of their often creative selves, which are dismissed as indulgent, or even a misuse of their time.

In coaching conversations I've helped clients develop CR by uncovering and coming to accept hidden talents such as art, dancing, love of playing music, or baking; what is nourishing, such as simply making and spending time with friends and enjoying nature. 'Anya', a junior doctor planning on specializing as a General Practitioner (GP) painted a river and hills, for example, while 'Jo' the paediatric registrar I mentioned earlier, baked a 'cake of joy'.

FIGURE 5.2   Creative outputs from coaching 'Anya' and 'Jo'

| Photograph 1: Painted by 'Anya', a Foundation Year 2 Doctor – planning to be a GP | Photograph 2: Cake of Joy baked by 'Jo', a Specialist Paediatric Trainee Year 2 |

For 'Jo', the cake captured her experience of coaching and the benefits she took away. Sadly I was unable to actually have a slice! 'Anya' had been experiencing 'a lack of confidence'. In just six sessions she rediscovered her love of painting, which she had sadly neglected as a result of the stressors of continual assessments and examinations. The river in her painting became a metaphor which she used as an anchor at any time she became anxious. For example, a particularly anxiety-provoking task for her was asking people in each placement to complete questionnaires that are essential to the 360-degree (multi-source) feedback process as they provide the information needed to evidence her developing competence.

The importance of the painting became central to 'Anya's' feeling of wellbeing. I recall in one of our sessions introducing her to the Greek philosopher Heraclitus, and inviting her to do a search and find out why what he had to say might be useful to her. In the following session she'd reflected on his words and particularly the idea that 'You could not step twice into the same river; for other waters are ever flowing on to you.' This had a very profound effect, providing her with a language that was important in strengthening her resilience. She decided that Heraclitus was 'a very wise man'. Such was the realization of the importance of her painting to her wellbeing, and the inspirational words of Heraclitus, that 'Anya' incorporated these into her resilience toolkit. In realizing just how much engaging in her art was a source of nourishment to balance the stressors of being a trainee, she was able to accept her creative self and integrate this into her way of being, into a re-storied self-narrative. What I found particularly touching in working with her was her telling me that the picture that she had created was going to be placed on the wall of her first office as a qualified GP, to remind her that, when faced with crises, she couldn't step twice into the same river.

The reason I include the stories of 'Danny' and his dancing, 'Anya' and her painting, and 'Jo' and her baking is that Muncey (2010) describes such snapshots and metaphors as the way in which we create autoethnographies, or in the context of this book, narratives about ways in which we work with our clients to enable them to journey through crises and transition, to re-story their sense of self, their relationships with the world, to recreate their autoethnography. However, to work in this way involves being courageous and taking a risk (Whitaker, 2009) – and moving beyond mastery of techniques.

Now let's look at some of the lessons from neuroscience for coaching for CR.

Value of creativity in coaching for compassionate resilience: lessons from neuroscience

What Whitaker (2009) states and I suggest here is that not all the work we do with clients can be expressed in verbal form, even if this is the 'stuff' of our schooling and at the heart of our practice. With very few exceptions (eg Whittaker, 2009) I see little in coaching textbooks that takes us into the creative realm, to help us move beyond mastery. Perhaps it's because as coaches, like our clients, we need to, as Whittaker observes, uncouple creative activities from possible early negative memories. Yet in employing creative methods we can open up new possibilities and encourage a more expansive mode of thinking. This is certainly the case with clients 'Anya', 'Danny' and 'Jo' and coaching practitioners 'Fiona', whose poem started this chapter, and 'Jane' and 'Lesley', whose work you'll read later.

Although there might be some 'talking therapies' that regard interventions such as those I've outlined above as 'business as usual', coaching isn't therapy. And for me, as a coaching psychologist in particular, there is a dearth of literature in theory and in practice that illuminates ways in which to use creative approaches in my work. Second, coaching psychology is informed by an evidence base that is largely inspired by a positivist paradigm, rather than qualitative approaches, drawn from the arts. As the past Chair of the Special Group in Coaching Psychology within the British Psychological

Society, Sarah Corrie (2014), observes, as a field of practice, it hasn't achieved the recognition it deserves. I'd argue this is in large part due to the lack of creative approaches in the parent discipline that underpins and informs the field.

An AE approach to coaching to build CR offers that potential; AE coaching demands the type of conversations, coach presence and awareness informed from what we are beginning to know from neuroscience (and elaborated on in the next chapter of this book by Paul Brown). It requires compassionate conversations, because as Newberg (2012) says:

> When you use compassionate communication... Something quite surprising occurs: both your brain and the brain of the person you are talking to begin to align themselves with each other... A phenomenon known as 'neural resonance' and in this enhanced state of mutual attunement two people accomplish remarkable things together. Why? Because it eliminates the natural defensiveness that normally exists.

The application of findings from neuroscience suggests that operating in the mode 2 system of thinking ('doing mode of mind' – Segal *et al*, 2013) is insufficient. We need, as coaches, new ways of working with our clients that nurture system 1, the 'being mode of mind', as illustrated in Figures 5.3 and 5.4.

FIGURE 5.3   The Two Minds Model

Analytical Mind (System 2)	Intuitive Mind (System 1)
Narrow bandwidth	Broad bandwidth
Effortful processing (long road)	Automatic processing
Step-by-step analysis	Whole pattern recognition
Conscious	Unconscious
'Talks' to the language of words	'Talks' to the language of feelings
Recent	Ancient
Features on management education and training	Ignored by most education and training

Adapted from Sadler-Smith/CIPD Report 'Fresh thinking in learning and development, Part 3: Insight and Intuition', 2014

FIGURE 5.4   Characteristics of each mode of mind

Doing Mode (System 2)	Being Mode (System 1)
Judging	Letting be
Goal setting and problem solving	Accepting 'what is'
Conceptual	Direct experience 'here and now'
Focus on the past and the future	The present moment
Automatic pilot (out of awareness)	Intentional (act with awareness)
Actions: Avoid and escape	Action: Lean into experience with curiosity
'Thinking about experience'	'Being with' our experience

Adapted from Segal *et al* (2013)

AE is a philosophy and an emerging coaching practice that speaks to me, in particular because it requires a commitment to relational ethics '... wherein the rights of others who might be present in the stories are respected' (Kidd and Finlayson, 2010, cited in Chapman, 2014). AE means at the outset making explicit in our writing our own narrative and how that shapes and informs our practice. Here I've done this through the cases of 'Danny', 'Anya' and 'Jo' and from my research 'data' – the poetry of advanced coaches 'Fiona', 'Jane' and 'Lesley'. These 'stories' illustrate the coaching values, beliefs and frameworks that inform my work, which is underpinned by neuroscience and my discovery that in a VUCA world we need to do research and practice differently. This will increasingly mean our being 'applied neuro-coaches' and drawing on creative approaches, to engage both system 1 and system 2 'modes of mind'.

Resilient individuals or resilient organizations?

That which doesn't kill us, makes us stronger

Nietzsche

Coming back to de Haan and Kasozi, these colleagues note that resilience and, as I reiterate here, building on strengths are antidotes to leader hubris. They highlight how resilience is defined in different ways and in different contexts. A full exposition of that literature is beyond the scope of this chapter; nonetheless to illustrate the size of this literature for example, I put the search term 'resilience' into Google Scholar and this generated 1,090,000 hits. Here is an illustration of the diversity to which de Haan and Kasozi refer.

Concepts include seeing resilience as synonymous with:

- mental toughness;
- hardiness;
- psychological and biological strengths required to successfully navigate change;
- a process of disruption and reintegration.

And resilience is seen as a set of individual traits which include:

- creativity;
- the ability to tolerate pain;
- insight into ourselves and what we are going through;
- independence of spirit;
- self-respect;
- the ability to restore self-esteem;
- capacity for learning;
- the ability to make and keep friends;
- freedom to depend on others, with the skill to set proper limits on depth of that dependency;
- view of life that gives a measure of purpose and meaning. (Drawn from Frach, 1997)

And even personal qualities such as:

- openness to new ideas (good listeners, keen learners and prepared to try different approaches);
- assuming the best rather than the worst of others;
- find opportunity and risk equally fascinating (recognizing the crucial link between the two for success);
- embrace positive change;

- see what needs to be done and be happy to lead the change;
- prefer dealing in transparency and honesty rather than obscurity and deceit.
  (Adapted from Clarke and Nicholson, 2010)

In positive psychology, resilience is seen as:

- a key attribute to attaining happiness and satisfaction in life;
- a set of traits that we can learn to cultivate to make us more resilient;
- acting for the benefit of others to serve as a greater internal motivator.

In the context of this book, resilience is the resource upon which we draw when faced with setbacks. It's a fundamental capability that enables an individual to survive, thrive and flourish in a VUCA world. It's our ability to learn and grow from adversity and to flex and bend, without breaking, and to spring back. Put simply it's our 'bounce-back-ability'.

It's not all about the client

I echo what de Haan and Kasozi observe. I've witnessed amongst the client group with whom I work how different clinical placements, with different peers, teams and leaders make a substantial difference to their resilience, wellbeing and performance. That is, they might experience being resilient in some settings, yet stressed and depleted in others. In organizational psychology this intersection between the individual and the organization is described as the person–environment (P–E) fit. This idea is one at the core of my thinking as a coaching psychologist. I see resilience as the outcome of the interaction between individual differences and the specific organizational, cultural, context, and compassionate resilience as that which is extended to the individual. It's this relationship that impacts on our ability to bounce back. Where one individual might find an environment stressful and depleting, another may find it stimulating and nourishing.

Compassionate resilience: the 21st-century 'take' on bounce-back-ability

A world characterized by VUCA puts a premium on resilience, yet this idea isn't new. It was the philosopher Nietzsche who noted how new beginnings can come through adversity. In a similar vein Klein wrote in 1944 that: 'the resilience of the human organism is even more amazing than its vulnerability' (in Newman, 2004). More recently Stephen Joseph, inspired by Nietzsche, has called for a move away from seeing life-changing experiences as negative events to opportunities for post-traumatic growth, that is, 'to find new meanings, create new webs of understanding and incorporate these into an ongoing narrative of one's own life' (Joseph, 2012), and in Chapter 4 of this book, Liz explores this theme too. This re-authoring of self-narrative is at the heart of the call to a turn to AE in coaching.

Informed through a philosophy that centres on relationship and dialogue, compassionate resilience seems just what's needed to thrive in a VUCA world, not just resilience. My position is shaped through my research into the impact of mindfulness on a coach's resilience and inspired by what I heard at the United Kingdom's All-Party Parliamentary Group (APPG) meeting in 2014 that explored the potential of mindfulness in the workplace (Houses of Parliament, 25 November 2014). At this meeting, Geoff McDonald, former global Vice-President of Unilever, stated that all too often the need for resilience is placed on the individual and not in transforming the organization. This echoes what de Haan and Kasozi argue – that whilst there is increasing interest in the topic of resilience, few organizations are implementing strategic resilience-focused interventions. System-level changes are required to bring about what McDonald calls for; the much-needed transformation in the leadership and organizational culture: the 'rules, roles and processes that describe the "way we do things around here"' (Peters and Waterman, 1982).

> Resilience is the process of adapting well in the face of adversity, trauma, tragedy, threats or significant sources of stress – such as family and relationship problems, serious health problems or workplace and financial stressors. It means 'bouncing back' from difficult experiences.
>
> (American Psychological Association)

In addition to the notion of a need for CR, another source of thinking that underpins my practice is discussed in the seminal *Harvard Business Review* publication *Building Personal and Organizational Resilience* (2003). It still has currency. Interestingly, in that book, Diane Coutu talks of resilience as the new 'buzzword' and her exposition of how resilience works is useful: 'More than education, more than experience, more than training, a person's level of resilience will determine who succeeds and who fails. That's true in the cancer ward, it's true in the Olympics, and it's true in the boardroom' (Coutu, 2003).

As I write this now, her words are both prophetic and still highly relevant. In her assertions I find she echoes another key influence on my work, Carl

Rogers, who was writing some 40 years earlier than Diane Coutu. Here in a piece entitled *Freedom to Learn for the 80s* Rogers talks about the interpersonal relationship in the facilitation of learning:

> The only goal if we are to survive, is the facilitation of change and learning. The only 'man' educated is the 'man' who has learned how to learn, to adapt and change and who realizes that no knowledge is secure and that only the process of seeking knowledge gives a basis for security. Changingness, reliance on process, rather than upon static knowledge, is the only thing that makes any sense as a goal... in the modern world.
>
> (Carl R Rogers, 1993, cited in Thorpe, Edwards and Hanson, 1993)

Rogers argues that our role as facilitators (what we 'do' as coaches) is to free up our client's curiosity; to unleash a sense of inquiry and encourage them to question and pursue their own interests in the spirit of creativity. These ideas are at the heart of an AE approach which employs creative methods to help clients 're-story' their experience of loss, change and transition to recreate an ongoing self-narrative. This is achieved in the context of a co-created dialogue that goes beyond mastery of techniques in which we can develop compassionate resilient individuals and help them become what Rogers calls 'creative practitioners'. This cannot be achieved purely through a cognitive form of knowing, but requires developing embodied (experiential) gut-level learning integration of the whole person. Continuing the theme set out earlier in this chapter, our role as coaches is to help heal the split, between heart and mind, body and soul and for clients to achieve a balance between doing and being.

Developing self-compassion in coaching resilience starts with the coach: the Case of 'Jane'

Now I will share stories from my research with advanced coaching practitioners exploring their experiences of mindfulness training through poetic inquiry (Chapman-Clarke, 2015). The study involves participants (as co-researchers in the language of AE) taking part in an eight-week Mindfulness in Coaching Research (MICR) programme adapted to suit the contexts in which they work – executive emotional intelligence (EQ) coaching. Participants were invited to engage in a mindfulness practice each week, based on a theme explored such as that I describe here, 'facing difficulties'. After each practice the coach then engaged in free-writing through using a tool I developed called 'Playing with Nine Words' (Figure 5.5 shows the steps involved and how you might adapt this in your work).

FIGURE 5.5   Playing With Nine Words

1. Taking the word that first came to mind after the first practice, write for three minutes, not letting the pen stop.

2. Now, skim read what you have written and highlight three words; select one word.

3. Write for a further three minutes, without stopping.

4. Skim read again, and highlight three more words; select one more word.

5. Write for a further three minutes, again without stopping.

6. Skim read and highlight three more words.

7. You should now have a total of nine words.

8. Write these nine words as a list, each on a separate line.

9. Play with these nine words – you can add words – and, for this exercise, using the title:
   'Compassion is...'

10. Create a poem from the nine words.

© Chapman, 2014

To help coaches with the process, this was the guidance given:

- keep to a time limit;
- keep your hand moving;
- don't cross out;
- don't worry about spelling, punctuation, grammar;
- go with the flow (lose control – freely associate, let your 'unconscious' do the talking: 'creativity cannot be explained by conscious processes alone' (Boden, 2004, quoted in Evans, 2013));
- don't think or get logical;
- 'Go with where the energy takes you, notice and be compassionate if it feels a little "scary"' (Evans, 2013).

From these nine words the coach created a poem that captured their embodied experience ('felt sense') of the mindfulness practice. They were then invited to reflect on their experience, using a process of self-inquiry outlined below.

This mirrors the 'inquiry dialogue' that is a core element in the eight-week mindfulness-based stress reduction (MBSR) programme from which the MICR is adapted.

Self-inquiry

When I read this:

- I notice...
- I am surprised that...
- I realise that...

When I read this:

- I am aware that...
- I feel...

Here is an illustration of the process in action, the case of 'Jane' below (cited with permission).

CASE STUDY 'Jane'

'Jane' is an advanced coach and after a successful career in executive education in the Further Education sector has been in private practice for three years. She became involved in the MICR to explore how mindfulness might be incorporated into her practice, particularly as she had been impacted through the work of Sandy Newbigging and Mind Calm. Although not able to participate in the weekly face-to-face sessions nonetheless she followed the programme which included Williams and Penman's (2011) workbook. She followed the home practice set for each week and engaged with the 'Playing with Nine Words' exercise.

One of the significant outcomes from her involvement with the programme was discovering her talents in writing poetry, something she (or any of co-researchers) had not previously done. Through the creative writing process 'Jane' came to an increased level of awareness, specifically, as in the case of 'Danny', how hard she could be on herself. One characteristic of this 'inner critic' was reflected in her not being able to accept positive feedback from clients.

The nine words which arose from the 'Nine Words' exercise for 'Jane' were: feelings, compassion, sadness, loneliness, self-doubt, warmth, softness, calm, peaceful. Below is her poem.

Befriending: A Statement:

> Turmoil and stomach churning
> not at all discerning
> Sadness, loneliness is part of learning
> To be compassionate towards oneself
>
> Feelings soften when widening the net
> to bring those dear to you to suffer less
> Strangers, neighbours deserve the same Compassion,
> Along with warmth and peace in their lives
>
> So now in this moment a calmness descends
> To get on with the day's demands
> We all shall be free of loneliness and self-doubt
> And feel the love that is being dished out

In her reflections she notes:

> *Having compassion for one's self is not easy, especially when the emotions that are manifested, are not necessarily telling the true story. Feelings of distress bring about irrational thoughts, which then lead to feelings and emotions that govern our next move or action. To seek the freedom from these emotions, I want to engage in mindful meditation, allowing myself to tap into happiness and joy that is so richly deserved knowing that emotions and thoughts are just temporary and not necessarily the truth at all.*

[and continues...]

> *I am more and more coming to accept what is... and acceptance gives me peace from worry and emotions even if it's only for a short time!*
> ('Jane', Advanced Coaching Practitioner in Chapman-Clarke, forthcoming)

'Jane' reports that she is now more able to bounce back; accept client feedback and enjoy what she describes as her 'mindful moments', meaning the time spent engaging in practice: 'I may not be able to get on my cushion for half an hour, but just stopping and noticing when I am getting bogged down in the story is invaluable; it may not be reality at all, just thoughts.'

For this coach, poetry is now an integral part of enabling her to find a 'voice' for making sense of her mindfulness practice. And, in terms of her development as a coach, 'Jane' has since shared the 'Nine Words Exercise' with clients and other coaches, who have similarly been impacted by the process and see the value of creative writing in their own and their clients' ongoing journeys to EQ.

Before we conclude, let's look at some steps you can take to develop CR as a coach. These are adapted from ideas for developing compassionate resilience in health visitors included in a document from the UK Institute of Health Visitors (2014).

FIGURE 5.6 Ten steps for developing compassionate resilience as a coach

1	Maintain a work–life balance, approaching this holistically, taking into account your physical, emotional, relational and spiritual needs.
2	Identify your values as a coach and your purpose – what do you enjoy or find rewarding in your work; which strengths do you draw upon?
3	How do you prepare for potentially stress-provoking situations? What forms of support are available? What needs to be included in your compassionate resilience toolkit?
4	Reflect on how you manage your 'hot buttons', the situations that you find stressful. What is your signature stress response? How do you balance nourishing and depleting tasks? Can you remember a time when you have 'surfed the waves' as Jon Kabat-Zinn describes periods of crisis (previous stressful situations)?
5	Practise how you can respond positively to a stress-provoking event; for example, using what we know about the brain and strategies for soothing, breathing, rhythm, compassionate imagery, self-compassion and mindfulness (see Chapter 10 in this book).
6	Accept life is challenging, focus on what you can control, influence and let go of what you cannot change – *mindfully*.
7	Harness the support of peers, supervisors, friends, someone with whom to share your feelings; coach or mentor.
8	Build an 'A' team (Chapman, 2011) – a constellation of support, with people who can provide you with different resources (eg make you laugh).
9	Keep a compassionate/reflective journal. Note your thoughts, feelings and behaviours, using cognitive-behavioural coaching methods to identify the inferences between your thoughts, feelings and expectations. What did you expect to happen? What happened? What was the difference? What have you learned and what would a compassionate friend say to you?
10	In your reflective journal, note down one positive moment daily, engage in intelligent kindness by simply being attentive to perhaps what you don't notice.

Conclusion

This chapter began and ends with a poem because poetry is indicative of my 'turn to AE', an emerging approach in coaching research and practice. It's already embraced by sports coaches and is finding its way into organizational research and leadership practice. It reflects a subtle but important shift that has the potential to impact dramatically on the way we work, to take us beyond mastery. It is radical in that it incorporates the 'I' of the coach into the 'we' of coaching. It is about the coach and the client in a co-created and shared experience. For me 'the call for a turn to AE' represents an authentic and relational quality that speaks to the current zeitgeist increasingly informed through applied neuroscience.

Creative approaches can yield 'epiphanies'; 'aha' moments that are not accessed through system 2, doing mode but arise from interventions that engage system 1, being mode. The 'doing' is what we and our clients do superbly well, the 'being' is much harder, and being compassionate to ourselves, whether coach or client, is harder still. To build compassionate resilience means that we as coaches need to extend compassion to ourselves in order to facilitate compassion in our clients.

My hope is that with this chapter, and those of my peers captured in this book, you have the resources that will inspire and encourage you to take a risk and sustain you in your own creative exploration, because, as advanced coach in the MICR 'Lesley' states:

You hear my soul through my poetry...
You hear my brain through my spoken choice of words
('Lesley', Advanced Coaching Practitioner in Chapman-Clarke, forthcoming)

References and further reading

Adams, T E, Holman-Jones, S and Ellis, C (2014) *Autoethnography: Understanding qualitative research*, Oxford University Press, New York

American Psychological Association (2015) The Road to Resilience, *APA Help Center* [online] http://www.apa.org/helpcenter/road-resilience.aspx [accessed 30 November 2014]

Bolton, G (2001) *Reflective Practice: Writing and professional development*, Paul Chapman Publishing, London

Boyle, M and Parry, K (2007) Telling the whole story: the case for organizational autoethnography, *Culture and Organization*, **13** (3), pp 185–90

Chapman, M (2011) *The Emotional Intelligence Pocketbook*, 2nd edn, Management Pocketbooks, Arlesford

Chapman, M (2014) Discovering autoethnography as a research genre, methodology and method for exploring coaches' experiences of mindfulness training, unpublished paper submitted in partial fulfilment of Doctorate in Practice (Applied Psychology), The University of Derby

Chapman-Clarke, M (2015) Exploring coaches' experience of mindfulness training using poetic inquiry: An Autoethnographic Study, unpublished doctoral thesis, The University of Derby, Derby

Clarke, J and Nicholson, J (2010) *Resilience: Bounce back from whatever life throws at you*, Crimson Publishing, Richmond

Corrie, S (2014) Report on the special group in coaching psychology, *International Coaching Psychology Review*, 9 (2), pp 216–18

Coutu, D L (2003) How resilience works, in *Harvard Business Review on Building Personal and Organizational Resilience*, Harvard Business School Press, Harvard

Doherty, D (2009) The discovery of 'writing as inquiry' in support of coaching practice, in Megginson, D and Clutterbuck, D, *Further Techniques for Coaching and Mentoring*, Butterworth-Heinemann, Oxford, pp 77–91

Evans, K E (2013) *Pathways Through Writing Blocks in the Academic Environment*, Sense Publishers, Rotterdam

Frach, F (1997) *Resilience: The power to bounce back when the going gets tough!* Hatherliegh Press, New York

Gearity, B T (2014) Autoethnography, in Nelson, L, Groom, R and Portrac, P (eds) *Research Methods in Sports Coaching*, Routledge, Abingdon

Gustin, L W and Wagner, L (2012) The butterfly effect of caring – clinical nursing teachers understanding of self-compassion as a source to compassionate care, *Scandinavian Journal of Caring Sciences*, doi: 10.1111/j.1471-6712.2012.01033. [online] https://webspace.utexas.edu/neffk/pubs/nurseselfcare.pdf [accessed 15 May 2014]

Harrington, A L (2012) Numbers, words and anonymity in 360-degree feedback: a qualitative study, unpublished PhD thesis, Loughborough University

Institute of Health Visitors (2014) Developing compassionate resilience, *IHV* [online] http://www.ihv.org.uk/uploads/GPP_%20Compassionate%20 Resilience_V3.pdf [accessed 15 June 2015]

Joseph, S (2012) *What Doesn't Kill Us: The new psychology of posttraumatic growth*, Piatkus, London

Kempster, S and Iszatt-White, M (2012) Towards co-constructed coaching: Exploring the integration of coaching and co-constructed autoethnography in leadership development, *Management Learning*, 44 (4), pp 319–36

Kempster, S and Stewart, J (2010) Becoming a leader; A co-produced autoethnographic exploration of situated learning of leadership practice, *Management Learning*, **41** (2), pp 205–21

Kidd, J and Finlayson, M (2010) Mental illness in the nursing workplace: A Collective Autoethnography, *Contemporary Nurse*, **36** (1–2), pp 21–33

Law, H (2013) *The Psychology of Coaching, Mentoring and Learning* (2nd edn), Wiley-Blackwell, Chichester

Leavy, P (2009) *Method Meets Art: Arts-based research practice*, The Guilford Press, New York

Muncey, T (2010) *Creating Autoethnographies*, Sage, London

Neff, K D and Costigan, A P (2014) Self-compassion, well-being and happiness, *Psychologie in Österreich* [online] http://self-compassion.org/UTserver/pubs/Neff&Costigan.pdf [accessed 2 March 2014]

Newburg, A (2012) Six lessons to strengthen compassionate leadership [online] http://www.fastcompany.com/1840226/6-exercises-strengthen-compassionate-leadership [accessed 1 March, 2015]

Newman, T (2004) *What Works in Building Resilience?* Barnardos, London

Paice, L (2012) The New Coach: Reflections on a learning journey, Open University Press, Maidenhead

Peters, T J and Waterman, R H (1982) *In Search of Excellence: Lessons from America's best run companies*, Harper Business

Pitsis, A (2014) *The Poetic Organization*, Palgrave Macmillan, Basingstoke

Rogers, C R (1983) The Interpersonal relationship in the facilitation of learning, in Thorpe, M, Edwards, R and Hanson, A (eds) *Culture and Processes Of Adult Learning*, Routledge, London (pp 228–42)

Sadler-Smith, E /CIPD (2014) Insight and Intuition, Research Insights 'Fresh Thinking in Learning and Development' Part 3 of 3, [online] http://www.cipd.co.uk/binaries/fresh-thinking-in-learning-and-development_2014-part-3-insight-intuition.pdf

Segal, Z V, Williams, J M G and Teasdale, J D (2013) *Mindfulness-Based Cognitive Therapy for Depression* (2nd edn), Guilford Press, New York (pp 63–77)

Sparkes, A C and Smith, B (2014) *Qualitative Research Methods in Sport, Exercise and Health*, Routledge, Abingdon

Williams, M and Penman, M (2011) *Mindfulness: A guide for finding peace in a frantic world*, Piatkus, London

Whitaker, V (2009) Offering creative choices in mentoring and coaching, in Megginson, D and Clutterbuck, D, *Further Techniques for Coaching and Mentoring*, Butterworth-Heinemann, Oxford (pp 100–15)

Useful resources

For questionnaires based on strengths-based/positive psychology:
www.authentichappiness.sas.upenn.edu/

On implications of behavioural science for coaching and learning, CIPD:
www.cipd.co.uk/hr-resources/behavioural-science.aspx Report Series:
www.cipd.co.uk/hr-resources/research/neuroscience-learning.aspx
(Pt.1 Learning and Neuroscience, Dr. Paul Howard-Jones; PT.2 Cognition,
Decision and Expertise, Dr. Adrian Banks; Pt.3, Insight and Intuition,
Dr. Eugene Sadler-Smith – all are downloadable in PDF and via podcasts)

For the interim report The Mindful Nation go to:
**http://oxfordmindfulness.org/wp-content/uploads/mindful-nation-uk-
interim-report-of-the-mindfulness-all-party-parliamentary-group-
january-2015.pdf**

For self-help resources (from which the PPQS is adapted) go to:
www.getselfhelp.co.uk

Insights from neuroscience

06

PAUL BROWN and HELEN LEEDER BARKER

In this chapter we explore the pivotal role played by the brain in both the client's and the coach's capacity to successfully navigate crisis and transition.

To adapt effectively to meet the demands of a situation, the client must first risk change with a brain that continuously harnesses its emotional system to direct familiar action; the primary functions of the brain being otherwise to make sense and to manage relationships. As we can see in the story below, the coach can provide the ongoing relationship that stabilizes situations, facilitating changes in the client's brain. Meaning and sense-making are crucial to this process.

CASE STUDY   David's story

David's coach noticed how agitated he was almost as soon as they sat down. Early on they had established a process of 'checking in' at the start of each session and this helped her to quickly zero in on what was going on. 'I'm such an idiot, I feel like I've got it written on my forehead – I just can't seem to get anything right – I'm going to resign, before they fire me – I don't think I could bear the humiliation,' he said despairingly. David had been recently promoted to Finance Director of a division of a large multinational logistics firm. This was a big step for him and required him to operate outside his comfort zone in areas including making quarterly presentations to the board, which he found particularly stressful. Before the first one he had endured a week of sleepless nights. Despite being visibly nervous (and enormously tired) he had 'done OK', but received feedback that he needed to be more concise next time, and deal with questions more confidently.

His 'second shot' had occurred the previous week and David explained that whilst he had managed to cut down his content in practice runs, he had 'waffled uncontrollably' when it came to the questions and answers; so that eventually one of the board members had stepped in to cut him off. He felt intensely ashamed afterwards.

For his whole life David had sought to ensure the details were right. This ability had been highly useful to his accountancy career until now, when it needed to shift to the background in terms of how he presented himself. The coach talked to David about the brain having software: that it can only work on the coding – in Transactional Analysis terms, the scripts; in neuroscience terms, the pathways – it has embedded. It was an analogy especially helpful to David in lessening feelings of shame and guilt for 'not being able to get it right'. Through biographical enquiry the coach helped David understand more of the origin of his way of behaving, the anxieties that generated it as well as the pleasures and satisfactions that maintained it, and to frame it in the context of his brain 'doing the best it can based on current programming'.

Given that he had been running his software system for more than 40 years David was able to see how skilful he had become at being a certain way. However, in responding to new executive challenges, his assumption that he could immediately fix this issue was unrealistic and so he became 'kinder' to himself. He began to look at embedding the possibility of some 'new programming' as like building a muscle group at the gym, something that could be done through concerted, regular effort over time. Through imagining himself in context in order to start creating new coding pathways in the brain, and then rehearsing them whenever he had a chance, David was able to both improve his ability to tune his brain into the needs of his audience, and to cut down on his waffle. When he sensed that he might be in danger of 'running the old script' he worked with his coach to create an array of 'tools' at his disposal to keep him on track. He started to enjoy aspects of his new role and to accept the possibility that he did not in fact 'need to know everything'. He realized that far from not knowing everything risking him getting fired, 'the ability to allow others to know the answer rather than me is the key to doing this job well'.

The concepts about the working of the brain that the coach used were neither extensive nor profound. But they were scientifically as well as metaphorically true and were used with a level of certainty that made them real to David, who valued professional certainty in others. They gave David a working model linked closely to his own knowledge of computers through which he could direct his own new learning and assess his progress. And the exploration of childhood and adolescent anxieties had allowed him to reassess them in the light of his own successes as an adult, see them more to do with the past than allowing them to intrude in the present, and so reframe his sense of himself.

Individual and professional transitional opportunities

The very extensive research into the brain that is now being funded world-wide has two main objectives. The first is to try to define how the brain works as a whole, not just work out what each bit does. The second is to see if it is possible to create an artificial brain of sufficient verisimilitude to make experimental work on a computer-simulated 'live' brain possible. Achieving this would make it possible to conduct research in a way that, on the living and embodied brain, is impossible.

Laboratory-based neuroscientists are, in general, not especially interested in the whole human being. They are focused on the brain. As coaches it is generally the human being in the shape of the client sitting before us upon which we focus, not the brain. But what is becoming very clear is that the brain is the master controller of everything to do with our behaviour. It follows, therefore, that if we professionally hold ourselves out to know something about individual change and development it might be profession-ally responsible to understand the mechanisms that make those possible. The profession of coaching has the opportunity to integrate the science of the brain with the art of coaching.

We believe the choice of whether or not to exercise that option will deter-mine the future of the profession and its underlying knowledge. So behind this chapter is an awareness also that coaching as a profession is potentially in a transitional process with which it may or may not engage. Does it wish to be a profession based upon scientific knowledge – or, like psychotherapy, rely only upon descriptive models that can never become explanatory? Transitions badly managed usually create crises.

So what do we know about the brain?

The brain cannot be disassembled in the laboratory into its constituent parts as (relatively) easily as can, say, the genome, for the single main reason that the key mystery of the brain is how it manages to function as a unitary whole. Understanding the interconnectedness of 86 billion brain cells creating between them 10^9 possible interconnections through the electrical stimulation of neurochemicals crossing extremely small synaptic gaps between cells (gaps of around one hundred nanometers) and present-ing that as a seamlessly functioning organ busy integrating sensation into making meaning is a daunting as well as hugely exciting, worldwide, investigative project.

Despite the huge resources being deployed, however, the results are unlikely, within the foreseeable future, to offer to coaches an accurate and working model of the brain that is of much practical use in a coaching session. For that, it is necessary to go back 40 years.

Modern neuroscience started in 1848 in Vermont, United States, when a railway blasting foreman, Phineas Gage, was using an iron tamping rod of just over a metre long and somewhat over an inch in diameter to compact an explosive charge prior to the fuse being lit and the rock blasted. The metal rod struck the rock, creating a spark that ignited the explosive powder and blasted the iron rod through Gage's left cheek and up through the top frontal part of his skull, landing some 80 feet away. Gage remained conscious, was carted off to the local small town, and there was able to sit and wait for medical attendance and to tell the incredulous doctor who attended him what had happened.

Penetrating head wounds of such a kind with subsequent survival were extremely rare at the time. Gage survived 12 years longer, displaying at first a marked change in character. From having been a highly responsible man, much valued by his employer, he became feckless and irresponsible. Medical attention was drawn to the site of the injury – left frontal lobe especially – and the change in personality. Some four years after the injury, however, there had been sufficient stabilization for Gage to become the driver of a coach-and-six in Peru after a brief fairground career in the United States exhibiting himself and his iron bar as an object of paying interest. However, he started having epileptiform seizures so returned to the United States to the care of his mother and sister, and subsequently died after a severe fit.

The Gage case is important not only for the remarkable fact of survival after such an injury in the septic conditions of the time but because it made it possible for the medical profession to start speculating about the relationship between the structure of the brain and the specificity of function.

The increasingly dominating questions for neurologists and neuroanatomists became not 'What does the brain look like?' but 'What do the bits of it do?' though the capacity to actually see the detail of the structure and systematically explore what each bit did was severely limited. In the mid-1870s, however, an Italian physician named Gogli developed a technique for staining brain tissue, showing its cellular and neuronal structure in great detail. By the end of the 19th century, crude techniques had developed for electrically stimulating animal brains to see what specific effects electrical current had upon muscular activity.

Beginning to understand function

Between 1930 and 1950, American-Canadian neurologist and neurosurgeon Wilder Penfield started mapping in great detail the specificity of the surface of the human brain via systematic electrical stimulation. He was very surprised to find that focal point stimulation could elicit complex verbal and emotional memories and speech as well as reflex motor activity. At around the same time (1949), Canadian psychologist D O Hebb made the imaginative leap to propose that the brain was essentially an associative learning device, with pre-synaptic cells having the capacity to stimulate post-synaptic cells and so create neural pathways. All subsequent thinking about the brain relies implicitly and explicitly on the separate work of Penfield and Hebb, though – as with Newtonian physics having to take on board that there is another universe of observation and explanation called quantum physics – it should not be assumed that remarkable discoveries about the way the brain is organized are not still to be made.

The technology of the brain sciences is now creating extraordinarily detailed images of the brain and, in the new science of connectomics, how its parts might be connected. But, as with deep-space telescopes, producing new pictures makes it possible initially only to start asking more detailed questions. In any case, rather than developing a detailed understanding of the structure of neural pathways and what they each relate to, as the connectomics neuroscientists are so painstakingly and brilliantly doing, it is more useful for coaches to understand how our brain, in relationship with the client's brain, can best enable the client to achieve their goals. In crisis this need is heightened for a number of reasons that we will go on to explore, but first let's ensure that we have a shared understanding and a working model of the way our brains function.

Understanding the way the brain works through the way it evolved

US physician and neuroscientist Paul D MacLean was the first to give systematic thought to the evolutionary development of the brain. After four decades of research he published a pivotal book setting out a working model of the brain that, despite academic dissent, has not been superseded for its practical value (MacLean, 1990). He defined what has become known as the Triune Brain – a brain of three parts that developed sequentially in the evolutionary record, and that gives humans a capacity that no other member of the animal kingdom appears to possess. That is, the capacity to think about thinking, wonder about feelings, and pass the results of that thinking and wondering on to other members of the same species through infinitely adaptable languages and arts.

The oldest part of the evolved brain is the reptilian or snake brain. It sits at the top of the spinal column, buried in the underside and back of the brain, and regulates all the basic bodily functions, such as breathing, sleeping, waking, salt levels, respiration, and so on and so on. Its workings are rarely noticeable to consciousness except when it is malfunctioning or especially stressed. In humans this reptilian brain is the first part of the brain to develop embryonically in utero.

MacLean's special insight about the brain arose from asking himself the question, 'What happened to the brain when mammals first appeared in the evolutionary record?' – about the same time that the dinosaurs, great reptiles that they were, died out. The fact that mammals have live young led MacLean to infer that the brain must have developed a special capacity to manage the relationship necessary to ensure the survival of the young into the development of effective independence, and that longer periods of dependency would necessarily presuppose more extensive or complex brain structures to cope with this.

This proved to be a profoundly accurate inference. The central part of the brain, the limbic system, frequently referred to as 'the mammalian brain', came into being in mammals. In the embryo it develops after the snake brain. It deals especially with the emotions and memory. It includes the almond-shaped structures, the amygdala, that lie on the inner surface of each of the temporal lobes.

The amygdala assess the significance of all stimuli, including those internally generated as thoughts and feelings, for their emotional loading. If danger is apparent the amygdala mobilizes everything to deal immediately with the danger. The body will respond within 80 milliseconds to a danger signal, though the evidence of that response will not get into consciousness for 250 milliseconds. In crisis it is this area that is mobilized, leading to the fright, fight, flight, freeze or, at worst, fainting responses that are the familiar reactions to threat. This amygdaloid response directs behaviour before we can engage rational processes. So we see that the brain manages the body, rather than the other way around, and it is a bottom-up structure. The middle part of the brain, the limbic system, evaluates incoming signals first of all for their emotional significance. Only then – though very very quickly – does it assign the signal to its appropriate pathway.

The third area of the brain to develop embryonically as well as in evolution – rather like a house that has been added on to over centuries, and that has a composite structure and integrity of its own individuality without having been originally designed as a unitary whole – is the cortical, or cognitive, brain that has the capacity to manage thought and language. Meaning is created, therefore, by an event (a stimulus) of whatever complexity being received by one of the five senses or generated by thought, assessed by the amygdala, its emotional significance established, routed on to an already established pathway (from the accumulation of experience) if there is one, sent into the cortex, attached to language, and consequently given the opportunity to be understood. A stimulus may be so ambiguous it is not understood, too far below the threshold of perception, or too far outside the range of experience to be properly appreciated.

The two halves of the brain are crucial too

The brain is also busy integrating the two halves (hemispheres) into which it is divided. McGilchrist (2009) notes the fact that the left brain manages focus and fact while the right brain manages possibilities and potential. In crisis the left brain will be the more active as it seeks the certainty of what is known. To create the transitional shifts necessary to resolve the crisis, though, the right brain has to come into play.

Recent work at the University of Pennsylvania on more than 1,000 brain scans of boys and girls, men and women, has produced compelling evidence that male and female brains operate differently (Ingalhalikar *et al*, 2013). The male brain appears to be focused within each hemisphere – pointing and propositional, good for solving problems; whilst the female brain seems to be working between the two halves very much more strongly, integrating and seeking solutions. The implications of this very recent knowledge for managing crisis and transition are as yet far from clear. Accepting that men's and women's brains are different is going to take a long time after nearly six decades of erroneous assumption, supported by much legislation and corporate practice, that men and women are essentially the same. The fact that many women have learnt to operate corporately like men does not mean that that is their spontaneous, natural or most effective style. What it is possible to conjecture with some certainty from this new knowledge is that women have a special capacity for facilitating.

All of this raises the interesting possibility that our brains are much more in charge of us than we are of our brains. Two consequences for coaching arise from this and they are observations of especial importance during crisis when the brain needs to be at its most flexible to manage transition but is at its most rigid.

All behaviour and all sense-making relies on emotion to create meaning

The first consequence is that we can begin to see the brain not so much as the organ of rationality as the organ of rationalizing. That is to say, it is making sense to us and for us of what is happening to us (so that we can convey that sense to ourselves as well as to others) but we did not consciously direct what is happening to us. We are finding out what is happening to us. Not infrequently a client facing a crisis says that he or she cannot make sense of what is happening. Yet the brain is struggling to make sense, and is stressed until it has done so. In such circumstances a coach is like an auxiliary brain, making sense for the client in the client's terms.

The second consequence is the certainty that all behaviour is underpinned by emotion. It is emotions (or the infinite combinations of emotions called feelings) that give significance to experience, as experience and emotion attached to words create meaning. So the coach needs to understand the way the individual client's emotional/feeling system works in order to be able to help the client read situations accurately, with the added knowledge that the feelings a client is having will be from within the range of the client's, not the coach's, experience.

A working understanding

A comfortable understanding of some certainties about the brain is a starting point for the coach being able to rely upon a professionalism that has an objective body of knowledge underneath it. Brown and Brown (2012) have set out six propositions that, in the present state of knowledge, are true about the operating of the brain. They form the essence of the body of knowledge that should underpin the coach's use of, and understanding about, the workings of the client's brain – see box.

The operating of the brain: six principles

The brain:

- is an integrated system with many specialized, highly differentiated areas. For practical coaching purposes it acts as a unitary system.

- manages the inputs and the outputs from the five senses and also what is internally generated by thoughts and feelings. Internal signals are the same to the brain as external signals – pieces of data to be assessed and made sense of within the system.

- both regulates and is regulated by its emotional system.

- is the organ for making sense and for managing relationships, and is a remarkable neurochemical factory.

- has no original templates, only possibilities.

- hates change, but is very good at adapting.

So what does this mean for clients in crisis?

From a brain-based point of view, the primary coaching task is to create in clients the optimal conditions for brain change. In doing so we need to understand the following key points:

- The coaching relationship is the foundation for the work of the client's brain in making sense of their unique situation. The attachment emotions of trust and joy facilitate change. The survival emotions of fear, anger, disgust, shame and sadness inhibit change. Surprise creates possibility and potential.

- The coach needs to manage energy in the coaching session in order to create shared 'sense making'. Mindfulness training is one especially good way of doing this (Hall, 2013). It allows the brain to start functioning in such a way that the mind can entertain a 'plane of possibilities' (Siegel, 2010) that makes transition possible, overcoming the confusion or rigidity that is characteristic of a mind grappling with crisis.

- The brain's preference not to change can be overcome through the triangulation of
  - The coaching relationship.
  - Energy management creating a shared sense-making between coach and client.
  - Imagining and then experimenting with new behaviours and ways of being starting inside the coaching sessions; and then testing and refining the new behaviours in between the further coaching sessions.

Change that will last originates in the limbic system through emotions being fired that will create and support the neural pathways upon which change depends. The emotions are especially aroused during crisis, and during transition they need consolidating in new pathways.

The coach's brain is where the client's change starts. So start, perhaps, with the coach's brain

Coaching relies upon the effectiveness of the coach not only to have appropriate knowledge but also to be able to manage the coaching encounter so it maximizes the likelihood of an agreed outcome. If the brain is the organ of relationship, it behoves the coach to manage their brain in such a way that the coaching relationship is of maximum benefit to the client.

There are two brains in the coaching session, each trying to make sense of the other. The client may not have the language to describe the activity of the coach's brain, but the client's brain certainly has all the non-conscious skills in assessing another that have got the client to the point in life s/he has reached. It is a truism now to say that the brain that got you 'here' will prefer to stay the same, as being the best bet for the brain to get you wherever 'there' is. Making change is an energy-demanding job, and the client's brain needs to be facilitated by coaching skill to make as economically as possible whatever development is required by the coaching goals.

The amygdala of both the client and the coach are busy assessing each other's signals, especially in the early stages of a coaching assignment. The amygdala want to work out what the emotional deal is. The client in crisis may well be particularly sensitive to signals from the coach's amygdala, due to the increased fear-based emotions so often aroused by the unfamiliarity or tension in their current situation. Therefore if the coach is not managing her own limbic system effectively then this may unwittingly reinforce, rather than reduce, the client's current state of crisis.

As another's face and everything connected to it is of special consequence to the way the brain of the perceiver of the face assesses the situation non-consciously, it is a professional responsibility of the coach to make sure that his or her visual, and especially facial, signals are effective. Looking in the bathroom mirror on any morning that contains a coaching session and asking oneself, 'Is this a face I want to meet today?' will help to structure the coach's self-presentation. The coach needs to learn to let oxytocin, the neurochemical of attachment, make the eyes shine, and to abolish the dead-eyed or haunted look of cortisol, the stress hormone; becoming more aware of his or her own brain's functioning as well as the client's.

Tuning to the coach's brain

A coach in a coaching session can very easily slip into familiar patterns of organizational hierarchical relationships, especially with a very senior client who is extremely well-practised in setting the style of any interpersonal encounter. It is the coach's professional skill to tune the client's brain to the coach's brain, not the other way round. And the client may present in initial sessions as sceptical about the value coaching can bring. If the coach's limbic response to this is anxiety-driven, the client's amygdala will recognize this and trust will be much harder to establish. It will be the client's amygdala creating resonant anxiety with the coach, not the coach's amygdala sending out signals of certainty and self-trust (confidence) to which the client's brain can tune.

The coaching encounter is, for many clients, a remarkable use of corporate time, allowing them to have self-reflective and analytic time 'uncontaminated' by other demands. So the coach has a special responsibility to so tune his or her own brain that the client's brain is regulated by – tunes to – the coach's brain. That is the skill that makes managing crisis and transition especially effective. The story below illustrates the key role the coach's brain has in providing the basis for a secure coaching relationship to be fostered; and that in so doing the possibility for the client to successfully navigate crisis and transition is greatly increased.

CASE STUDY   Rose's story

Rose, a senior oncologist, sought help from a coach as she was going through a personal crisis in her working life. She had just missed out on 'the promotion of her career'. She had been passed over for this role once already and this time had felt sure it was hers; the head of department had even intimated this to her at a recent meeting. However, she had found out subsequently (through another colleague) that it had been offered to a peer whom she considered junior to her in experience and ability.

Rose came to her coach in a state of confusion, anger, and profound self-doubt. The coach resisted (with some difficulty) the temptation to jump into the presenting problem of the missed promotion and instead worked at building a secure attachment in the coaching relationship upon which future insight could be built. Initial sessions were spent in mutual, supportive exploration of Rose's life history, establishing a shared understanding in which she felt supported, accepted, understood and, most importantly, not judged. This enabled her limbic system to experience a level of calm in sessions, and role-modelled a relationship based on total acceptance that was unfamiliar to her (and so an important learning experience in its own right).

Gradual small changes were made, such as the reduction of her addiction to caffeine, and other 'self-care' mechanisms, including daily ten-minute meditation. These allowed some 'quick wins' in mood stabilization in high-stress situations at work. From this relational foundation the gradual process of self-understanding grew and Rose was eventually able to see how her rigid attachment to her work status as the key determinant of her feelings of self-worth – old patterns that had worked to get her where she was but were now keeping her stuck – was causing her to act in a judgemental, critical and hyper-vigilant way at work. From this window of insight, Rose and her coach were able to work together to shape an alternative conception of herself, from which new hope (and also work behaviour patterns) ensued.

It is not only the coaching relationship, however, that needs to be considered. As we saw with Rose, the client's brain needs to access the plane of possibilities, through connection with the limbic system into the cortex, and the coach has an important role in enabling that.

In times of crisis, though, there may not be much opportunity to be reflective and analytical. Taking an analogy from battlefield surgery, what happens in the operating conditions of a mobile surgical headquarters dealing with the first-stage trauma of severe injury is different from the reflective work of reconstruction surgery well away from the battlefield. Nevertheless, the good battlefield surgeon will have somewhere in mind the later work that will have to be done and will, so far as is possible, integrate that awareness into the immediate demands of a life-threatening situation.

So it is with the coach. If a special skill of a coach is to understand a client very effectively through having conducted a biographical enquiry that established the emotional patterning of accumulated experience, that skill may not be appropriate in the immediate circumstances of coaching a client in crisis. But knowing that it is important and picking up clues for later reference is invaluable.

The coach's auxiliary brain

In many crisis situations the coach's essential professional task is to provide the client with an auxiliary brain. The brain of the coach needs not only to be able to read its way into the client's situation, which mirror neurons make possible (Rizzolatti *et al*, 2002), but also to define courses of action that are intuitively appropriate to the uniqueness of the client, not just appropriate to the particularities of the situation.

'Uniqueness of the client' is a crucial statement. For what the client needs, above all in crisis, is a solution or solutions that resonate with his or her own range of options. The client in crisis wants to hear a statement that makes it very apparent that s/he, the client, has been understood. And that understanding is, in crisis, a very considerable imaginative act on the part of the coach and relies upon a correct reading of the emotional system backed by the language facility and skill to make it conscious to the client.

For in all coaching the coach is working with and upon the clients' understanding of themselves. In crisis the Self gets immobilized. If clients hear proffered solutions that do not take sufficient account of/are not informed by sufficient imaginative insight into the individual nature of their own sense of Self, then whatever it is that the coach is offering will not make much sense to them, and be no use.

'Mistakes' as crises

Clients may not infrequently chastise themselves for making errors that have led to the current crisis, generating a state of pervading shame, fear, regret or blame that prevents them from activating themselves effectively to create solutions. Or they may well in the normal course of coaching describe such circumstances from the past.

But the brain does not make mistakes. It is inconceivable that we would have a brain that evolution designed to make mistakes. At any point in time the brain will always make the right decision – the only decision at which it could arrive – based upon its own uniqueness. It might be that the moment a decision is made, the individual utterly regrets the decision; or it has damaging consequences for the wider system in which he or she operates and that had not been properly assessed. But had the brain in question been capable of making any other decision at the time it made the one just made, then it would have done so.

This observation can be immensely helpful in coaching a client for whom, in the coaching conversation, a previous decision of some consequence has become identified as 'a mistake'. From knowledge of the way the brain works, the coach can be certain, whatever the decision, that it could not, at the time at which it was made, have been a mistake. This can be immensely liberating for a client, for it then opens up the possibility of understanding why, at the time, the decision seemed to be adaptive but subsequently proved not to be so; and upon what, within the individual, the decision was pre-dicated. This opens up the prospect for the client of not being the victim of their own decision-making process but the architect of whatever happens, and so engages again the plane of possibilities within the brain.

It may also be helpful to observe that, in general, individuals do not learn from their mistakes. Indeed, they are very likely to repeat them, for the brain that made the original 'mistake' clearly has within it the likelihood of coming to exactly the same conclusion again, having come to it once already. The brain remembers what, for it, worked. So we can become destined to repeat 'crises' in our work or personal lives, leading to a seeming 'Groundhog Day' of depressingly familiar, unhelpful reactions. The client who experiences this scenario can find surprise – and so the possibility of change – in understand-ing that his or her brain is not malfunctioning. It is in fact behaving exactly as it should in seeking out the familiarity of what it knows, even if what it knows is ultimately unhelpful to the client. One example of this is the leader who leaves one organization based on a perceived 'personality clash' or lack of fit only to find himself back in the 'old situation' in a new environment.

The players and the context have changed, but the crisis repeats. In Transactional Analysis terms, the plot stays the same. In neuroscientific terms, old pathways are more easily activated than new ones.

Individuals adaptively learn from experience that has been properly considered in all its emotional underpinnings. Facilitating this process – consolidating experience in all its meaning – is a special skill of a brain-based coach. This then enables new adaptive learning. The brain remembers what works.

Often overlooked, for lack of a working knowledge of the emotional system and the way it drives behaviour, is the valuable acquisition that when new or difficult emotions are aroused through changing behaviour, the client has gained the modelled resources to recognize and deal with these. The capacity to read emotions and feelings properly creates data that makes new meanings. In a crisis this is of particular relevance, as ambiguity is often heightened and the prevailing conditions for experimentation may seem inclement.

Tears in crisis

A special situation arises in many coaching situations when the client suddenly becomes tearful, which can also surprisingly occur when there is no immediately apparent crisis or transitional process presenting. This is what happened with Mark:

CASE STUDY   Mark's story

Mark's coach took a deep breath as she walked into her first session with this new client at a large London law firm. The brief had been scant. Mark, the Senior Partner, had requested a new coach after only a few sessions with his previous male coach. He was described in feedback from his team as tough, no nonsense, ambitious and often demanding of others. The coach was therefore somewhat surprised when, around 10 minutes into the first session, just after the coach had finished introducing herself and her background, Mark's face contorted and he began to sob. The coach's surprise moved swiftly into anxiety at the thought that this could be a reaction to something that she had said and that she would become another coach the senior partner didn't want. Totally missing the opportunity for connection, insight and change that the tears presented, the coach rooted around in her bag for tissues whilst trying to manage her own anxiety. Upon finding out that the one time that she actually needed tissues there were none, she dashed out to the canteen area opposite to grab a napkin (and momentarily flee the scene). By the time she got back Mark had composed himself somewhat and was ruefully apologetic about the outburst.

A social response of finding tissues, offering to make coffee, feeling embarrassed, suggesting a brief break in the session, or similar actions, is the mark of a coach who has no idea what is really happening within the client and yet for the development of whose Self the coach is professionally responsible.

The body can only send signals of the kind that it can itself command. The body cannot command language, but it can command a very substantial repertoire of non-verbal signals. The submission or suppressed rage response of blushing is one. Tears are another.

So far as tears are concerned, what is being displayed is something that is fluid. What tears mean is that the Self has, at that moment, become very fluid. Its boundaries have, for the moment, lost their sense of certain identity and individuality. In whatever has immediately preceded the tears, a trigger to past experience has been activated that, in the present, is offering itself to being reconstructed. So whatever the coach says or does next has profound possibilities within it. The social responses and their type as described above will simply push the old boundaries back into place. What the client is signalling is an opportunity – request is too strong a word – for the re-organizing of some aspect of themselves. Tears are, in the best possible sense, a cry for understanding.

So in this very specific crisis situation in a coaching session what the coach says or does next has profound implications. It is where art supersedes science, though science has made possible the observation that the highest form of art is, at that moment, especially necessary.

CASE STUDY   Mark's story continued

Mark's coach, still feeling slightly shaken, quipped, when she had returned to the room, 'My life story doesn't often have that effect on clients,' eliciting a slightly rueful but sympathetic smile from Mark and helping her to stay with his sadness long enough to talk about it together. So she re-entered his neurobiological system, even though she had initially lost the immediate potential benefits of responding to the tears by papering over the issue entirely. All was not lost, however. She noticed that the tears had subtly altered the dynamic in the room. She gathered her courage to enquire further as to the feelings behind the tears.

It emerged that Mark had recently lost his mother and was also in the process of getting divorced. This was putting significant psychological pressure on him and he had become depressed and was now at an all-time low though trying hard not to show it at work. The safety of the coaching session, and the presence of a woman who was there for him, not leaving him, released pent-up emotions. Over time the coach was able to enable Mark to commence sessions with a psychotherapist with whom he could work through his grief and the issues surrounding his divorce. He continued with the coaching, focusing on his self-awareness and emotional management with others. A 360-degree feedback two years later created reports from team members and colleagues indicating clear change.

Energy focused in crisis

Many forms of psychotherapy and the coaching practices derived from them – Gestalt, psychosynthesis, integrationist, psychodynamic, to name but four – have used a general concept of energy. It is usually not clear whether this refers to psychological or physical energy or, indeed, to cultural or spiritual energy, and what those forms of energy might be. What has become apparent in the neurosciences, however, is that the brain is an energy-hungry system and that the management of energy makes for the effective operating of mind.

The energy supply to all parts of the body has, at its core, the transport by the blood of oxygen and glucose. In electrical terms the body runs off about 95 watts of energy, of which the brain demands between 20 and 25 watts. As the brain is at most only 4 per cent of body mass it can be seen that it is a very energy-hungry system.

Although it is not entirely clear yet how the brain actually manages its energy, it does so by shunting the available energy supply to where it is most needed at any moment in time. It does not generate more when the demand on the brain increases, like turning up the gas jet on a cooker. Turning up the heat would fry the brain.

Metaphorically, if the energy within the brain is thought of as a squad of six soldiers, they can be in one place or another doing whatever has to be done but not in two or more places at the same time – except by halving or further dividing their energy, making less available in any one place. This is the way the brain works.

This, then, is the clue to the management of crisis and transition from an applied neuroscientific point of view. Energy has to be made available to the brain where it is most needed. That is the coach's task, which is most facilitated by the depth of trust between coach and client. Once effected, the brain has a remarkable capacity to find its own answers and to create the new pathways that it needs. Without the supply of energy appropriately available, it cannot do that practically however much the person might want it.

It is the emotions (e-motions: energy = action) that carve the pathways in the brain or find the new connections that are needed to create new insights. So the first task of the coach is create the conditions where the emotions are focused in effective play. And the means of doing that is through relationship. Both the test and the purpose of an effective relationship is trust. And the purpose of establishing trust is to create the conditions where the brain functions at its most adaptive.

States of mind

Siegel (1999) describes the brain's capacity to operate in one of the three main modes. The first is chaotically which, at its extreme, is a manic state. The mind can appear to be extremely busy but in fact is functioning on the basis of very short bursts of attention and is not properly focused anywhere. Many highly creative people function spontaneously somewhat chaotically, the more successful having the capacity to have longer periods of focus. Rebecca was one such client:

CASE STUDY   Rebecca's story

Rebecca, a senior Marketing Executive, had been meeting with her coach for six months but was still struggling to set clear goals or to experience any change. Both felt that they were not making the progress that they had initially hoped for. They would settle into a session on an area of focus, about which Rebecca would leave feeling highly enthused and excited, only for her to reappear in the next session having been too busy to take the actions to which she had apparently committed with great enthusiasm.

Rebecca was in her mid-thirties with what looked to be, on paper, a highly successful career, having moved around the world on a series of expatriate assignments for a series of well-known management consulting firms. However, in contradiction to the highly confident image that she projected to the world, she felt unsure, unclear and in her own assessment, 'stuck'. Whilst she saw that her mobility, flexibility and ability to work under often significant amounts of pressure had allowed her to build a career and move up the corporate ladder, they had also reinforced a somewhat erratic pattern of mental functioning. Year on year she moved to new locations and departments where she 'shook things up', generated a stream of great ideas then moved on leaving others to deal with the process of implementation.

The second mode is rigidity which, at its extreme state, is obsessive-compulsive disorder. In this state attention is very fixed, adaptability is poor, and perceptual shifts are hard to come by. Organizations that are process-driven suffer from imposed rigidity. It is not that order and discipline are to be done away with; quite the contrary. But they should be in the service of the strategic and operational goals of the organization, not the goals in themselves that they so easily become.

CASE STUDY   Peter's story

Peter worked for a large engineering firm in Project Management. He led a large team and had been asked to work with a coach by his manager who had received feedback from a number of Peter's team members that they felt intimidated by him. They reported that Peter was obsessed by the details of their work, and the rigidity and regularity of his need for reporting and updates on progress was getting in the way of them completing their 'day jobs'. Peter was open to getting a coach as he saw this as an investment in his development by the organization, but became very particular about getting the right one. He worked with HR over a period of six months and met with four coaches but none was 'quite the right match'. By the time he finally found one he could settle on working with, two of his team had quit and his own stress levels were through the roof.

The third mode is where the brain is flexible and functioning within the plane of all its possibilities. This is a state that mindfulness, well-trained and practised, can readily induce. The energy of the brain is available to be focused by its frontal lobe cognitive functions.

CASE STUDY

Rebecca, the management consultant described above, was in fact 'busy being busy'. Coaching needed to get her brain working more within the plane of possibilities. In their work to find activity-based goals for change that they could work on together the coach had been unwittingly playing into her unhelpful pattern of functioning. In this case the coach, through supervision, was able to see the pattern and dynamic that was at play and to reflect on this openly and frankly in the session with Rebecca. Whilst initially taken aback, but with a great degree of non-judgemental, shared exploration, Rebecca started to gain insight into how her current way of functioning in her life and work was affecting her. Together they were able to identify an area of her life in which Rebecca showed the capacity for much longer and more consistent focus: playing the piano. She had done this since she was a child but over recent years had stopped playing. She purchased a keyboard and began to practise daily. This experience allowed her brain to release its manic state and to focus for longer and longer periods – eventually working up to half an hour a day. This experience, along with the experience of the coaching sessions where the coach role-modelled a flexible, open energy, was able to give her 'windows into another possible way of functioning' which provided the first building blocks for change.

Bearing these three elements in mind, coaching in crisis and transition sets out to mobilize the state in which the plane of possibilities begins to function, allowing the brain to engage its own resources in the best possible way.

CASE STUDY   Gianni's story

When Gianni came into coaching his whole world was in turmoil. The company he worked for had recently been taken over by a venture capital firm and he was under significant pressure to meet unrealistic targets and to make drastic cuts in his team. He had recently been arguing almost constantly with his wife, and his teenage daughter wasn't speaking to him. To top it all his mother had recently been diagnosed with Alzheimer's and he urgently needed to find a care home for her. He didn't know where to start and was feeling totally hopeless. His coach noticed how she left the first session with him feeling 'utterly drained' and how she almost dreaded the second meeting as – like Gianni – she was starting to feel anxious and overwhelmed in the face of his list of issues.

So the coach realized she needed to work hard on her own energy management in the lead-up to their second meeting. She was to be especially focused on remaining calm, present and resourceful for Gianni. If she wasn't able to do this, she reasoned, how would she ever be able to encourage and support him to do the same?

During their hour together she helped him to connect to the emotions he was feeling, empathizing and affirming his reality without judging or urging him to move to solutions. She watched his shoulders drop, his face relax and the worry lines gradually soften. In his third session Gianni told his coach that these sessions were 'the best time for him, the thing that kept him going through the weeks'. A few months in he was able to start to make sense of the issues he was facing and had found workable solutions to the matter of redundancies in his team as well as having repaired his relationship with his daughter. He was a clever and resourceful person for whom the crisis of so many problems arriving at once had been preventing him from coping effectively.

The relative calm that he was able to experience in sessions through 'tuning' to the coach's brain both role-modelled a new way of 'being with himself' and enabled him to redirect his energy to seeing possibility and therefore options in a situation which had previously seemed debilitating in its awfulness. The coach had engaged his right ventro-lateral pre-frontal cortex through managing her own energy and creating the conditions where Gianni could keep his own focused so that energy could flow to the creative/adaptive structures of the brain instead of being totally consumed by anxiety and doubt. What had previously been chaotic functioning of his brain had settled itself into his brain being able to operate within the plane of possibilities. The coach, knowing enough of Gianni's background to know that he had the capacity within him that he needed, had created the conditions under which his brain did the necessary work by itself.

It is axiomatic, of course, that getting the client's brain into the state described as 'the plane of possibilities' is not possible if the coach's brain is not in such a state; the client's brain will be hyper-sensitive to any signals emanating from the coach that echo the uncertain or disturbed state of the client.

And not forgetting the organization too can be in crisis

Those of us working in organizational settings are of course not just engaging the client's brain, but those of other key stakeholders in the organization. It is therefore important that we recognize the organization as an integrated system and the client's place within that system. It is not unhelpful to conceptualize the organization in its entirety as sharing many features in common with the single brain: an energy-hungry system that exists in relationship and makes sense based on shared meaning. The organization in crisis is likely to be exhibiting similar features as the brain in crisis – reduced capacity to inhabit the plane of possibilities due to one, if not all, of the adaptive emotional responses to crisis: flight, fight or freeze. Awareness of this will enable the coach to work more effectively with their client in changing not just their personal situation, but influencing enhanced functioning in the organization as a whole.

A model of leadership helps too

It is also a part of modern corporate life to be intensely focused on leadership. The coach needs to have at least one effective working model of what leadership is about, one that makes sense in neuroscientific terms and is not simply another descriptive endeavour; and that can be especially deployed at times of crisis and transition. There are two models that we find helpful.

Torbert's (Rooke and Torbert, 2005) Leadership Development Framework (LDF) metric relies essentially on meaning making. The nature of making meaning creates nine different stages of development. The LDF metric locates the person's developmental level within the stages and particularizes not only the current level of functioning but what would have to be done to achieve the next level.

Among Torbert's nine stages one is especially relevant to transitional times. It describes a shift from being an expert achiever to becoming a strategist through becoming an individualist. That is to say, it sees leadership as being a shift from someone whose task is make everything as certain as possible at the highest possible level of skill (the expert achiever) to someone who can tolerate uncertainty and ambiguity by managing their own uncertainties whilst staying flexible and aware. Torbert was without the benefit of modern neuroscience when he was developing his model. Nevertheless, he describes states in which the certainty/rigidity of the expert achiever can, at its best, be replaced by the capacity to create the state of being in the plane of possibilities by making the journey of becoming an individualist. The latter is a person who trusts his or her own judgement when there are high levels of uncertainty, and as such can create the resonant state in others, enabling them to function without becoming either too rigid or too impulsively chaotic.

The significance of attaching this thinking to a leadership model is that the individual undergoing a transitional period has, in the first place, to be a leader to him or herself. Without the capacity to regulate one's own internal states it will not be possible to regulate the states of others.

The second model states this more simply. It has been described by Brown and Brown (2012) as 'the limbic leader' and has six elements attaching to it. The limbic leader is able to connect with others, is courageous, is clever enough, walks their own talk, inspires others, and appears to others to be worth following. In the first five of these she trusts herself. In the sixth, she is trusted.

So having either, or preferably both, of these models in mind gives the coach a structure from within which the client can be viewed and the observations being made fitted into the appropriate framework. This is especially helpful in transitional periods. Both these models relate to the way the brain works – the first developmentally/culturally, the second in terms of the way the core Self has learnt to trust itself.

Conclusion

Using knowledge about the brain is not to require of a coach that s/he abandons other models of coaching intervention. It is to adopt a body of knowledge that underpins all human behaviour however that behaviour is otherwise described. By adopting that knowledge and becoming conversant with it the coach has not only a way of explaining behaviour to the client that has a scientific basis to it but can have a much clearer understanding of the means of creating behaviour change in pursuit of the coaching goals. The shift the coach is making professionally is from descriptive to explanatory under-standings of the client's behaviour and, at the same time, a deeper certainty as to the kind of coaching intervention to make.

It is almost certain that the first quarter of the 21st century will be remembered as the period when the brain was essentially understood, even if all its myriad connections have not been entirely mapped. In consequence the descriptive models of human behaviour that populated the 20th century, and the 'schools' of psychology that supported them, will give way to an agreed understanding of human behaviour that will go on developing. Coaching, as a profession, has the opportunity to adopt neuroscience as its shared underpinning common body of knowledge. That is a transitional option for the executive coaching profession that is worth deep consideration as a way of preventing an eventual crisis of the profession being founded on too little scientific substance. Barbers and surgeons became independent of each other in the 16th century. In the 21st century executive coaches, by analogy, might need to ask whether professionally they want to be barbers or surgeons.

With shared scientific knowledge, executive coaching as a profession may be able to avoid the crisis that psychotherapy has got itself into through developing different schools of theory and practice but having no common ground about the whole person. Enough understanding of brain and behaviour gives the coach a body of professional knowledge that has worldwide applicability as the underpinnings of coaching technique and method. And applied neuroscience offers coaches the opportunity to become the coach not only to the individual or team but, as an expert in brain and (emotionally driven cognitive) executive behaviour, to the whole organization.

References

Brown, P T and Brown, V (2012) *Neuropsychology for Coaches: Understanding the basics*, McGraw-Hill / Open University Press, Marlow

Hall, L (2013) *Mindful Coaching: How mindfulness can transform coaching practice*, Kogan Page, London

Ingalhalikar, M *et al* (2013) Sex differences in the structural connectome of the human brain, *Proceedings of the National Academy of Sciences of the United States*, **111** (2), pp 823–28

MacLean, P D (1990) *The Triune Brain in Evolution: Role in paleocerebral functions*, Plenum Press, New York

McGilchrist, I (2009) *The Master and His Emissary: the divided brain and the making of the western world*, Yale University Press, New Haven and London

Rizzolatti, G *et al* (2002) From mirror neurons to imitation: Facts and speculations. in Meltzoff, A N and Prinz, W (eds) *The Imitative Mind: Development, evolution and brain bases*, Cambridge University Press (pp 247–53)

Rooke, D and Torbert, W R (2005) Seven transformations of leadership, *Harvard Business Review*, April

Siegel, D (2010) *The Mindful Therapist: A clinician's guide to mindsight and neural integration*, WW Norton & Company, New York

Siegel, D (1999) *The Developing Mind: How relationships and the brain interact to shape who we are*, The Guilford Press, New York

Executive coaching in times of organizational change:
a vital support and developmental mechanism

07

ANTHONY M GRANT and SEAN A O'CONNOR

Organizational change and the resultant turbulence have become part of the everyday experience in organizations in the contemporary commercial world. Organizational turbulence can be understood as non-trivial, rapid, and discontinuous change in an organization, brought about by events such as restructures, mergers and acquisitions, or downsizings, the effects of which are often experienced as disconcerting and stressful (Cameron, Kim and Whetten, 1987). Organizational turbulence can be distinguished from purposeful pre-planned change such as specific organizational cultural change initiatives or systematic leadership development programmes.

In the past organizational change has tended to be part of designated mergers and acquisitions or pre-planned cultural development initiatives, and certainly these in themselves are often difficult for organizations to deal with (Gaughan, 2010). However, since the year 2000 the rate and unpredictability of organizational change appear to have escalated, resulting in organizational turbulence placing even greater demands and stresses on the shoulders of managers and executives. Such uncertainty and turbulence have been especially evident since the Global Financial Crisis (2008), and there have been resultant significant increases in levels of stress in organizations worldwide.

Not surprisingly, the executives and employees who work in such unstable organizational contexts all too frequently struggle to develop the psychological and behavioural skills that they need in order to deal with the uncertainty of change whilst simultaneously remaining focused on reaching their organizational or work-related goals. Indeed, the ability to build, manage and maintain effective teams and deliver on work-related goals during periods of organizational turbulence or disruptive change is considered to be one of the most important attributes of effective leaders. Additionally, cognitive flexibility, innovation and creativity can often be particularly important during times of turbulence as tools to meet the needs of rapid unexpected change. However, these kinds of skills come naturally to only a few; for most, some kind of assistance in the form of executive coaching may well be an effective supportive approach. The focus of this chapter is on examining whether executive coaching can indeed help executives and managers during times of organizational turbulence and change. This chapter builds on and extends previous research in this area (eg Grant, 2014; O'Connor and Cavanagh, 2013), examines the extant literature and explores the processes by which executive coaching could be helpful to executives in dealing with change. After summarizing the findings of an executive coaching intervention which was conducted during a period of organizational change and turbulence, the chapter outlines key points from a previously published study (Grant, 2014), and using this as an example case study then presents a range of suggestions for the practice of executive coaching in times of organizational change.

Overview of the literature on executive coaching and organizational change

Executive coaching is frequently used by corporations to help executives develop their capacity to deal with turbulence and change, to provide a framework for leadership development as well as supporting executives in reaching their organizational or work-related goals. Executive coaching can be understood as a helping relationship formed between a client who has leadership, managerial or supervisory authority and responsibility in an organization, and a coach who uses a range of cognitive and behavioural techniques in order to help the client achieve a mutually defined set of goals. These goals may typically include the aim of improving his or her leadership skills, professional performance, wellbeing and the effectiveness of the organization (adapted from Kilburg, 1996).

The academic literature on executive coaching *per se* has grown over time. A search of the database PsycINFO (part of the American Psychological Association) conducted in March 2015 using the keywords 'executive coaching' found a total of 635 citations, with the first published paper being Sperry's (1993) landmark discussion article describing the needs of executives, and how psychologists can best engage in consulting, coaching, and counselling. Between 1993 and 1999 there were a total of 31 citations, between 2000 and 2005 there were a total of 99 citations, between 2006 and 2010 there were a total of 268 citations, and between 2011 and March 2015 there were a total of 237 citations. (For a detailed review and critique of the literature on executive coaching see Grant *et al*, 2010.)

The anecdotal use of coaching by practitioners and consultants as a methodology for helping executives deal with a range of change-related issues is echoed in the peer-reviewed academic literature. Cross-indexing the terms 'executive coaching' and 'change' in PsycINFO in March 2015 identified a total of 144 citations. That is to say that 22.68 per cent of the executive coaching literature in PsycINFO is in relation to issues to do with change. However, of these 144 citations 120 are opinion articles discussing, for example, ideas on how to best facilitate organizational cultural change (Steed, 2013); how systems approaches can facilitate organizational change (Sher, 2013); or how integrating Acceptance and Commitment Therapy into coaching methodologies can help leaders develop a repertoire of crisis resiliency and value-directed change management skills (Moran, 2010).

Limited empirical research on change-related executive coaching

Of the identified 144 citations only 26 were empirical studies. The majority of these (17) used a case study methodology or retrospective survey approaches that explored the effectiveness of executive coaching in relation to organizational change.

This emerging evidence base suggests that executive coaching may well be effective in times of organizational change, although, clearly, far more empirical research is needed to evaluate the effects of executive coaching, particularly in times of change.

Understanding the dynamics of executive coaching in times of change

The above research summary makes apparent that there is limited research exploring explicitly the dynamics of executive coaching during times of change. There is little known about the extent to which coaching helps develop personal change readiness – the capacity to cope with, or the ability to recover from, the uncertainties that organizational change introduces into one's work life. Nor is much known about the extent to which coaching helps develop leadership self-efficacy, resilience, or workplace satisfaction. The cognitive behavioural psychological mechanisms by which executive coaching may help executives deal with organizational turbulence have rarely been discussed in detail in the coaching literature to date. These are important issues if we are to understand the utility of using executive coaching during times of organizational change and turbulence.

Uncovering these issues is not an easy endeavour. The research to date has been primarily qualitative or exploratory in nature. Whilst qualitative and exploratory approaches can give rich insights into individuals' lived experience, they fail to provide the quantitative data required for many standardized assessments. Both qualitative and quantitative data are needed in order to comprehensively develop the knowledge base. Such mixed-methods approaches allow testing of specific hypotheses whilst also exploring the broader and unforseen impact of coaching through qualitative interviews or self-reports.

This chapter will now discuss such psychological mechanisms and will outline the relevance of executive coaching in times of organizational turbulence, using one of the few mixed-methods studies to explicitly explore these issues (Grant, 2014).

The cognitive and behavioural mechanisms of executive coaching

There are a broad range of theoretical frameworks that inform executive coaching practice, from the solution-focused, cognitive behavioural through to psychodynamic and systems theory. Irrespective of one's preferred theoretical approach, there are a common set of principles underpinning executive coaching and these include:

- collaboration;
- accountability;

- awareness raising;
- responsibility;
- commitment;
- action planning;
- action.

In short, regardless of theoretical preferences, the coaching relationship is one in which the coach and client form a collaborative working alliance, articulate goals and develop action steps designed to facilitate goal attainment. The client's responsibility is to enact the action steps, whilst the coach's role is to help keep the coachee on track, helping them to monitor and evaluate their progress over time, as well as providing an intellectual foil for brainstorming and facilitating the process of examining issues from a range of different perspectives.

There are three key underlying cognitive and behavioural mechanisms underpinning the process of executive coaching:

- First, having a confidential and supportive professional relationship from which to reflect and gain perspective on one's personal and professional issues can relieve stress and anxiety and enhance one's capacity for reflexivity.
- Second, the process of setting personally valued goals, and then purposefully working towards achieving them can build self-efficacy, enhance wellbeing, as well as develop solution-focused thinking (Sheldon and Houser-Marko, 2001).
- Third, systemically engaging in such processes whilst being supported in dealing with any setbacks can build individual resilience and enhance self-regulation, which are both vital factors in successfully dealing with change (Baumeister *et al*, 2007). As a result coachees may well experience greater self-efficacy, change readiness, job satisfaction and wellbeing as well as being better equipped to deal with change and workplace stressors.

The utility of coaching in times of organizational change

Given the above description of the process central to coaching, there are several reasons why coaching might help executives function more effectively during times of organizational change or turbulence.

First, in order to deal more effectively with organizational uncertainty and ambiguity, executives need to be able to take time to stand back from the day-to-day cut and thrust of corporate life and engage in the flexible strategic thinking vital to understanding and constructively responding to emergent and unpredictable issues (Grant, 2014). Such reflexivity sits at the core of the coaching process. Second, the effective leadership of others requires leaders themselves to have good self-insight – an awareness of their own personal thoughts, feelings and behaviour (Gill, 2002) – and coaching has been shown to increase such insight (Grant, 2007).

Furthermore, problem-focused diagnostic and causal analysis may not be very helpful when dealing with problems emerging from complex adaptive systems (such as global businesses) that are in states of turbulence. Indeed, an overly diagnostic approach may even create further cognitive confusion, and hence impede goal progression. Additionally, leaders are often embedded in multiple networks of relationships within which change can be dramatically unpredictable (O'Connor and Cavanagh, 2013). In these kinds of situations, leaders need the ability to focus on constructing solutions rather than getting stuck in problem analysis. They also can benefit from being more transformational and adaptive in the way they work within their environments. For many this will require a change in mindset from a diagnostic or reductionist approach to a more holistic, solution-focused thinking style, and coaching has been shown to increase solution-focused thinking and transformational leadership behaviour. Furthermore, self-efficacy is a vital factor for individuals dealing with complex situations that are novel, volatile or stressful, and coaching has been shown to increase both self-efficacy and management skills – and management skills are essential in navigating successfully through turbulent times (Baron and Morin, 2010).

This chapter now presents a case study example of how one global organization utilized executive coaching in order to provide support and leadership development to executives navigating a difficult period of organizational change (Grant, 2014). The use of this case study example allows us to place the previous theoretical discourse into an applied, real-life practical context, and in doing so develop more specific and sophisticated ideas on how to best use executive coaching in times of organizational change.

CASE STUDY A example of how executive coaching can be helpful in times of change and turbulence

The organization concerned specializes in consulting and engineering in project delivery on a global scale. Founded in 1964, the business has grown significantly in the last 10–12 years. It now operates in 17 countries across Asia-Pacific, the Americas, Europe, the Middle East and Africa, employing some 7,000 people in 54 offices.

The organization had also undergone a number of significant changes in recent times. In October 2011, after a 15-year tenure by the previous leader, a new CEO assumed responsibility for the business. In addition to the organizational change and turbulence often associated with new leadership, a new business operating model was also introduced in July 2011. This model had a greater focus on collaboration across the business, requiring significant shifts in the way that various business sectors operated and interacted with each other. Such changes are known to be highly stressful as people negotiate new working relationships and find new places in the organizational hierarchy. The business had also undergone some recent restructuring. Additionally, during 2011 and 2012 it was in the process of exploring the possibility of a transformational merger to assist it in fulfilling its ambitious growth targets.

This depth of organizational change is typically highly stressful for both managers and employees, as they re-calibrate their working practices within a turbulent and shifting corporate landscape whilst simultaneously striving to achieve their designated organizational and role-related goals.

It is these issues that make this a useful case study in which to explore the impact of executive coaching in times of organizational change and turbulence.

The aims of the coaching programme

The programme aimed to be supportive on both professional and personal levels. On a professional level, the primary aims of the coaching programme included developing participants' ability to manage change, to navigate ambiguity and to help them to foster productive relationships across the business. In addition, on a more personal level, the programme was used to support participants in managing their own personal and career development through supporting greater clarity and a deeper understanding of their individual strengths, personal values and development needs.

The participants were 38 executives, and senior and middle managers from the organization's business units and functional areas. There were 30 men and eight women (mean age 42.7 years) from across 14 geographical locations including Adelaide, Auckland, Brisbane, Jakarta, Kuala Lumpur, London, Manchester, Melbourne, Newcastle upon Tyne, Perth, Santiago, Shanghai, Singapore and Sydney.

The programme consisted of positive psychology-based 360-degree feedback about their key perceived strengths, a 'best self' description (Roberts *et al*, 2005), potential developmental directions and four one-to-one coaching sessions. Prior to commencing coaching each coachee was matched with an internal organization business mentor to provide additional support to them throughout the coaching programme.

The executive coaching sessions

The coaching sessions were conducted by 14 experienced professional executive coaches. Twelve of these were registered psychologists and of the other two, one was a member of the International Coach Federation.

The coaching sessions utilized a cognitive-behavioural, solution-focused framework. This approach to coaching rests on the assumption that goal attainment can be best facilitated by understanding the reciprocal relationships between one's thoughts, feelings, behaviour and the environment, and by aligning these four domains in order to best support goal attainment. Incorporating a strong solution-focused perspective into a cognitive-behavioural modality helps orientate the coaching away from diagnostic problem analysis and towards the development of personal strengths and solution construction.

There were four, 90-minute one-to-one coaching sessions. Coachees prepared for each coaching session by completing a reflection log prior to meeting with their coach in which they noted any specific challenges they had faced in the preceding weeks, and their goals for the coaching session. Such techniques have been found to help individuals effectively enact purposeful change (see Gollwitzer, 1999).

All initial sessions were completed face-to-face. Subsequent sessions were face-to-face where the coach and coachee were based in the same city, with other sessions being held over the phone. In total 62 per cent of sessions were completed face-to-face.

To ensure that the coaching session remained goal-focused, each session started by setting a specific goal for the session. Such goals included: becoming less reactive and defensive in meetings; dealing with specific aspects of change; demonstrating better listening and communication skills whilst under pressure;

becoming more adept at delegating; and developing stronger relationships both in the business and with clients. Following goal setting, the coach and coachee then typically explored the reality of the current situation, before developing options for action and concluding with specific action steps that helped define the way forward (see Whitmore, 1992). The coach's role was to provide a personal reflective space, to help the coachee think from different perspectives, and to work with the coachee to brainstorm and develop potential options and action plans. Each coaching session concluded by delineating specific action steps to be completed prior to the next coaching session. Such iterative goal-focused processes maximize the chance of real change occurring and ensure that each coaching session builds on the work of the last.

Additional organization support was provided through four- or five-way meetings with the coach, coachee, their manager and/or internal sponsor, their mentor, and their Human Resource business partner. The objective of this meeting was to review progress, and ensure alignment between the key coaching themes and the provision of ongoing support mechanisms with the aim of maintaining behavioural change over the longer term.

Determining the impact of the programme

The issues deemed to be of most importance by the organization in determining the effectiveness of the coaching programme in helping the coachees adapt to the changing organizational context and the associated organizational turbulence were:

- the extent to which the coachees achieved their goals;

- changes in solution-focused thinking styles;

- changes in change readiness;

- changes in leadership self-efficacy;

- changes in personal resilience.

In order to gather some qualitative data on participants' experience of the coaching programme they were asked to respond to the following open-ended questions on its completion:

- What specific benefits (if any) has the coaching had on your leadership abilities?

- What specific benefits (if any) has the coaching had on other areas of your life?

The use of an open-question methodology is an important point in this study because it allowed the participants themselves to determine the various aspects of the coaching experience that they considered to be of most benefit.

Results and outcomes of the coaching programme

Participation in the coaching programme was associated with significantly increased goal attainment, enhanced solution-focused thinking, greater ability to deal with change, and increased leadership self-efficacy and resilience. (For full details of assessment processes, details of measures and data sets and statistical analyses see Grant, 2014.)

All participants gave responses to the open-ended questions. Key themes were identified in the participant's written responses. The following categories were ordered by frequency of inclusion (note: some participants made more than one response).

Impact on leadership abilities

1   Increased self-awareness and increased clarity of thought: 18 responses.

2   Helped build leadership brand and build leadership skills: 12 responses.

3   Helped achieve organizational or professional goals: 9 responses.

4   Greater awareness of career possibilities: 5 responses.

5   Helped achieve better communication within organization: 3 responses.

6   Higher levels of confidence and trust in team: 3 responses.

Impact on other areas of life

1   Better work–life balance: 15 responses.

2   Better relationships with family; less stress and more calm: 7 responses.

3   Greater sense of purpose in life and awareness of personal values: 5 responses.

4   Feel better about self and life in general: 4 responses.

5   Able to use programme insights in other areas of life: 3 responses.

Comments from participants often represented a number of the above categories. This can be seen in the representative examples provided below of responses from participants:

> *Opportunity to discuss ideas and issues in a neutral forum and realized the important of reflection. I've developed deeper trust in the team and developed more patience in meetings and a greater degree of listening and engagement. I now have more awareness of my goals, other peoples' perceptions of me and the things that trigger me.*

Another participant wrote:

> *The coaching sessions have been very beneficial; I feel that my sessions have focused me on my developmental themes, as well as helping me understand more about myself.*

In relation to the impact the coaching had on other areas of life one participant wrote that the coaching:

> *Provided impetus to change some of my behaviours that were causing stress, worry and negativity. I now have an increased commitment to exercise, health and reconnecting with friends, neighbours and family.*

In summary, this case study suggests that executive coaching during times of organizational change is associated with goal attainment, enhanced solution-focused thinking, and improved flexibility in dealing with change, while also supporting increased leadership self-efficacy and resilience. Furthermore, the benefits from the coaching programme seem to generalize to other (non-work-related) areas in the coachees' lives. Such generalization is not unexpected (Yeow and Martin, 2013), with these self-reports providing additional data suggesting that executive coaching during change and turbulence has supportive utility providing both professional and personal benefit.

So what? Reflections on the outcomes of the case study example

The question now arises as to the importance of these outcomes and the relevance to executives, leaders and managers in organizations that are experiencing significant change or organizational turbulence. It is to these issues that we now turn.

Coaching enhances solution-focused thinking

Coaching was associated with significant increases in solution-focused thinking – a key skill in times of organizational turbulence and change. This is important because many leaders have a propensity to engage in analytical problem-focused thinking (Mumford *et al*, 2000). Of course, problem-focused analytical thinking is important. Problem-focused approaches assume attempts to understand the causal structure and aetiology of a problem will help to identify effective solutions or pathways to action. A problem-focused analytical approach can indeed be effective with relatively simple or stable problem states, where there is ample time to reflect on a specific problem, or when attention to detail and minutiae is required (Forgas and East, 2008). However, problem-focused approaches may not be so effective during periods of organizational turbulence when causal factors are not clear or too complex to lay out individually and identify specifically. The context is often changing too quickly and a more adaptive responsive process may be required (Stacey, 1996). Indeed problem-focused thinking at its extreme may even lead to a debilitating cycle of rumination – a persistent focus on one's problems. Such ruminative cycles have been linked to the onset of depressive experiences, biased negative memory recall, reduced creativity and, paradoxically, impaired problem-solving skills (Lyubomirsky and Nolen-Hoeksema, 1995).

Effective leadership requires cognitive flexibility (Chung, Su and Su, 2012) and the ability to apply a range of thinking styles including both problem-focused and solution-focused thinking where necessary. This cognitive flexibility is particularly important during periods of organizational change (Gill, 2002). A solution-focused approach tends to eschew explorations of causal aetiologies, and instead focuses directly on working out how to create a desired change state. In this sense, solution-focused approaches are essentially creative. Through identifying resources, developing approach goals and exploring different ways of achieving those goals, the repertoire of action possibilities is dramatically increased. Indeed, the ability to engage in a constructive style of thinking orientated towards the development of solutions is a crucial ability when working in systems fluctuating through change. Leaders embedded in these complex contexts need to be able to rapidly adapt to emerging problems from a range of different perspectives. This requires disengagement from the problem, the identification of specific goals, and the marshalling of resources needed to make positive change. These four facets are the core constructs of solution-focused thinking. The application of these facets was clearly evident from participants' qualitative comments. For example:

> [The coaching] has helped me to focus on areas of strength as a means to drive better performance... it helped me reflect on activities and achievements and prompted me to think about other ways of tackling problems. I was able to

look at the situation from different perspectives and come up with new and different solutions.

Changes in change readiness and leadership self-efficacy

The coaching in this case study also had positive impact on change readiness. Change readiness is a construct essential to job satisfaction; the ability to solve job-related problems, as well as the ability to constructively and proactively engage with challenges inherent to organizational change (Jones, Jimmieson and Griffiths, 2005). Given that the organization in our example was experiencing significant organizational fluctuation, the observed increase in change readiness was an important indicator that executive coaching can assist coachees to become more adaptive and confident in dealing with change and turbulence.

This type of confidence in times of change is important because it is a core component of self-efficacy. Self-efficacy is a domain-specific confidence in one's ability to perform a specific task. It is an important predictor of behavioural change, as one's individual's judgement of self-efficacy influences the cognitive decision-making process to engage in goal-directed behaviours, as well as the degree of effort and resilient persistence (de Vries, Dijkstra, and Kuhlman, 1988). Leadership self-efficacy can thus be understood as the level of confidence that a leader hold in his/her ability to successfully enact effective leadership behaviour. In times of organizational turbulence leadership self-efficacy would include belief in the ability to engage in behaviours related to setting directions and goals for followers and building organizational relationships supporting commitment to change processes, and then working with individuals to overcome potential obstacles to change (Paglis and Green, 2002). The importance of leadership self-efficacy in relation to motivating and engaging team members during times of organizational change is highlighted by one participant who wrote:

> It [the coaching] helped clarify my thoughts and aspirations into achievable outcomes, and this generated a greater sense of purpose, and my confidence has improved. I feel re-energized. By being more aware of my leadership behaviours and their impact on others and feeling more confident in my interactions with others, I have noticed stronger relationships developing between myself, my peers and my team, and I feel much better about dealing with the current situation.

These findings that coaching enhanced leadership self-efficacy provide supportive evidence of executive coaching as an effective organizational change-related intervention.

Impact on personal resilience

The coaching programme was also effective at enhancing resilience – clearly a vital factor in dealing with change. While resilience was not explicitly targeted within the coaching engagements, the observed increases in resilience make sense because as individuals work towards their goals there are inevitable setbacks and challenges to be overcome. Tackling setbacks is likely to improve one's resilience as individuals begin to experience an increased sense of personal mastery as they overcome such challenges. Indeed, coaching has been found to increase resilience and reduce depression in a range of populations including medical students (Taylor, 1997), high-school students (Green, Grant and Rynsaardt, 2007) and in the workplace with executives (Grant, Curtayne and Burton, 2009). Clearly the coaching process, through supporting individuals to autonomously engage and overcome difficult and trying circumstances, is providing an environment for resilience to emerge and be strengthened within the coachee. The coaching conversation in this sense becomes an environment in which additional resources (the coach and the coaching process) are available to the coachee to support a positive and adaptive change experience. Any identified successes or challenges overcome then become evidence to support perspectives of success over future challenges. In this way a positive flourishing feedback loop is created supporting continual growth and resilience building.

The role of reflexivity in developing leadership skills

Any change process requires iterative intentional processing. The opportunity to reflect, review and evaluate one's leadership approach and process has long been recognized as an essential part of any developmental change (Lewin, 1952). Alfes, Truss and Gill (2010) discuss the importance of individual and cultural change defined as shifts in collective values, beliefs and learned ways of behaving. Qualitative comments from participants in the current case study under analysis echo these points:

> Coaching has taken my leadership abilities to the next level, and has acted as a catalyst to deeper self-awareness and ultimately changes in behaviours, approach and outcomes.

Another wrote about the role of reflection in developing leadership skills:

> The coaching gave me important time to reflect on my activities and prompted me to think about other ways of tackling problems. I was able to reflect on my style of leadership. I have been able to stop and think about what I am doing

and where I am going. It has taught me (through self-reflection) to focus on my leadership strengths and what I am good at. The coaching and self-reflection have really helped me become more self-aware of my leadership abilities and then work more effectively with others.

The coaching sessions had an immediate impact for some:

I've rapidly come to see those areas of my style that were not helpful in developing stronger leadership relationships. The one-on-one coaching sessions allowed me to explore these issues of style in a safe environment and hone into the key specific and measurable activities that I could do to change my style.

Enhanced work–life balance: an unexpected outcome

Many participants experienced better work–life balance and relationships with family, a greater sense of purpose in life and awareness of their personal values, or an ability to use insights gained in coaching in other areas of their lives. This information would not have been identified without the use of open-ended qualitative questions. As one participant noted:

The coaching made me consider work–life balance in a more professional way. I have now given this a much higher priority and now I do not see this as a detriment to achieving my professional goals but rather a requirement of achieving them.

Another found the leadership techniques learnt in coaching to be useful in other areas of life:

I have been able to apply the same techniques to my family, especially my children and other relationships too.

What we can learn from this case study example

There a number of key learning points that can be gleaned from this example case study regarding the effective implementation and expected effects of executive coaching during periods of organizational change and turbulence:

- set broad issue parameters for the coaching intervention, but encourage coachees to determine their own goals;
- ensure the coaching is of both professional and personal relevance to the coachee where appropriate;
- encourage a strong solution-focused coaching style rather than problem analysis;
- foster reflectivity and enhanced perspective-taking in the coachee.

How to work with leaders during times of organizational change and turbulence

Coaching individuals who are embedded in complex, unexpected and sometimes turbulent change is a difficult undertaking. Such coachees are usually faced with difficult tasks under extreme pressure. It is easy under great stress and pressure to fall into patterns of behaviour that may have previously been successful under vastly differing circumstances. While this might be a well-known and comfortable approach for a coachee, it may not be the most appropriate given the turbulent circumstances at hand. When the need for adaptive function is most relevant, a shift in perspective is required and coaching is well placed to assist with this developmental pathway.

When coaching during times of organizational change, it is the task of the coach to provide a supportive environment that can allow a coachee to suspend their experience of stress and explore more adaptive possibilities that can assist them in reaching their goals. Coachees need to engage in this challenge while also supporting their team through difficult and unexpected circumstances. Working in this way under such circumstances creates tension between a leader's instinct to act quickly in familiar and known ways, and the time required to allow for more adaptive ideas for action to emerge. Helping individual coachees to remain for the requisite period of time at these points of tension in order to let creative possibilities to emerge is very challenging. This however is crucial, as it provides the conditions for coachees to identify adaptive possibilities for moving forward.

There are a number of things coaches can do in order to best set the conditions that encourage adaptive thinking even during times of organizational change. These include:

- creating a coaching climate of trust within the sessions;
- support the suspension of assumption and perspective taking;
- including multiple levels of a system within coaching conversations.

Coaching climate

The term 'coaching climate' refers specifically to the atmosphere and experience of the coaching process within and across each session. If the climate of a coaching session is one built on trust then a number of benefits become available for the coach and the coachee. This is particularly important in times of turbulent change, as the climate of the organization may have dramatically shifted. In most cases this shift in organizational climate is one geared towards urgency, risk aversion and potential negative expectations. These conditions create overworked and stressed experiences depleting of internal personal and organizational resources. In negative emotional environments, similar to that described here, an individual's ability to think more strategically becomes limited (Lyubomirsky and Nolen-Hoeksema, 1995). This is problematic as out-of-the-box thinking may well be what is most required in order for the leader to identify effective and adaptive opportunities to enact through the change.

If a coaching climate can be created in which the coachee feels they have the permission to explore ideas and can take risks, they will then have more opportunity to identify pathways for positive adaptation. A coach can support this by building trust and openness within the engagement. The coach should take on a large degree of responsibility for managing the space in which the coaching takes place. This includes the very basics of coaching, for example: ensuring that the booking of rooms is not a stressful process for the client; limiting interruptions and disturbances of daily regular work activities; and setting coaching engagements at times where the coachee might be least impacted and have more capacity for creative thought.

The creation of positive rapport between the coach and coachee is essential to building a supportive coaching climate. Coaches should focus on ensuring that all promises of delivery are kept. A coachee should not be chasing their coach for promised support or materials, for example. Another strategy might be to normalize stress and use appropriate personal sharing or disclosure to create more rapport and connection between the coach and client. Rapport is essential as without rapport there is no room for challenge, and challenge is essential for stretching coachees beyond their current frame of thought. This position brings us to our next important coaching behaviour to support adaptive function of leaders in times of change.

Supporting the suspension of assumptions and perspective taking

If a coach has created a supportive environment within which there is trust, a coachee will be more likely to explore alternative ideas and remain open to challenge. This is an essential part of the coaching engagement, particularly in times of turbulent change, as it ensures there is enough trust in the relationship in order for challenge to occur. Challenge and tension put relationships at risk and there needs to be enough trust built up to allow the coach to take risk in challenging the perspectives of their client. This is particularly the case when asking clients to challenge their assumptions around any given situation.

Assisting a coachee to suspend their assumptions and judgements allows them to develop new insights, often formulated from implicit information already held by the coachee. This in turn can provide possible adaptive pathways to solutions. The process of suspending assumptions can work through the reflective analysis of prior judgements. This can be challenging during times of change as pausing and reflecting may be the last thing on the mind of a leader trying to manage complex change. From this perspective, suspending assumptions is about broadening attention beyond the current state of awareness. This process strengthens the need for a positive coaching environment, as positivity tends to support a broadening of attentional capacity (Fredrickson and Branigan, 2005).

One suggestion made by Isaacs (2008) in his thesis on dialogue, useful for coaching engagements in particular, is that of externalizing thought – working with leaders through identifying challenging or unexpected situations in their experience and walking them through their thought sequences at the time. This process can help to identify judgements and assumption that are clouding their progress. The coach and coachee can work with these real-life scenarios to identify alternative thought sequences that might have been more helpful or productive and create action plans to enact these in similar situations. As a coach, it can also help to ask questions about alternative perspectives that might be held by others on the situation under investigation. These other perspectives may be of those present or of others who, if present, might have seen things differently. These identified useful perspectives can then be used to identify alternative pathways moving forward (Argyris, 2000).

This process may require coaches to actively challenge a leader's assumptions when required. This approach requires a great deal of rapport and finesse, particularly if the assumptions are strongly held and are part of an individual's leadership identity.

In order to encourage exploration and the process of perspective shift, it can be important to include multiple perspectives in analysing the coachee's goals and processes. This might include identifying respected leaders within or outside the organization and using these as a lens to analyse a given situation. This can provide the coachee with a tool to step out of their perspective. By stepping into multiple potential perspectives of a given situation a coachee can open up alternative ways of seeing events that can be chosen by the coachee and may provide multiple and alternative adaptive ways to move forward.

Including multiple levels of a system within coaching conversations

Supporting a leader through coaching to include a systems perspective within the coaching conversation is similar in many ways to helping a coachee explore multiple perspectives (O'Connor and Cavanagh, 2013). However, this process differs essentially in that each perspective available for exploration can also be applied at multiple systemic levels. Taking a systems approach also includes thinking about the relationships across a system more specifically and how these might influence processes and experiences, rather than just thinking about the potential perspective individuals might hold on a given situation.

A systems approach includes identifying important components of the coachee's network in strategic planning and solution finding. This might include identifying key players in a change process or organizational environment and analysing issues and challenges from their perspective or position. Often what seems most important from one position may have different value when reviewed from a different organizational level, position, team or individual (Sher, 2013). This can open up opportunities for action pathways and solutions previously unavailable to a coachee.

Finding leverage points through tension and relational connectivity

In order to recognize important aspects of a system that may help in identifying leverage points for perspective shift and/or actual change in the system, it may well be useful for coaches to help their coachees to explore tension in a more active fashion. For example, we have found it useful to ask questions about times when the coachee is feeling most uncomfortable or unsure of themselves, or about situations in which they are identifying unusual behaviour or responses in others. Once these tension points have been identified it can be informative to engage in a relational view of these situations. One way this can be achieved is by identifying what is most at risk, exploring the processes within relational exchanges, and examining how things (eg, power dynamics, emotional exchanges) may have shifted from previous relational states (Isaacs, 2008). In many cases, these experiences can often be about relationships that have been inadvertently damaged or an identification of a required relationship that doesn't exist. Relational connectivity is often a key concept for understanding systems-level experience, particularly within an organizational change process.

Coaches can explore with the leader the degree of interconnectedness between teams, organizational function and organizational members in order to identify the current active pattern of relationship. This information can then be used to ascertain any potential for benefit to changing the degree of connectedness at these different levels; are they too interconnected thus slowing down progress, or do they need more connectivity as information is being poorly shared? The question then becomes, what are the important and essential patterns of interconnection required for adaptive function in times of change? This analysis must include both the content of interaction required for adaptive function, and the quality of that interaction to take place.

Presenting problems are often clothed in previous experience and may seem insurmountable to leaders when under the pressure of unexpected change. This can lead to coachees falling into previous behavioural patterns; these may not be the most adaptive, and in the worst cases can actually be highly maladaptive or dysfunctional (Kets de Vries, 2004). When coaches create a supportive and trusting environment for their coachees, they can provide the conditions for new forms of adaptive thinking. Through challenging a coachee's assumptions, exploring multiple perspectives and engaging in a systems approach to analysis and engagement, a coach can assist a leader to open more pathways to the potential alternative actions required to function more effectively in times of organizational change and turbulence.

Summary

The example case study presented in this chapter provides useful evidence that executive coaching during periods of organizational change can indeed be an effective, if not vital, support and developmental mechanism. It is clear that executive coaching during times of organizational change can have a wide range of positive effects including facilitating goal attainment, enhancing solution-focused thinking, developing greater change readiness, and increasing leadership self-efficacy and resilience. In addition, it appears that the positive impact of executive coaching in times of organizational change can generalize to non-work areas such as family life. However, the implementation of these programmes requires planning and care if the possible benefits are to be made manifest. In this way, times of significant change and organizational turbulence can have positive impacts on both organizations and the people that work in them.

References

Alfes, K, Truss, C and Gill, J (2010) The HR manager as change agent: evidence from the public sector, *Journal of Change Management*, **10** (1), pp 109–27

Argyris, C (2000) Teaching smart people how to learn, *Harvard Business Review*, May–June, pp 99–109

Baron, L and Morin, L (2010) The impact of executive coaching on self-efficacy related to management soft-skills, *Leadership & Organization Development Journal*, **31** (1), pp 18–38

Baumeister, R F, Vohs, K D and Tice, D M (2007) The strength model of self-control, *Current Directions in Psychological Science*, **16**, pp 351–55

Cameron, K S, Kim, M U and Whetten, D A (1987) Organizational effects of decline and turbulence, *Administrative Science Quarterly*, **32** (2), pp 222–40

Chung, S-H, Su, Y-F and Su, S-W (2012) The impact of cognitive flexibility on resistance to organisational change, *Social Behavior and Personality: An International Journal*, **40** (5), pp 735–45

de Vries, H, Dijkstra, M and Kuhlman, P (1988) Self-Efficacy: The third factor besides attitude and subjective norm as a predictor of behavioural intentions, *Health Education Research*, **3** (3), pp 273–82

Forgas, J P and East, R (2008) On being happy and gullible: mood effects on skepticism and the detection of deception, *Journal of Experimental Social Psychology*, **44** (5), pp 1362–67

Fredrickson, B L and Branigan, C (2005) positive emotions broaden the scope of attention and thought-action repertoires, *Cognition & Emotion*, **19** (3), pp 313–32

Gaughan, P A (2010) *Mergers, Acquisitions, and Corporate Restructurings*, 5th edn, John Wiley & Sons, London

Gill, R (2002) Change management – or change leadership? *Journal of Change Management*, **3** (4), pp 307–18

Gollwitzer, P M (1999) Implementation intentions: simple effects of simple plans, *American Psychologist*, **54** (7), pp 493–503

Grant, A M (2007) Enhancing coaching skills and emotional intelligence through training, *Industrial & Commercial Training*, **39** (5), pp 257–66

Grant, A M (2014) The efficacy of executive coaching in times of organizational change, *Journal of Change Management*, **14** (2), pp 258–80

Grant, A M, Curtayne, L and Burton, G (2009) Executive coaching enhances goal attainment, resilience and workplace well-being: a randomized controlled study, *Journal of Positive Psychology*, **4** (5), pp 396–407

Grant, A M *et al* (2010) The state of play in coaching today: a comprehensive review of the field, *International Review of Industrial and Organizational Psychology*, **25**, pp 125–68

Green, L S, Grant, A M and Rynsaardt, J (2007) Evidence-based life coaching for senior high school students: building hardiness and hope, *International Coaching Psychology Review*, **2** (1), pp 24–32

Isaacs, W (2008) *Dialogue: The art of thinking together*, Crown Business, New York

Jones, R A, Jimmieson, N L and Griffiths, A (2005) The impact of organizational culture and reshaping capabilities on change implementation success: the mediating role of readiness for change, *Journal of Management Studies*, **42** (2), pp 361–86

Kets de Vries, M (2004) Organizations on the couch: a clinical perspective on organizational dynamics, *European Management Journal*, **22** (2), pp 183–200

Kilburg, R R (1996) Toward a conceptual understanding and definition of executive coaching, *Consulting Psychology Journal: Practice and Research*, **48** (2), pp 134–44

Lewin, K (1952) *Field Theory in Social Science: Selected theoretical papers by Kurt Lewin*, Tavistock, London

Lyubomirsky, S and Nolen-Hoeksema, S (1995) Effects of self-focused rumination on negative thinking and interpersonal problem solving, *Journal of Personality & Social Psychology*, **69** (1), pp 176–90

Moran, D J (2010) Act for leadership: using acceptance and commitment training to develop crisis-resilient change managers, *International Journal of Behavioural Consultation and Therapy*, **6** (4), pp 341–55

Mumford, M D *et al* (2000) Leadership skills for a changing world: solving complex social problems, *The Leadership Quarterly*, **11** (1), pp 11–35

O'Connor, S and Cavanagh, M (2013) The coaching ripple effect: The effects of developmental coaching on wellbeing across organisational networks, *Psychology of Well-Being: Theory, Research and Practice*, **3** (1), p 2

Paglis, L L and Green, S G (2002) Leadership self-efficacy and managers' motivation for leading change, *Journal of Organizational Behaviour*, **23** (2), pp 215–35

Roberts, L M *et al* (2005) Composing the reflected best-self portrait: building pathways for becoming extraordinary in work organizations, *Academy of Management Review*, **30** (4), pp 712–36

Sheldon, K M and Houser-Marko, L (2001) Self-concordance, goal attainment, and the pursuit of happiness: can there be an upward spiral? *Journal of Personality & Social Psychology*, **80** (1), pp 152–65

Sher, M (2013) *The Dynamics of Change: Tavistock approaches to improving social systems*, Karnac Books, London

Sperry, L (1993) Working with executives: consulting, counselling, and coaching, *Individual Psychology: Journal of Adlerian Theory, Research & Practice*, **49** (2), pp 257–66

Stacey, R D (1996) *Complexity and Creativity in Organizations*, Berrett-Koehler Publishers, New York

Steed, J (2013) Building a coaching culture in your organization, in Forman, D, Joyce, M and McMahon, G (eds) *Creating a Coaching Culture for Managers in Your Organization*, Routledge/Taylor & Francis Group, New York (pp 25–33)

Taylor, L M (1997) The Relation between resilience, coaching, coping skills training, and perceived stress during a career-threatening milestone, *Dissertation Abstracts International*, **58** (5), pp 2738–39

Whitmore, J (1992) *Coaching for Performance*, Nicholas Brealey, London

Yeow, J and Martin, R (2013) The role of self-regulation in developing leaders: a longitudinal field experiment, *The Leadership Quarterly*, **24** (5), pp 625–37

Leaders in crisis: attending to the shadow side

08

ERIK DE HAAN and ANTHONY KASOZI

In this chapter, we explore how we as coaches can help leaders become more aware of and address their shadow sides, which can manifest more strongly during times of crisis and transition, with potential high costs for individuals and those around them.

CASE STUDY Greg's story

The last nine months have 'been the most difficult of my life', Greg tells his coach. He's talking about his planned return to work after an enforced absence from his new role as Director and Chief Executive of a young offenders' rehabilitation charity. Although he talks now about being energetic and keen to get back to work, he's hesitant and uncharacteristically contemplative and apprehensive. His recent promotion to an executive leadership role has meant taking on a higher, more public profile, working harder and longer than ever and yet getting 'blamed for all my predecessors' errors, getting little thanks for my hard work, and destroying the confidence that many others had put in me'.

Much of what Greg was facing was unfortunate. The day he took over at the helm, the charity was confronted with the damning findings of a donor-instigated consultant's report. In the weeks that followed, Greg suspended and subsequently fired staff members, and two board members resigned. Greg was left working with a split acrimonious board and persisting accusations and counter-accusations between board and senior executives. Despite working longer, harder, and more relationally than his predecessor, Greg 'failed' to resolve the situation. Worse still, Greg fell ill at a 'critical time' suffering from severe asthmatic episodes, body pains and panic attacks. Six months into the new role, he'd been forced to take extended sick leave, a development which 'further estranged him from his feuding board and increased the sense of siege and embattlement' experienced by his executive co-team members.

Talking to his coach, Greg now acknowledges that he cannot go back and do more of the same. He feels that the hard-working, hard-pushing, quick-stepping approach is no more likely to work now than it had done the time before. Time away from work has given him space to think how better to use his strengths this time round. He is more aware of his limitations and less confident that he can ignore their 'foreboding presence'. As he contemplates going back, he feels like a 'wounded gladiator returning to the very arena in which he had last fallen'.

Greg's experience of the challenges of recovery is sadly one that far too often confronts us as coaches working with people in challenging roles. Often our clients have to step into situations of tremendous responsibility, at short notice, and with minimal support or preparation. They deal with multiple challenges driven by events and circumstances beyond their control. They face change and recurring crises for which they feel (and are sometimes held) accountable. Under these circumstances their best attributes are often engaged. They drive hard to achieve and may even enjoy significant and rewarding accomplishments. However, amidst it all, they also come face-to-face with unhelpful and unproductive patterns of their own behaviour. They face aspects of themselves which they may have hitherto relegated to the background, but may now feel overwhelmed by and unable to push aside. They feel unable to live without these aspects as they offer potential solutions to their problems. Yet they also cannot continue to live with them as they too often lead to personally and socially costly consequences. Somehow they have to find ways to embrace and integrate their challenging selves into new and effective ways of working. If they are unable or unwilling to contend with these challenging 'shadow aspects' of themselves, individuals may go into overdrive and become gripped by these shadow sides and patterns of being, doing, thinking and relating.

Supporting leaders in crisis or transition

As coaches we notice and may even share personal and previous experience of the challenges that create the situations that leaders like Greg face. These are common scenarios. As coaches, we need to acknowledge that, and improve how we engage with and support leaders facing challenges and crises. We need to rise to the challenges presented by clients seeking to find ways of attending to and embracing the shadow sides of leadership exposed by the conditions they face.

As we've repeatedly witnessed in our practice, seeing, and embracing, something mostly hidden and elusive is by no means easy. Yet our experience working in this area has shown us that it's not only useful but essential. The costs of failing to do so are very high – financially, socially, and in relation to physical and mental health. We've found that as in other areas of health, awareness precedes prevention and prevention delivers useful outcomes for those indirectly as well as those directly involved. However, we also know that awareness on its own doesn't necessarily lead to the choices and changes required to escape and/or change difficult patterns of overdrive. Leaders at senior levels, in fact all those responsible for others in the workplace, should sooner or later be learning about, and from, their shadow aspects.

Of course, the shadow side of leadership is not the only area to consider, and other chapters in this book suggest how to address other aspects of developmental experience.

What we address

Given the focus of this book we explore the reality and challenges of overdrive and hubris often experienced during times of transition and crisis. Our goal is to offer input that may help us to be more effective at working with senior executive clients addressing such challenges. We consider:

- **Contexts and challenges that leaders face** and the need for us as coaches to pay attention to and notice leaders' work realities, and why these matter to those we work with.

- **Nature of the leadership role (its attending shadow) and the tendencies to derailment (overdrive and hubris)**: what it is about leadership that triggers hubris, and what we should look out for when coaching high-performing and successful leaders.

- **When and how derailment typically expresses itself:** how we may recognize when leaders are facing difficulties, and how to work effectively with those facing the challenges of derailment.

- **Patterns and behaviours of leaders:** how we can use descriptive typology to gain greater insight into the behaviours and patterns of clients.

- **Coaching support leaders in overdrive may most need and benefit from:** how we can support leaders to attend to and to recover from overdrive.

The contexts that create the challenges leaders face

As coaches working with leaders in challenging fast-paced roles we're aware that they're often under tremendous pressure to be decisive. This is the case in organizational transformation or even crisis. Leaders tell us that major unavoidable changes in context and external events require them to be working through, living with, and leading and supporting others through recurrent episodes of crisis. The problems leaders have to deal with are constantly presented to them as needing deliberate, quick and intelligent action. In their decision making they're also asked to be cognizant of a multiplicity of factors such as the interests of a diverse set of stakeholders (internally and externally), regulatory requirements, standards of accountability, the scrutiny of critical media, and an informed, active and technologically connected public.

Not only do leaders' executive decisions often have to be made in an instant, soon after they are made, they are transmitted quickly across the globe, available for anyone to respond to or comment on. Executives today rarely have the time for long contemplation before deciding. They can no longer rely on having the luxury of isolated spheres of influence within which to test different strategies or study the consequences of a judgement or choice before making the next one.

Executives who we coach agree that they typically have to contend with a litany of challenges. They say that they have to be:

- Incredibly hard-working, decisive and intellectually, physically, and emotionally resilient, required to work across time zones, and to be on call at the ping of an e-mail, or the tinkle of a telephone even during evenings, weekends and holidays.

- Productive and seen to be productive with a strong strategic sense, but also able to switch mode and to quickly and effectively engage, deeply and constructively, with detail.

- Prepared to be visible and on display at all times, open to criticism and able to respond constructively to it. Flexible, comfortable with conflict, and adaptable to ever-increasing and complex demands *and* able to work well with ambiguity.

- Adaptable across cultures and across conversations within cultures. Highly self-aware, with a strong sense of self and preparedness to offer their values for inspection.

- A hard-working team player as well as a strongly independent individual. A motivator and a judge at the same time. Part of the organizational push, rush and tumble as well as a pace-setting runner, able to avoid the kerfuffle and venture out confidently ahead – to lead the way for others.

- Comfortable with knowledge working of all kinds; being on top of the facts about their organizational unit, allegiances, unwritten rules, present but changing 'no-go areas', and who needs to know what.

- Purposeful and knowing what their longer-term purpose is; which objectives they cannot compromise on but also those they are happy to be flexible about and to accommodate.

- Engaged and collaborative, as well as tough and uncompromising. Protecting the individual yet looking after the whole. Working at the core and yet felt as present at the periphery. Responsible for detail and at the same time staying out of the detail to imagine the future.

- Quick and available to troubleshoot; acutely aware of and prescient towards situations that could spiral out of control. Present and visible, and seen to address issues as they arise – wherever and whenever.

In summary, they have to be incredibly present to a great many people. They have to be erudite and action-oriented; reflective and initiating; flexible and warm in relationships yet decisive. Leaders of today have to embrace many paradoxes and transcend many contradictions. What is required of them appears superhuman, yet around the globe entire hierarchies of executives face exactly these challenges and demands daily. It is not surprising that so many leaders derail.

The nature of the leadership role (its attending shadow) and tendencies to derailment (overdrive and hubris)

Leadership at any level is a place of privilege, honour and distinction. Whatever the size of the organization, wherever in the hierarchy, to lead is to be elevated into responsibility for others and to be accountable for the activities and impact of those being led. The leadership role is therefore one of crucial importance for the team, organization and beyond as it seeks to achieve its aims.

At the same time, being honoured and set apart as a leader also always opens up a rift, between 'you', the 'leader', and 'them', the 'team'. This breach is the essence of what we call the leadership shadow: leadership by nature creates a split between a gesture and a response, or between intention and the ability to follow through. Such a rift, distance, or setting apart offers the leader the unique opportunity to help others to make meaning and to reconsider meaning: the split symbolizes and thus maintains a relationship, in which learning and development can take place, and action prepared. Any bid for leadership creates a certain tension in relationship, which is perhaps best expressed by the image of light and darkness, figure and ground, foreground and shadow.

A pertinent feature of the 'split' that leadership creates is an equivalent split within the leader. This is because as an active leader they often have to push the 'follower' boldly to the background, an endeavour which in itself entails in some circumstances a strong-willed, single-minded and bold leadership decision. More broadly there is in our view a 'shadow side' that is triggered the moment the leader conceives of him/herself as a leader. This is a hidden shadow that over time can become less accessible and lead to severe consequences for leadership effectiveness.

Seen like this, we contend that stepping forward into any act of leadership creates a rift within the leader; a rift between their sunny, active, constructive, or aggressive side that has the ambition to contribute, create and prove something, and their doubting, pessimistic, needy, vulnerable, careful and concerned side, which craves connection with oneself and others. The shadow side is therefore part and parcel of leadership.

For most executives it is very tempting to identify simply with their more 'sunny' side, the 'acceptable leadership' side of their public interventions. They tend to ignore the other side, the shadow side of their leadership for as long as they can. This can carry on for a long time while they 'grow' leadership presence and 'mature' in their leadership role. What the outside world sees is a healthy, mature, straightforward process of stepping into ever more senior leadership positions.

All of this works very well as long as nothing happens to trigger leaders to overstep the mark, go beyond their authority or take expedient steps and adopt behaviours that push beyond the boundaries of what is acceptable for them and for others. Once leaders face a mishap, make a mistake or fall into misfortune they inevitably enter a transition and encounter questioning or criticism of how they lead. This makes it clear that it's still very important for leaders to learn or to address the way they lead and relate/make meaning with others in the face of difficult circumstances. It is no longer sufficient simply to identify with their leadership strengths. They also have to contend with their leadership challenges and how these may manifest within their own lives and the organizations they're leading. In today's extremely fast-paced and demanding business environment these confrontational moments (when leadership strengths are insufficient) occur more frequently and are found more often within our privileged coaching conversations, as well as being exposed in the public arena via the media.

Derailment, overdrive and hubris

In order to understand and help professionals work through the unhealthy effects of such intense experiences including hubris and humility, it is necessary to understand the undercurrents that inform them.

Our coaching work confronts us, sooner or later, with managers and professionals overstepping the mark and going into overdrive. Clients are pushed or push themselves into a balancing effort that overshoots and that they have difficulty recovering from. This experience may be seen as unhealthy because it has an immediate negative effect on the quality of their work and relationships. It may lead to increased stress and burnout. In the extreme, it may result in a marked decrease in physiological and psychological resilience, and even a negative spiral featuring physiological and psychological illness or collapse.

Central to these rather extreme experiences of overreaching is the idea of hubris. Hubris may be described as a sense of overbearing pride, defiance or presumption not justified by the circumstances or the perceptions of others. Hubris, while being implicated in the spirals of unhealthy experience described above, is itself associated with a cycle of experience. In this hubristic cycle, excessive pride and pig-headedness are generally associated with public displays of overconfidence, which hide associated private and deeply held feelings of remorse and doubt. The oscillation between excessive pride, and deep shame and self-doubt, can become a repeating cycle spiralling out of control. This is evident when leader clients continue to be lauded and applauded in public while privately seeking help from us and others close to them to escape from and change what they're facing or feel trapped in.

What makes this process particularly challenging, assuming even that clients recognize the issues within themselves and subsequently address their causes and symptoms, is its association with other relatively healthy processes of noticing our own strengths and actively developing them. These are related and intermingled processes. One is a process of 'growing our talents' or 'growing our business', the other an intertwined process of 'growing our hubris'. The primary developmental task here is to grow one's talent without succumbing to the rupture, exhaustion, pride or stress that are the essential concomitants of the very process, leading to excessive and unfounded self-assertion. For growth and balancing to take place effectively we need to pay attention as objectively as possible to our progress and the influences of our changing roles and relationships. This requires the ability to face failure or the possibility of failure with deep self-awareness and fortitude whilst continuing to relate effectively with others. Learning to lead requires humility in the true and original sense of the word – being lowly and grounded including being in touch with what the base of the organization thinks and being open to personal experiences of incompetence (impotence) and 'over-competence' (omnipotence). Humility in this sense has little to do with a lack of self-confidence or with self-abasement and may be a quality that can support confidence as well as authenticity in leadership (Collins, 2001).

In the Greek myths a divine spirit of retribution, personified by the three Fates or by Nemesis, follows hubris. This haunting spirit metes out a divine punishment for the pride and presumption of the ordinary mortal. In our modern business world, this natural drive for balance or cleansing after hubris is often represented by some form of derailment, which can take the form of a very public 'outing' as well as ousting. In modern times it's as important as ever to restrain hubris and to bring back balance to the business of leadership.

When and how derailment typically expresses itself

We've found that senior executives may typically go into overdrive when faced with persisting stretch and challenge and when they perceive the stakes for them (and for those they lead) as being extremely high. Typically these transitions are characterized by changes in role, relationships and contextual challenges, for example, when:

- An executive is promoted into a new role that has challenges that they haven't faced before. In this instance, the executive has to raise their game quickly and take on new ways of working and behaving that need to be seen (by them and by others) to be productive quickly.

- A role that an executive is comfortable in unexpectedly takes on a new character. In these circumstances internal or external changes may create new and unexpected demands on the executive, such as suddenly being expected to engage in a different way or to achieve more stretching and different outcomes, for which they are ill-prepared.

- An executive finds him/herself in a role that has not existed before. This is possibly the most demanding of the three scenarios. In this instance the executive has to create a new focus and purpose for the emerging and therefore ill-defined role and deal with many demands and pressures, without historical precedent or guidance from a predecessor.

In addition to these scenarios, executives may obviously find themselves in situations where their circumstances and support networks outside work become challenging. This may be due to relationship difficulties, illnesses or bereavement. Under such circumstances executives may experience disruptions originating from their lives away from work but affecting their sense of stability and effectiveness in work too.

All these factors can lead to episodes of relational overdrive and myopia. Our experience is that overdrive episodes are not limited to particular types of organizations or settings; they can emerge amongst executives from any kind of cultural background and across sectors.

We do observe however that the risks and impacts of overdrive, relational myopia or hubris are most significant in large, complex, fragmented and global organizations, and where talented individuals are elevated to positions which nourish, reward and exploit strengths and at the same time fuel particular hubristic processes that their personal makeup and biography expose them to.

We consider that a leader can typically overstep the mark in several directions; upwards, towards higher authority, but also downwards by imposing decisions which limit the team's effectiveness or individual team members' contributions. The leader can also overstep the mark towards peers and wider society, violating ethical boundaries, and towards 'self', by forcing themselves to do things they're incapable of or can't sustain physically or otherwise.

Our role and how we can help as coaches

As coaches working with hard-driving leaders we need to be aware of the fact that we are within and part of the system that influences and can be influenced by the leaders' successes. We are also by virtue of our role often uniquely placed to notice, to be effective 'mirrors', thinking partners and change enablers. This requires us to be aware of when these leadership strengths develop patterns that are unhelpful and instances when they may go into overdrive. We also need to be able to develop our own awareness of when we may be ourselves enthralled and captivated by leaders' shadow aspects, and what we need to do to attend to them and support our clients to do the same. In our view, we as coaches need to start with being able to notice and understand the typical ways in which leaders may overstep themselves. Let's look at the ways of overstepping the mark we've identified, with some examples:

1 **Presumption towards authority or the larger organization**. Here the leader oversteps the mark with regard to the hierarchy or the institutional order. If done against oppression, then this kind of hubris could be very positive and in fact, heroic. For example, a new director of HR of a leading consultancy notices that interns and junior consultants work longer hours yet receive less acknowledgment. After repeatedly raising the issue with colleagues and being repeatedly ignored the leader cancels the intern and graduate recruitment interviews and refuses to sign any new intern contracts. He also awards all recently appointed junior consultants a 5 per cent pay rise.

2 **Presumption towards designated role and own team**. Here a leader suppresses the creativity or contributions from their team, using discretion to limit rather than enhance the team's effectiveness. Or conversely, when a leader caters to demands of key members of the team that go beyond the reasonable expectations laid down by the role, including ethical considerations. Faced with the risk that a report that the audit team is preparing will expose the weaknesses in the contracting process that he's just implemented,

the long-standing finance director tables a proposal to suggest to the board that it is time to consider a new audit firm, as the existing firm has a number of consulting assignments that expose them to a conflict of interest.

3 **Presumption towards own context.** This is when a leader oversteps the mark towards society as a whole, by engaging in non-ethical leadership practices such as abuse of office or fraud. Ahead of the upcoming social club management committee elections, the head of the existing management committee indicates to colleagues that he intends to defer the proposed increase in management committee compensation until after the elections. He further states that all members of the committee who were not putting forward their names for re-election may not be eligible for compensation, as compensation is unlikely to be backdated to any previous team members no longer serving.

4 **Presumption towards the self.** Here a leader exhausts themselves so that they are unable to function or cope. Faced with a punishing schedule of global travel and meetings negotiating new contracts with suppliers, a buying director fails to take medication to control his blood pressure and is signed off at his next scheduled corporate medical by the alarmed company doctor.

We can present these four types of hubris diagrammatically in a single figure (Figure 8.1). In this figure the space opened up by managerial discretion and power wielded is represented by a square. However, if a leader truly uses up all the space that he has in terms of managerial discretion, and allows his or her decisions to stretch all the way to the edge of that field, then very real occasions of hubris with serious consequences are to be expected. A wise leader therefore stays well within the bounds of his or her discretion, within a self-imposed new square as drawn below, as the 'impact zone' (Figure 8.2).

This turns leadership into an art, the purpose of which is to stay inside the box voluntarily, restraining oneself whilst using one's managerial discretion to help the team become more effective. This sounds straightforward but is, in practice, quite difficult. This is because the leader's own desire to be successful, personal assumptions about what success looks like and is driven by, as well as the behaviour and reinforcing/challenging behaviour of others around him, are all forces that pull the leader into the 'hubris zone'. All these forces make it much more difficult for leaders to recognize significant boundaries that they need to be observe. In positions of power and leadership it's easy to overstep the mark.

FIGURE 8.1   Leadership power or managerial discretion encompasses four areas where a leader could transgress but needs to hold themself back

FIGURE 8.2   Managerial discretion in a rectangle with different 'zones' of hubris enclosing the (self-imposed) freedom of the manager

Figures 8.1 and 8.2 from de Haan and Kasozi, 2014. Reprinted with permission from Kogan Page

In our experience, working at the edge and stretching to change and to challenge existing norms can be remarkably effective at creating new opportunities or turning around fossilized, tired and failing organizations. Yet we do also find that overstepping and going too far is a real risk. Many leaders succumb and fail; some recover and learn from experience(s) in order to have another go. Indeed many successful entrepreneurs and leaders point to earlier failures as being significant in enabling their future successes. Post-crisis growth is a topic covered elsewhere in this book.

Some however may never learn and appear fated to repeat and to pay and make others pay for repeated errors. For example, Edward, a retail buyer known for his hard negotiation and tough dealing with retail suppliers, had a reputation that followed him from company to company. Despite being cautioned and even coming close to losing his job a number of times, he managed repeatedly to change roles before being disciplined. He often insisted on complete loyalty from those working with him and even expected that they demonstrate similar behaviour. In a number of his roles he was often accused of having a 'bullying' tendency towards junior staff. These accusations led one of his HR Directors to insist on offering him a coach as a precondition for his being considered for further career advancement. In the first conversation with his self-chosen coach he unrepentantly wanted to focus on how he could be more influential and persuasive of people who just didn't have a sense of urgency, for example the HR Director.

Descriptive typology to gain greater insight into the behaviours and patterns of leaders

It is possible to elaborate a descriptive typology that we as coaches can use to gain greater insight into the behaviours and patterns of leaders, in their daily 'effective' work and also when they go into overdrive. Such a typology can serve us as an instrument for studying how non-problematic and ostensibly healthy relationships may be transformed into less helpful and problematic ones, often simply by increasing the pressure and challenges faced.

Below we present 11 personality adaptations which characterize patterns of behaviour (de Haan and Kasozi, 2014). We indicate how these personality adaptations when in overdrive border on known personality disturbances in medical diagnosis. We also indicate how some of their overdrives may be linked with known behavioural drivers (Kahler, 1975) going overboard.

In coaching, the descriptions are best used as a stimulus for reflection, a possible route to greater insight in conversations with executives, between coaches, or between coaches and groups of executives working together to make sense of a challenging context. As coaches it is essential to invite our clients as individuals or in teams to step outside the fray and to reflect, away from the task and the work, on what they are doing when they are at their best and what that 'best' looks like or becomes when overcooked or pushed too far. In these conversations, leaders may themselves describe or identify some of the patterns we outline here. As coaches we can help them avoid the simple stigma of classifying and unhelpfully pigeonholing themselves, whilst naming and recognizing patterns prevalent in their behaviour and the implications this may have for them, those they lead and their organizations. The patterns we offer are listed below and characterized as follows:

Personality adaptations

Leadership as doing – where assertiveness comes to the fore, doubt and vulnerability go into the 'shadow':

- *Charming Manipulators*, whose actions may brush up against the rules and mould them to their own design. In this style, strict accountability may go out of the window, because their accountability may be relegated to the 'shadow'.

- *Playful Encouragers*, whose influence is felt mainly indirectly. Full responsibility taking for their actions may be difficult, as their responsibility may be relegated to the 'shadow'.

- *Glowing Gatsbies*, who influence from the front and bask in their successes. In this style it may be easier to criticize others but harder to look at themselves in a similar way, as their humility may have been relegated to the 'shadow'.

- *Detached Diplomats*, whose actions remain largely in their own world, disengaged and disconnected from those around them. It may be hard to keep the organization's issues and people in focus, as their ability to reach out may be relegated to the 'shadow'. In fact, when this pattern is highly developed, leadership interventions themselves may go under and the leader seems very absent.

Leadership as thinking – where knowledge comes to the fore, trust goes into the 'shadow':

- *Responsible Workaholics*, whose stamina is admirable and who can take up a vast array of leadership agendas. However, they may find it difficult to see the forest for the trees, because their ability to prioritize and make a firm stance on a controversial issue may be relegated to their 'shadow'.

- *Impulsive Loyalists*, who are very involved but may be subject to mood swings. They may find it very hard to hear bad news about how the business is going, because some of their tolerance and self-confidence may be relegated to their 'shadow'.

- *Brilliant Sceptics*, who are scrupulous and alert but may focus more on the negatives. They may think that people are for or against them, and in particular suspect that they are against them, because their trust and safety may be relegated to their 'shadow'.

- *Creative Daydreamers*, who always have fresh thinking to offer but they may try to be different just for the sake of it, or their thinking bears no relationship to issues at stake. Consequently, some of the creative thinking may be not very applicable or plain wrong for the future, because dry realism and utility may be relegated to their 'shadow'.

Leadership as feeling – where empathy comes to the fore, assertiveness goes into the 'shadow':

- *Virtuous Supporters*, who try to look after their people and are liked by everyone. They may find it hard to look after their own interests or assert themselves when they have something to offer, because their own personal power may be relegated to their 'shadow'.

- *Accomplished Thespians*, who generously offer their own feelings and ideas but may over-occupy the centre of attention. They may enjoy the limelight a little too much and become obsessed with their public image, because their natural self-affirmation may be relegated to their 'shadow'.

- *Simmering Stalwarts*, who are reliable and ambitious yet afraid to make decisions that might involve risk. They may be concerned or hesitant because of what other people might think or do, because their self-confidence may be relegated to their 'shadow'.

We introduce and work with these patterns through reflective conversations that start with an appreciation of executives' challenges and strengths. As we've argued before, leaders' shadow and bright sides are intimately connected but drift apart upon taking up a leadership role, so coaching needs to consider both systematically. In the next section we give some ideas for exploring and even making use of what is going on in the client's (and our own) shadow.

We emphasize that the summary representation we make here holds the idea of a personality 'type', 'character' or 'caricature' lightly. We could after all argue that there are as many 'types' as there are people in this world. We could also argue that all the so-called 'types' can be found within a single person, even within every single person. In addition it may be noted that the relational matrix around us may bring out the 'type' we become. So organizational manifestations of 'types' may very easily change when people change jobs, or when there is a merger or a different composition of working teams. And conversely, hiring a fresh leader into a stable workforce may bring out traits that are primed in that workplace, such as traits of the previous person holding that job. We have chosen these particular patterns instead, because they have a long history in psychiatric literature and because they each have been well-researched. Over the past two decades they have even been operationalized as a psychometric instrument for leaders in organizations, in the form of the Hogan Development Survey (HDS) (Hogan and Hogan, 1997), so that any executive or coach can undertake a personal positioning exercise on the same 11 patterns. The 11 patterns that we have chosen to elaborate on are from the fourth edition of the *American Diagnostic and Statistical Manual* [DSM-IV] (American Psychological Association 1994). Table 8.1 sets out the patterns in detail.

It is very rare to see the personality 'disorder' in extreme textbook form and highly unusual to see one of the 'caricatures' played out exactly as described above. Yet we regularly encounter aspects of various overdrive patterns in stressful situations and in demanding careers.

The personality patterns usually play out at work in a 'neurotic' way, not completely outside socially acceptable norms, and just strike us as rather intense or unusual. Privately, during 'down time' with the family or at late solitary nights in the office, the patterns may become distinctly beyond the socially acceptable. Similarly, in the privacy of the coaching room, where the spotlight and empathy is entirely on the executive and their 'patterns', the presentation may also be more extreme – with more direct recognizable behaviour and pronounced open expressions of emotions associated with the overdrive behaviour characterized and described above.

In order to complement and take the typology presented further we also present in Table 8.2 all 11 personality patterns, making use of Ware's (1983) terminology. Specifically we include here Ware's terms of:

1 'open door' (the channel through which the particular person can be reached best);

2 'target door' (the channel through which the particular person can find new ways of working, insight or personal change and growth); and

3 'trap door' (the channel which is usually closed to the person as it is kept hidden behind the other two channels).

TABLE 8.1   A Descriptive Typology of Patterns of Leadership Overdrive

Movers and Shakers		
• Four 'overdrive' patterns in leaders related to patterns that focus on action or paradoxically and actively withdrawing from (productive).	1. The Charming Manipulator	• We have linked this 'type' to 'anti-social' characteristics – moves to charm and dazzle you and to engineer a very impressive performance.
• These four leadership patterns give primacy to 'behaving' above 'thinking' and 'feeling'.	2. The Playful Encourager	• Linked to 'passive-aggressive' characteristics – moves to encourage others and find encouragement, being both sensitive to motivation and reluctant to act when not motivated.
• They can be approached and worked with most straightforwardly through thinking about behaviours and actions, employing to-do lists, specific goals, and practising new forms of action.	3. The Glowing Gatsby	• Linked to 'narcissistic' characteristics – moves to propel themselves forward into a glorious future, impressing everyone around them.
	4. The Detached Diplomat	• Linked to 'schizoid' characteristics – distinguishes themself by not being moved in those occasions where other people would be: their main characteristic is a stoic, tough or detached form of 'non movement'.
Rigorous Thinkers		
• Four 'overdrive' patterns in leaders, which are related to the leader's cognitive style or way of thinking.	5. The Responsible Workaholic	• Linked to 'obsessive-compulsive' characteristics – ruminates about his every action and doggedly carries it out with rich detail and self-monitoring.
	6. The Impulsive Loyalist	• Linked to 'borderline' characteristics – ruminates in a more excited way, vacillating between optimism and pessimism.

TABLE 8.1 *continued*

• These four leadership patterns give primacy to 'thinking' above 'behaving' and 'feeling'. • They can be approached and worked with most straightforwardly through thought, cognitions, deliberations, considerations, insights and the like.	7. The Brilliant Sceptic 8. The Creative Daydreamer	• Linked to 'paranoid' characteristics – is a critical thinker, full of suspicions about other people's motives. • Linked to 'schizotypal' characteristics – is a creative thinker with endless supplies of great ideas that, however, rarely get executed.
Sensitive Carers • Three 'overdrive' patterns in leaders, which are related to the leader's care and attention to emotion and feeling. • These three leadership patterns give primacy to 'feeling' above 'behaving' and 'thinking'. • They can be approached and worked with most straightforwardly through empathy, understanding, and personal support.	9. The Virtuous Supporter 10. The Accomplished Thespian 11. The Simmering Stalwart	• Linked to 'dependent' characteristics – feels for other people and wants to be a good team player for them. • Linked to 'histrionic' characteristics – overflows with feeling, particularly their own private feelings. • Linked to 'avoidant' characteristics – also overflows with feeling, but more in a concerned and troubled sort of way.

From de Haan and Kasozi, 2014. Reprinted with permission from Kogan Page

TABLE 8.2 Personality patterns

Personality pattern	Personality 'overdrive'	'Open door'	'Target door'	'Trap door'	Working style and drivers	Antidote / permission
The Charming Manipulator	'Antisocial'	Behaviour	Thinking	Feeling	Leader believes the rules are made to be broken Be strong and please others	Respect others more: your rule-breaking strategy is one day going to catch up with you It's OK to be vulnerable
The Playful Encourager	'Passive-aggressive'	Behaviour	Feeling	Thinking	What leader says is not what they really believe Try hard and be strong	Just do it, or else be upfront about your resistance
The Glowing Gatsby	'Narcissistic'	Behaviour	Feeling	Thinking	Leader thinks that they're right, and everyone else is wrong Be perfect and be strong	You look pathetic a lot of the time, being the only one not seeing that you cannot and will not be able to know or do it all Be less dependent on others' praise

TABLE 8.2 *continued*

Personality pattern	Personality 'overdrive'	'Open door'	'Target door'	'Trap door'	Working style and drivers	Antidote / permission
The Detached Diplomat	'Schizoid'	Behaviour	Thinking	Feeling	Leader is disengaged and disconnected Be strong	Try to engage more with others Feelings are helpful and human
The Responsible Workaholic	'Obsessive-compulsive'	Thinking	Feeling	Behaviour	Leader gets the little things right and the big things wrong Be perfect, be strong and try hard	Think big picture as well. It's okay to make mistakes, and it is important for learning too
The Impulsive Loyalist	'Borderline'	Thinking	Behaviour	Feeling	Leader is subject to mood swings Be perfect and hurry up	Try to count to ten and relax
The Brilliant Sceptic	'Paranoid'	Thinking	Feeling	Behaviour	Leader focuses on the negatives Be perfect and be strong	Relax: there will always be a more charitable explanation

TABLE 8.2 *continued*

Personality pattern	Personality 'overdrive'	'Open door'	'Target door'	'Trap door'	Working style and drivers	Antidote / permission
The Creative Daydreamer	'Schizotypal'	Thinking	Behaviour	Feeling	Leader tries to be different just for the sake of it Be strong and try hard	Try to listen and connect with other stakeholders
The Virtuous Supporter	'Dependent'	Feeling	Behaviour	Thinking	Leader tries to win the popularity contest Please others and be strong	Try instead to look after yourself more It's OK to want something for yourself and it is OK to disagree
The Accomplished Thespian	'Histrionic'	Feeling	Thinking	Behaviour	Leader needs to be the centre of attention Please others	Relax about how other people see you
The Simmering Stalwart	'Avoidant'	Feeling	Behaviour	Thinking	Leaders is afraid to make decisions Try hard	Worry less about what people will think

From de Haan and Kasozi, 2014. Reprinted with permission from Kogan Page

This table can be used by coaches for their own reflection and preparation as they work with a client. For informed and self-aware clients who may have already noted the role of drivers in their behaviour and interaction with others the coach may find it helpful to share edited versions of the table – focusing on working styles and permissions.

Coaching

While many self-aware people may recognize the challenges they face in transition, addressing these challenges and balancing them effectively is difficult. Leaders need support to find the help they need and to develop meaningful insights they can work with and adopt. Coaching helps them to find out what to do and be to maintain balance and to avoid becoming unbalanced.

In this section we offer four ways to identify the degree of risk and thus balance hubristic patterns with counter-measures.

The ancient Greeks called the antidote to hubris *sophrosyne*, which means healthy-mindedness. Sophrosyne also stands for humility, restraint, self-control and temperance; in short, anything that brings us back from the abyss of hubris and that placates the nemesis of retribution, so that we remain capable of offering the very best of our leadership.

In our view these are the starting points for sophrosyne:

A Owning, realizing and reflecting on our weaknesses or vulnerabilities.

B Building up our strengths and resilience.

C Balancing our strengths with our weaknesses by finding the strengths or challenges in our weaknesses.

D Truly focusing on our team and other stakeholders, in a generous and even self-effacing way.

These four are complementary and can therefore be practised coherently, mindfully and simultaneously.

A. Know thyself: own your vulnerabilities

'Know thyself' is an ancient motto in the temples of Luxor and Delphi, and seems to have had a connotation of knowing our boundaries, ie knowing where we might overstep the mark and invoke the wrath of the gods. Knowing ourselves is a balancing act; by understanding our vulnerabilities we can acknowledge and own them, and in true sophrosyne sense, begin to apply moderation and restraint, cultivating ego strength. We actively try to stay away from acting out our vulnerabilities, by not giving in to temptation and restraining managerial discretion.

As a coach we can guide executives towards a more effective and in-depth way of doing this with the help of a more personalized programme, using psychometrics, feedback instruments, executive coaching and other forms of leadership development. As described above, this may best be done as part of a reflective and developmental as well as appreciative conversation away from frenetic and pressurized leadership work – for example as part of a retreat, end of year review and/or contracting or re-contracting discussion.

Part of knowing yourself honestly is taking on board your real and true resistance to doing something about your limitations. Schein (1993) says that for any learning to happen we have to find a balance between two countervailing anxieties:

- The 'fear of learning', which testifies to the acute pain and frustration which can accompany learning, where we know what we need to give up and change but do not know what we will get in its place. As a result of this fear, most of us will try to suppress any information and avoid any action that confronts us with the fact that we have not yet learned something.

- The 'fear of survival' or the fear of not learning, which is often associated with feelings of despondency and powerlessness. If this fear gets the upper hand, we will be forced to make an effort to learn.

Executives are not immune to these fears and can face significant internal defences to overcome to know themselves better, defences that protect and often mask their vulnerabilities, shame and frailties. To balance those defences it is very helpful to cultivate an ongoing interest in learning about themselves and others. This means being open to new experiences and views, in particular upward feedback in terms of their performance as leader. And it means taking every opportunity they can to expand their repertoire of understanding and insight as well as action. Leaders who are good at learning relate positively to the possibility of finding out something new that helps them to engage better with their reality and with their team. They learn from immediate experience and are also able to take a step back and reflect on wider experience that might inform and change their assumptions and frames of reference.

B. Work on your resilience: build up your strengths

As work environments become increasingly challenging and uncertain, resilience is receiving a great deal of interest among those responsible for performance and wellbeing in organizations. In the main, however, resilience-focused selection and development interventions are still quite limited, and there is so much more that the scientific study of resilience, wellbeing and performance has to offer the organizational practitioner (Flint-Taylor and Robertson, 2013). Resilience has been defined by psychologists in a variety of ways across a number of settings, including 'the ability to bounce back or recover from stress, to adapt to stressful circumstances, to not become ill despite significant adversity and to function above the norm in spite of stress or adversity' (Carver, 1998; Tusaie and Dyer, 1994). Resilience involves three vertices (de Haan and Kasozi, 2014); an internal, an external and an 'in-between' vertex:

- key individual characteristics (such as ability, personality, attitude, mood);
- the experience of pressured situations or challenges;
- the productive coping that occurs as a result of that experience (bouncing back, keeping going, learning, driving forward etc).

It is important when helping leaders develop resilience that attention be paid to individual factors, but equally so to understand how these individual factors interact with the situations they're encountering and finally how we can capture the outcome at individual, team and organizational levels. In his work at Ashridge Business School, our colleague Alex Davda has identified six key areas of resilience, which he describes as 'resilient attitudes' which have been shown to affect how an individual thinks about, feels and then responds to pressured or stressful situations (Davda, 2011).

These six attitudes are:

- *Emotional control*: Controlling emotions and taking personal responsibility for thoughts, feelings and behaviours.
- *Self-belief*: Belief and confidence in the self and personal capabilities.
- *Purpose*: Setting and organizing goals and identifying a broader meaning from these.
- *Adaptability/adapting to change*: Adapting readily to change and responding to uncertainty in a positive and developmental manner.
- *Awareness of others*: Demonstrating self-awareness and an understanding of other people's situations and perspectives.
- *Balancing alternatives*: Generating and managing alternative options, opinion and choices.

Whilst these resilient attitudes are generally found to be helpful for those under pressure, each can become counterproductive if it is 'overused' or used in the wrong situation.

Developing resilience takes work and time, but there is now growing evidence of how resilience training (and in our view, with additional and sustained follow-on coaching) can boost individual and organizational success (Proudfoot *et al*, 2009). The Comprehensive Soldier Fitness programme (Seligman and Fowler, 2011) also gives a clear example of a large-scale resilience-development intervention that is beginning to show benefits for individuals and whole organizations.

From our point of view, developing resilience involves:

- An awareness of the characteristics already possessed and whether they help or hinder under pressure. (For example, is the leader extremely organized, finding adapting to uncertainty and ambiguity difficult, as may be the case for an obsessive-compulsive pattern?)

- An intention or motivation to develop a resilient attitude towards pressure that can either help someone overcome certain individual predispositions or build on their strengths. (For example, can a naturally pessimistic person develop a more optimistic approach by focusing on what can be learnt from situations when they reflect on them?)

- An understanding of what is difficult about certain situations and which resources are needed to manage them.

- An ability to consider a number of outcomes that may be experienced as a result of certain situations.

C. Find value in your own 'dark side': balance strengths and weaknesses

Self-knowledge and understanding of one's vulnerabilities is one thing. Strengthening resilience is quite another. It is very clear that both together do not alone make a 'character', a well-balanced, mature and mindful leader. Well-developed toughness and resilience can make for a great champion, and profound self-knowledge can make for an eminent sage. However, if the two are not balanced then the champion will suffer from dark areas that are out of consciousness or out of grasp, such as momentary pride, arrogance, addictions, or weakness. Or conversely the sage will recoil into introspection, experiencing moments of being unable to face the world or act in the marketplace. What makes for a truly mature leader is a certain balance in strengths and weaknesses, a sense that the greatest strengths are allowed to look silly and weak, and the greatest weaknesses bear some hidden treasure.

One aspect of balancing strengths and weaknesses is the process of taking back projections to counteract a process that happens very frequently under stress, and in particular for leaders. It is the process of splitting one's own strengths and weaknesses and, in order to build up a positive identity (Petriglieri and Stein, 2012) or to feel safer and less anxious, attributing strengths to oneself and weaknesses to others. Leaders can be supported to develop their own (perceived) weaker sides so that they balance their strengths, and so work against the ubiquitous pattern of splitting and projecting in response to pressure.

Consequently strengths become more marked and moderated by substantial challenges, so that hubris or excessive pride are much less likely.

D. Lead without the self: truly focus on the team

As we have been focusing on the leader and what they can do to face up to hubris, derailment and overdrive, we have forgotten slightly the task and definition of leaders. If we take the core task of leadership as being about growing the effectiveness of the team then it is essential that the leader 'leads' themself specifically for the purpose of enabling and supporting the team in its quest for success. A grounded, selfless leader will focus on the very ordinary aspects of their team (Binney, Williams and Wilke, 2005); the everyday challenges of strategy formation, operations and people. Such a leader, who is perhaps less self-conscious and less central to his or her own leadership, will run a smaller risk of overdrive and hubris. The well-intentioned, focused and active busy bee has less time and fewer opportunities for overstepping the mark than the redolent and self-referencing queen bee.

We believe it is possible to grow compassion in equal amounts to energy, drive, focus and toughness. For many executives this is however almost like a Copernican revolution, in which they move away from placing themselves and their ambitions at the centre of the universe, and start paying full attention to others' ambitions and growth. Coaching can help open their minds to the interests and drives of others, and to discover that the world does not actually revolve around them but around other people and their interests and needs. Like the task of an executive coach, a leader's task is fundamentally altruistic and selfless. It is to intervene so that others can perform.

Regaining balance: you do not have to do it alone

The one thing that all leaders in overdrive seem to struggle with is a certain lack of compassion, sometimes a lack of compassion for themselves and perhaps more often a lack of compassion for others. The four ways of balancing that we have introduced here all endeavour to grow compassion and acceptance, for oneself, for others, and for the consequences of difficulties, disappointments, and loss.

The best place for a leader to grow compassion and to address the excesses of hubris and relational overdrive is in a tailor-made, confidential and personal relationship, such as can be established in the privacy of executive coaching. By working in such a personal one-to-one helping relationship other relationships can be brought under scrutiny, and overdrive and derailment patterns can be observed and explored in depth. The coaching relationship can be used as a preventive intervention but also as a remedial intervention, provided the executive can feel safe enough to talk freely about very sensitive areas, which are possibly burdened by shame or frustration.

Leaders in transition often face challenges that are difficult to deal with unsupported. This is because the challenges arise out of complicated interplays of events, personal predispositions, patterns and splits, inherent in leading in change and uncertainty. As leaders push to deal with what they face they may go into overdrive(s) that are difficult to recover from. As coaches we can be of most help when we support clients to develop the awareness, relationships and practices needed to deal with overdrive episodes as they arise.

Over time it is also important to help clients develop their resilience. This requires coaches to help them develop resilient attitudes. Resilient attitudes, well-cultivated and practised, equip clients to be more emotionally balanced, self-aware and purposeful, whilst relating well with others and with the realities faced effectively. This enables leaders and those they work with to face transitions with realism and creativity, adopting behaviours that are most helpful for themselves and their organizations.

References

American Psychiatric Association (1994) *American Diagnostic and Statistical Manual*

Binney, G, Wilke, G and Williams, C (2004) *Living Leadership: A practical guide for ordinary heroes*, FT Prentice Hall, Harlow

Carver, C S (1998) Resilience and thriving: Issues, models and linkages, *Journal of Social Issues*, **54** (2), pp 245–66

Collins, J (2001) Level 5 leadership: The triumph of humility and fierce resolve, *Harvard Business Review*, **79** (1), pp 66–76

Davda, A (2011) Measuring resilience: A pilot study, *Assessment and Development Matters*, Autumn, pp 11–14

de Haan, E and Kasozi, A (2014) *The Leadership Shadow: How to recognize and avoid derailment, hubris and overdrive*, Kogan Page, London

Flint-Taylor, J and Robertson, I T (2013) Enhancing well-being in organisations through selection and development, In R J Burke and C L Cooper (eds), *The Fulfilling Workplace*, Gower, Farnham (pp 165–186)

Hogan, J and Hogan, R (1997) *The Hogan Development Survey Manual*, Hogan, Tulsa, OK

Kahler, T (1975) Drivers: The key to the process scripts, *Transactional Analysis Journal*, **5** (3), pp 280–84

Petriglieri, G and Stein, M (2012) The unwanted self: projective identification in leaders' identity work, *Organisation Studies*, **33** (9), pp 1217–35

Proudfoot, J G *et al* (2009) Cognitive-behavioural training to change attributional style improves employee well-being, job satisfaction, productivity, and turnover, *Personality and Individual Differences*, **46**, pp 147–53

Schein, E (1993) How can organisations learn faster? The challenge of entering the green room, *Sloan Management Review*, Winter 1993, pp 85–92

Seligman, M and Fowler, R D (2013) Comprehensive soldier fitness and the future of psychology, *American Psychologist*, **66**, pp 82–86

Tusaie, K and Dyer, J (2004) Resilience: A historical review of the construct, *Holistic Nursing Practice*, **18** (1), pp 3–8

Ware, P (1983) Personality Adaptations, *Transactional Analysis Journal*, **13**, pp 11–19

The role of coaching in supporting organizations to address mental health issues

09

ANDREW KINDER and TONY BUON

This chapter will explore the contribution that coaching can make towards supporting organizations through the many challenges presented by mental health issues and potential triggers for these issues such as conflict and workplace change.

When addressing mental health issues, it's particularly important to respect professional boundaries, yet coaching in the workplace is often confounded by its lack of a clear definition and its use often confused with other interventions such as counselling, mentoring and training. At the same time, not all coaches have psychological knowledge and training and may struggle to recognize when to refer on. In this chapter, we'll explore the impact of mental health issues at work, delineate coaching from mentoring and counselling, and offer pointers to coaches and coaching sponsors for how coaches can safely contribute in this arena.

The demands of a competitive business environment, the emergence of a more transformative approach to leadership, and the emphasis placed on employee empowerment, have all resulted in a growth in the use of coaching in workplaces worldwide. As Bartlett (2007) stated, 'coaching is one of the fastest-growing techniques for human resource development'. Coaching has been utilized as an effective response to issues including leadership development, succession planning and executive 'burnout' (International Coach Federation, 2013).

For most people, the workplace is significant as they spend a substantial proportion of their lives there and it offers meaning, structure and a sense of belonging to many of them. Waddell and Burton's influential review 'Is work good for your health and wellbeing?' (2006) found that work is generally good for physical and mental health and wellbeing, and can be therapeutic for people with common mental health problems.

Workplace mental health

The premise that work has some inherently protective characteristics is not, however, the whole picture. It's also the case that work-related stress can result in mental health issues within the workplace, and that these can have negative impacts on individuals and fellow workers. Combining all those with a stress-related or mental health issue at work amounts to 14 per cent of the working population (Adult Psychiatric Morbidity Survey, 2007), while as many as one in five employees have an existing or potential problem with alcohol or other drugs (Buon and Compton, 1994). Against such a backdrop, it's imperative that coaches have some understanding of mental health issues, and of when it is appropriate or inappropriate for them to offer support.

It's very apparent that stress and mental illness at work are significant when calculating the cost for business. The Centre for Mental Health (2010), for example, estimates that if you combine the total economic and social cost of mental health problems in the United Kingdom, it amounts to £105 billion per year that includes a significant human cost.

Work-related stress and situations where mental health issues aren't appropriately handled can be linked to declining work performance, an increase in accidents, lost quality, impaired problem solving, absenteeism and presenteeism. Other impacts may include wasted management time, poor workplace relationships and the associated costs of retraining and recruitment when people leave.

Mental health conditions are well defined within the Diagnostic Statistical Manual of Mental Disorders (Version V), which explains the criteria that psychiatrists and psychologists follow when diagnosing and classifying such conditions. However, mental health is better seen as a continuum from the severe end (schizophrenia, bipolar affective disorder, psychosis) to the mild/ moderate end ('stress', low mood, less severe forms of anxiety/depression). In terms of the workplace, it's the mild to moderate end of the continuum which produces the highest number of sickness absence cases and also provides the biggest challenge for organizations. The reason is that these health problems are most often multifactorial, with work-related, social-domestic and psychological factors all playing a part. To the line manager within an organization it can present quite a confusing situation to manage.

Given all these factors, there's an urgent need for organizations to address mental health issues within their workplaces and ample opportunity for coaches to contribute to this endeavour. Coaches can help individuals feel supported and able to deal with the challenges in today's organizational environment, assisting with areas such as helping clients extract significance and meaning out of the job, providing support through change and crisis, and assisting with and managing conflict at work. Weinberg and Cooper (2012) recognize that speaking with family or friends can be problematic and that having someone truly independent, such as a workplace coach, can be of real benefit in becoming more resilient during turbulent times. They conclude that:

> If we're facing uncertain or challenging situations insider or outside work, then seeking support and advice is particularly helpful, as otherwise we can feel alone in having to deal with such circumstances... even if we have doubts about our resilience in turbulent times, we need to recognize there are core parts of our psyche which are designed to adapt. Our mission – which as a species we have chosen to accept over tens of thousands of years – is to recognize our potential psychological strengths and deploy them to meet the challenge at hand (p 139).

However, it's vital that the coach be able to recognize when to refer on to counsellors (and psychologists). This is outlined later in this chapter and some of the red flags to watch out for are set out in Table 9.1 further on. To be able to know when to refer on requires an appreciation of what coaching is and is not, which we look at next.

Delineating coaching from other interventions

There's often confusion and overlap in the use of the terms coaching, counselling, and mentoring in the workplace context. Given that these are all about personal change and self-development there's bound to be overlap both in terms of practitioner competencies and ways of working. While the coaching practitioner will have similar underpinning skills with counsellors and mentors, it's important to be clear about their different uses and roles within an organizational context. The next section will outline coaching before turning to mentoring and then counselling.

Workplace coaching

Coaching is rapidly gaining respectability within organizations and one way of seeing its relevance is to hear from John Russell, Managing Director, Harley-Davidson Europe, who says:

> 'I never cease to be amazed at the power of the coaching process to draw out the skills or talents that were previously hidden within an individual, and which invariably find a way to solve a problem previously thought unsolvable' (quoted by Williams, 2008).

Yet increasingly, when looking at who provides coaching at work there can be confusion due to who is carrying out the coaching. For instance, some coaches are counsellors who offer coaching services while some coaches appear to involve themselves in psychotherapy with coachees, whether or not they're qualified to do so. And there have been many debates in the coaching literature about potential boundaries between coaching and therapy (eg Horner, 2011). Also, some managers or supervisors claim they're coaching their team but have limited training (or insight into the coaching process), including within the psychological arena.

Then, when looking at how counselling/coaching is viewed more widely, some people (especially men) may prefer to disclose to others that they are seeing a 'coach' and shy away from using the term 'counsellor' or 'therapist' (Kinder and Boorman, 2010). This will, therefore, impact how programmes are communicated within the workplace and further confuse what is being delivered.

Although there's a lack of agreement among coaching professionals about definitions, there are some agreed characteristics that seem universal to workplace coaching (adapted from Schwenk and Kinder, 2012), and which may have implications for coaches deciding what falls outside their professional boundaries (and vice versa):

1 Coaching is a skilled activity that should be delivered by appropriately trained and supervised professionals.

2 Coaches require advanced communication skills and specific coaching skills, which include the principles of adult learning (pedagogy).

3 Individual coaching goals should be aligned with organizational goals and competences/skills development.

4 The individual receiving coaching should be psychologically well and not require counselling intervention.

5 Personal issues may be discussed if relevant to coaching goals, but the emphasis should be on work issues.

6 Follow-up and effective feedback should be part of any coaching plan.

Mentoring

The relationship between the mentor and mentee can be longer term than coaching and some view it as about more general life transitions. In the workplace, it can be seen to have a wider focus than coaching. Clutterbuck (2008) positions it as helping the mentee with their 'lifestreams' such as job, career, family, health and fitness, intellect and spiritual wellbeing. He also positions a mentor as someone who can help the mentee work out priorities in life, decide the amount of effort to expend to reach those priorities, manage guilt from making decisions around this, negotiate this with others and develop greater skills in developing an effective work life balance (Clutterbuck, 2008). Increasingly, however, coaches will work in these areas too, although the length of time available can be based on the budget available, with mentors often internal with therefore less budget constraint.

Mentoring in the workplace is sometimes organized and formally conducted by the employer or individuals themselves may seek out their own 'independent' mentors who they feel have the requisite skills and experience at work – they have 'seen it and done it all before'. Like coaching, mentoring is aimed at complementing other learning and development activities such as formal training, short courses, self-study, career planning activities, secondments, etc.

More specifically, mentors can support their mentee with a number of strategies, including:

- assistance in constructing career development plans;
- guidance on the knowledge, skill and attitude necessary for a particular position;
- help with learning and development contracts;
- guidance on dealing with workplace politics;
- general guidance with formal and informal learning;
- assistance with specific personal development areas.

Depending on how the coaching is set up, these aspects can also be a focus for the external coach to explore with their client.

Workplace counselling

Workplace counselling, provided internally through staff support or externally through Employee Assistance Programmes (EAPs), is a hybrid form of counselling that is both therapeutic in the sense of traditional counselling yet sufficiently workplace focused to fit alongside the needs of the organization. This particular form of counselling is often time-limited, with a specific therapeutic focus and with an eye to the organizational impacts including work–life balance (Kinder *et al*, 2013).

So, one perspective on the differences between workplace counselling, coaching and mentoring within an organizational context is to think of an employee on a continuum (see Figure 9.1) between −1 (the employee is not coping and distressed), 0 (an employee is functioning at work, 'meeting expectations') and +1 (an employee is excelling, 'exceeding expectations'). Workplace counselling sits at the −1 end of the continuum and focuses on moving the employee from this point to 0. On the other hand, coaching or mentoring sits at the other end of the continuum and helps the employee change from 0 to +1. This also explains the overlaps at the 0 point.

FIGURE 9.1   Continuum of helping (Schwenk and Kinder, 2012)

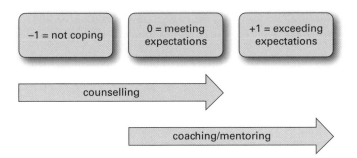

The workplace counsellor will therefore often work with employees who have a common mild to moderate mental health condition which could result in sickness absence whereas the workplace coach/mentor will often work with employees who are at work but not particularly excelling or feel that they are stagnating. There may be times and scenarios in which experienced coaches do intervene with clients towards the −1 to 0 end of the spectrum, and we are seeing more coaches becoming involved in wellbeing programmes which are targeted at stressed employees, but this needs to be done with caution, as we have stressed elsewhere.

An Employee Assistance Programme (EAP) is a proven strategy for assisting employees with many of the problems that affect their work performance. The International Employee Assistance Professionals Association (EAPA) defines an EAP as a workplace programme designed to assist: (1) work organizations in addressing productivity issues, and (2) employees in identifying and resolving personal concerns, including health, marital, family, financial, alcohol, drug, legal, emotional, stress, or other personal issues that may affect job performance (EAPA, 2015).

An EAP is based on a concern for the high cost to industry and the community in both human and financial terms when these problems manifest themselves in the workplace in the form of absenteeism, accidents, turnover or poor productivity.

For an EAP to be effective it should include:

- A clear statement on confidentiality so that even though it is paid for by the employer, the employees who use it can rely on it being a completely independent and confidential service which provides offsite professional counselling and onward referral as required. Coaching may also be included (Kinder and Hughes, 2012).

- Access for supervisors and managers to professional support to discuss any staffing problems.

- Information and guidance on work-related issues affecting psychological aspects of occupational health and safety issues.

Table 9.1 sets out some of the differences between coaching, mentoring, and workplace counselling. We will then look briefly at some of the similarities.

TABLE 9.1   Comparing coaching, mentoring and counselling

Coaching	Mentoring	Workplace counselling
Focuses on the individual or team	Focuses on the individual	Focuses on the individual, but can involve others
Short-term relationship	Ongoing long-term relationship	Is often short but long term can be made available

TABLE 9.1 *continued*

Coaching	Mentoring	Workplace counselling
Structured (although can be informal)	Informal	Generally structured
Focus can be on specific skills development but also on career and personal development, depending on 'contract'	Focus is on career and personal development	Focus is on personal development and/or healing
Can be direct manager or colleague, sometimes a professional coach	Normally not a direct manager but may be a colleague	Counselling should not be done by line manager or a colleague (though they may refer to counselling)
Focused on present and future	Focused on future	Focused on past, present and future depending on the model
Agenda set by client, the individual and usually the manager too	Agenda set by mentee	Agenda mutually discussed
Usually does not advise	Can provide advice	Does not advise
Often related to work performance issues although can be developmental	Normally does not address work performance issues	Can focus on work performance issues
Uses advanced communication skills and additional training if professional coach	Uses advanced communication skills	Uses advanced communication skills with additional therapy training

TABLE 9.1   *continued*

Coaching	Mentoring	Workplace counselling
May discuss stress management issues if disclosed and their impact on work but needs to refer on to others for mental health	May discuss stress management issues if disclosed and their impact on work but needs to refer on to others for mental health	Can treat or assist with mental health issues
Confidentiality important but exact nature depends on who provides the coaching and the 'contract'	Confidentiality important	Highly confidential
Other people often involved	Does not normally involve others	Rarely involves others (exceptions group, couples or family therapies)

The similarities between coaching, mentoring and counselling

All three helping professions provide the client with a safe, boundaried place in which to carry out an aspect of personal development. Although there are differences in terms of the focus for each profession, when viewed more widely they share a greater number of skills and approaches:

- **Therapeutic relationship** – this is central to all activities.
- **Providing a safe and non-judgemental space** – this reduces the defences that the client has and enables them to open up and set realistic goals.
- **Reflective practice** – observing how the client responds to questioning, assessments, agreed tasks or 'homework' can help identify further development objectives.

- **Creativity** – energy and change often come from thinking and behaving differently.
- **Review** – this involves evaluation and reflection on the effectiveness of the support provided and to ensure goals set are achieved.
- **Limits of competence** – practitioners need to know the boundaries of their competence and know how to and whom to refer on.
- **Thinking systematically** – this is an important aspect within the workplace so that the individual and the organization are considered (Schwenk and Kinder, 2012).

Personal problems

When an employee's personal problems affect their performance or that of the work group, the manager must intervene; referral to professional counselling may be appropriate. Counselling may be offered internally by a professional counsellor or externally, perhaps by an EAP. Table 9.2 sets out some scenarios and behaviours which might require referring on.

Rather than offering internal support, some organizations try to get around this by using local community services from a company referral directory. However, this requires the manager or coach to diagnose the employee's problems (eg is this employee drug dependent or do they have marital problems?), something they may not be qualified nor entitled to do. In addition, trying to keep such a directory updated is difficult and time-consuming.

TABLE 9.2   Examples of behaviours or situations where the coach should consider referring on to a mental health practitioner

History	<ul><li>Past attempts at suicide or self-harm</li><li>Past psychiatric history including severe and enduring mental health conditions</li><li>Current suicidal ideation</li><li>Sense of hopelessness and helplessness</li><li>Symptoms of traumatic stress including flashbacks to an incident, intense emotions feelings and avoidance</li><li>Psychological distress which is impacting social and economic status</li><li>Taking (prescribed, herbal, self-prescribed) medication for anxiety, depression or other mental health issues</li></ul>

TABLE 9.2   *continued*

Behaviours	• Increased or uncontrollable use of alcohol or other drugs (illegal, legal and/or prescription)
	• Physical behaviours such as shaking, slurring of words, unable to sit still, being in a highly agitated state
	• Obsessional checking and elaborate rituals/routines
	• Dramatic deterioration in personal hygiene
	• Workplace violence
	• Difficulty performing familiar work tasks
	• Excessive withdrawal from others
	• A significant loss of interest in work or projects and significant (out-of-character) apathy
	• Dramatic changes in sleep patterns (too much or too little)
	• Significant weight loss or gain, appetite loss, or overeating
	• Increased risk-taking behaviour
	• Uncharacteristic, 'strange' behaviour
	• Excessive social withdrawal
Thoughts	• Hearing voices
	• Catastrophic thinking
	• Incoherence and not being able to follow thought processes/irrational
	• Uncharacteristic disclosure of personal or intimate information
	• Problems with logical/critical thought and speech that cannot be explained
	• Difficulty concentrating, remembering things, or making decisions
	• Unusual or exaggerated beliefs about being able to control other people or specific situations
	• Uncharacteristically pessimistic or dark thoughts shared with others including suicidal ideation
Emotions	• Sudden outbursts of emotions without any obvious trigger and appearing out of control

NOTE: Having one or even a few of these symptoms does not indicate a mental illness. But a person experiencing several together that are causing them problems in the home and/or worklife should be assessed by a qualified mental health professional.

It is easy to envisage how much valuable time is wasted by managers or coaches trying to deal with something they are neither trained for nor competent to handle. The legal ramifications of the manager's action can also be called into question, as the manager has a duty of care to prevent damage to the employee resulting from their 'support' (Buon, 1992).

Duty of care

Duty of care is a legal concept which states that a person who suffers harm as a result of the actions (or inactions) of someone who has a duty of care towards them may be able to take action against that person (and their employer) for negligence (Buon, 2005). If a manager or a coach is engaged in an activity that any reasonable person would realize calls for care to prevent damage to an employee, then that manager or coach has a duty of care to the employee who may rely on their claimed knowledge and skill. It could be suggested that if a high level of skill is required when dealing with complex issues such as mental health (such as with counselling), then a greater duty of care is demanded.

Therefore in the case where an employee follows the advice of the manager or coach and this results in the employee suffering harm or loss as a consequence, the manager or coach and the organization could face legal action. Even if the manager or coach is strictly within the legal requirements for duty of care, they may still be outside the ethical standard of duty of care. It's worth noting that professional counsellors carry malpractice insurance whereas managers, internal coaches (and HR professionals) often do not (Buon, 2005). However, many coaches do abide by the ethical codes set out by the professional coaching bodies they belong to, which an organization providing coaching should ensure are fully in place.

A further problem is that the manager or workplace coach can lose focus as they get involved in the employee's complex personal or mental health problems; their focus moves from the performance decline to the employee's problems which may not be the job they are paid to carry out. It is important that professional coaches receive supervision, and that coaching buyers enquire about this when selecting external coaches and/or ensure internal coaches get supervision.

Since the passing of the Health and Safety at Work Act in 1974 in the United Kingdom, for example (and subsequent legislation from the European Union), employers have had a clear statutory duty of care, and generally, employers all over the world have a duty of care from an ethical stance. The United Kingdom's legislation, for example, requires workers' health and safety to be protected 'as far as reasonably practicable' and is reinforced by additional regulations that require employers to be proactive in identifying and reducing risks. These duties extend beyond physical issues of risks and include issues of a psychosocial nature including mental health issues (Kinder, 2004).

The United Kingdom's Health and Safety Executive (HSE) recommends a five-step risk assessment process, supported by management standards to identify stress hazards, and this can be used by coaches too to help them assess risk, potentially nipping problems in the bud and tackling them appropriately:

- identify hazards;
- decide who might be harmed and how;
- evaluate the risk and take action to avoid or reduce;
- record the action plan;
- monitor and review to ensure remains effective.

The HSE approach seeks to reduce the likelihood of workplace stressors causing work-related illness that include common mild to moderate mental health problems such as anxiety and depression. However, as has been highlighted, distress within the workplace is not uncommon and the costs already highlighted make it worthwhile for organizations to invest in and ensure access to effective employee support services which include coaching/counselling interventions (see Boorman, 2008). In addition, workplace coaches need to have an awareness of where their interventions fit within the overall organizational system and how they can raise concerns about the prevalent organizational culture which may be impacting upon the employees they are trying to help.

Workplace conflict

There are many individual and organizational precursors or contributing factors in the development of workplace conflict. Any given conflict situation may have been caused by one or a combination of these factors and so the nature of that conflict situation may be straightforward or more complex. A summary of the most frequently reported precursors or factors can be seen in Table 9.3 below.

TABLE 9.3 Individual and organizational precursors in the development of workplace conflict

Individual factors	Organizational factors
Physical or mental health problems	Inappropriate management/leadership style
Poor communication skills	Flexible working practices
Lack of negotiation and/or assertiveness skills	Lack of performance management systems
Diversity and differences	Poor or lack of delegation
Competing needs and goals	Lack of team leadership
Misperceptions and misunderstandings	Office politics/power issues
Inappropriate use of personal or group power	Ineffective conflict resolution processes
Underdeveloped emotional competencies	Over-reliance on e-mail communication
Internal emotional states	Blame and shame workplace culture
Personal problems outside work	Overly competitive workplace culture
Lack of job satisfaction	Physical environment
Low self-esteem	Poor decision-making practices
Alcohol or other drug-related problems	Lack of organizational due process
Relationship problems	Scarce resources
Language difficulties	Poor morale

SOURCE: Buon (2008, p 251)

An employee's experience of workplace conflict can be both negative and positive, and the factors that contribute to whether it is one or the other or a mixed experience are complex and multifaceted. In any conflict situation, there will be elements of both unmet human needs and the material or negotiable issues. As a conflict becomes more intensely felt over time the challenge in creating a resolution is to assess these elements as accurately as possible and then adopt the most appropriate approach that addresses both of these aspects (Buon, 2008).

Where conflict isn't responded to in a timely and effective way or where it has escalated over time or has become entrenched it becomes dysfunctional rather than functional. As a result, a whole range of negative effects can be experienced at an individual and/or organizational level.

At an individual level, unresolved conflict can result in a loss of commitment to the job or the organization; frustration, stress, anxiety or depression including physiological symptoms; strained or dysfunctional working relationships; increased use of prescribed medication or alcohol and other drugs; and a decrease in personal work performance (Buon, 2008).

At an organizational level, where conflict isn't responded to appropriately the impact on the organization can be significant. Buon (2008) has suggested this can include:

- employee turnover;
- reduced productivity and performance;
- absenteeism and presenteeism;
- increased formal grievances and investigations or claims;
- acts of sabotage or revenge;
- increased injuries and accidents;
- increased occupational health claims;
- loss of creativity and innovation;
- employee relations problems;
- loss of management time;
- customer/client dissatisfaction.

Responding to workplace conflict

An individual's or organization's capacity to respond effectively and positively to conflict is dependent upon the internal personal and organizational resources available to create and support that response. Clearly there is no one correct way to respond to all workplace conflict as each conflict situation will present its own unique set of issues and challenges. There must then be an ability to be flexible and adaptable if our responses and interventions are going to be consistently effective.

The following list (Buon, 2014) provides a brief overview of some of the key resources that are utilized in response to workplace conflict:

1 **Self-awareness:** An understanding of self and personal 'triggers' can be a very valuable resource in understanding conflict and its impact.

2 **Resilience:** Some of the factors that contribute to resilience are a positive attitude, optimism and the ability to regulate emotions.

3 **Social and interpersonal skills:** Active listening skills and the ability to remove barriers to communication can all assist in resolving conflict.

4 **Leader/manager intervention:** The employment relationship has an inherent power imbalance and so all employees need to know that natural justice is enshrined in an organization's policies, procedures and management behaviour.

5 **Policies and procedures:** It is essential to have in place a robust and meaningful set of complaint or grievance handling procedures.

6 **Employee assistance or welfare support:** As conflict can be rooted in personal problems (or can cause personal problems) it is important to have an EAP available.

7 **Mediation schemes:** Mediation is the intervention into a conflict situation by a third party. This person usually has no decision-making powers but simply assists the parties in conflict to resolve the issues they are facing. These schemes (both internal teams and the use of external mediators) are becoming increasingly common in the workplace and are reporting impressive success rates (Roberts, 2013).

A workplace coach should be aware of the key resources listed above and introduced where appropriate. The coach can then discuss with the client the implications, advantages and disadvantages of each approach.

However, in the first instance it is always best to try informal problem-solving processes. Most company grievance procedures will contain an informal stage, but most organizations do not indicate how this informal stage should work (Buon, 2008). The most effective way of preventing the incidence and escalation of conflict, and of empowering employees to find their own solutions is to develop and utilize good informal and problem-solving processes and interpersonal process skills; very much the territory of coaching, of course. We need to get past the fears of 'walking on eggshells' with respect to our differences from each other at work and of making a mistake as managers, accepting that responding well to conflict means being open to learning about ourselves and our organizations (Buon, 2008). A coach can be invaluable in this approach.

Workplace change

Change is a fact of life in all organizations. There are different levels of change, which range all the way from a minor change in a work procedure to a major revamping of the organization structure. Most people would suggest that significant or dramatic changes are the most complicated to handle but experience shows that even the apparently simplest of changes can produce complex and sometimes costly consequences (Buon, 2014).

Change can come in many and varied forms from, at one extreme, cataclysmic world events to, at the other extreme, a simple adjustment to a filing system. However, no matter how large or small the change is, the same dynamics are present and the impacts can be seen on individuals (Buon, 2014).

In spite of the good intentions of employers, the majority of change initiatives fail because of the failure by an organization to address properly the people factors. In the long run, these factors can be critical to the success or failure of such initiatives. Research indicates that too much attention is given to process issues, such as changing structures and systems, at the expense of the people factors (Buon, 2014). Elsewhere in this book, models and frameworks for understanding and working with change and transition are explored.

The failure to communicate the need, or make the case for change, can result in employees not fully understanding why the change is necessary or even in suspicion or lack of trust, to the extent that employees may believe that information is deliberately being withheld or distorted. Further, organizations often fail to take account of individual differences; for example, some people can cope with change and others find it more difficult.

Workplace coaching (as well as mentoring or counselling through EAPs) can assist individuals through the change process and support the overall change initiative. While developing a coherent strategy and having decided on an effective approach to change are essential components of the process of managing change, neglecting the people issues can be a recipe for disaster (Buon, 2014).

To illustrate this, Williams (2008) outlines that 'people today need connection with a mentor/coach/guide more than ever before due to the rapid pace of change, difficulty in creating sustainable relationships, desire to live one's life purpose, and many other reasons' (p 287). He predicted that workplace coaching had a unique contribution to make to helping employees manage change, as well as other organizational issues:

We are on the verge of a fundamental shift in how the workplace ensures employee retention, team cohesiveness, sales and production increases, and overall employee effectiveness and satisfaction. Coaching is on its way to becoming bigger and more successful than any other form of organizational investment in the future (Williams, 2008).

Conclusion

We started off this chapter highlighting the relevance of the workplace to most of us given that we spend a lot of our waking hours at work and suggested it's necessary to differentiate coaching, mentoring and counselling from one another, particularly where addressing mental health issues is concerned. While the coaching practitioner may possess similar skills with workplace counsellors and mentors, it's important to be clear about their different roles within an organizational context including some of the pitfalls of overstepping boundaries.

We outlined how the workplace coach has an important contribution to make to improve employee and organizational wellbeing alongside mentors and workplace counsellors. However, this contribution should be made with a deep understanding of the complexity of the workplace environment. The workplace coach faces many of the issues that the first workplace counsellors experienced when entering the workplace. These include the need for an understanding of organizational development, employee relations, power structures and the challenges of the 'dual-client' relationship (Grange, 2005).

Mental health, stress at work, conflict and change are all common within organizations and they can cause real problems for managers who try to 'bury their heads' and deny that they exist. However, there is a growing appreciation among more balanced and progressive organizations that there are benefits to facing these real issues and to investing in programmes that include workplace coaching.

Taking a world view, coaching has established itself as a useful learning and development tool, which can improve employee performance, embed skills and empower employees, and also has a part to play in boosting employee wellbeing and tackling stress in the workplace. However, there remain some confusion and contradictions in the coaching field that are potentially damaging the full adoption of coaching into organizations, and coaches and those purchasing coaching need to be aware of boundaries.

References

Adult Psychiatric Morbidity Survey (2007) *The NHS Information Centre for Health and Social Care*

Bartlett, J E (2007) Advances in coaching practices: A humanistic approach to coach and client roles, *Journal of Business Research*, 60, pp 91–93

Boorman, S (2008) Employee support strategies in large organisations, in Kinder, A, Hughes, R and Cooper, C (eds), *Employee Well-being Support: A workplace resource* (2008) John Wiley & Sons, Chichester, UK

Buon, T (1992) Employee counselling and performance management, *Journal of Occupational Health & Safety – Australia and New Zealand*, 8 (1), pp 59–67

Buon, T (2005) Employee counselling and performance management, *Counselling at Work*, Summer, pp 18–19, BACP, Lutterworth

Buon, T (2008) Perspectives on managing workplace conflict, in Kinder, A, Hughes, R and Cooper, C (eds), *Employee Well-being Support: A workplace resource* (2008) John Wiley & Sons, Chichester, UK

Buon, T (2014) *The Leadership Coach*, Hodder & Stoughton, London, UK

Centre for Mental Health (2010) *Long-term conditions and mental health. The cost of co-morbidities*, UK

Buon, T and Compton, B (1994) The Development of alcohol and other drug programs in the workplace, in Stone, R J (ed), *Readings in Human Resource Management* (2) pp 240–52, John Wiley, Brisbane, Australia

Clutterbuck, D (2008) Mentoring and employee well-being, in Kinder, A, Hughes, R and Cooper, C (eds), *Employee Well-being Support: A workplace resource* (2008) John Wiley & Sons, Chichester, UK

Clutterbuck, D and Megginson, D (2005) *Making Coaching Work*, Chartered Institute of Personnel and Development, London. Available at: http://www.cipd.co.uk/bookstore

Diagnostic Statistical Manual of Mental Disorders (5th edn) (2013) American Psychiatric Association, US

EAPA (2015) Definitions of an employee assistance program (EAP) and EAP core technology, updated 10/11, *EAPA* [online] http://www.eapassn.org/About/About-Employee-Assistance/EAP-Definitions-and-Core-Technology [accessed 26 April 2015]

Grange, C (2005) The development of employee assistance programmes in the UK: a personal view, *Counselling at Work*, Summer, BACP, Lutterworth, UK

Health & Safety at Work Act in 1974, 1974 Chapter 37

Horner, C (2011) A hazy notion, *Coaching at Work*, **6** (5)

International Coach Federation (2013) *2013 ICF Organisational Coaching Study*

Kinder, A (2004) Stress audits, what are they are why bother? *Counselling at Work Journal*, Winter, BACP, Lutterworth, UK

Kinder, A and Boorman, S (2010) Tackling stress in the workplace, in David Conrad and Alan White (eds) *Promoting Men's Mental Health*, Radcliffe Publishing, Oxon, UK

Kinder, A and Hughes, R (2012) *EAP Guidelines*, UK Employee Assistance Professionals Association, Derby, UK

Kinder, A, Nind, K, Aitchison, D and Farrell, E (2013) Counselling and personal development, in Lara Zibarras and Rachel Lewis (eds) *Work and Occupational Psychology: Integrating theory and practice*, SAGE Publications, London, UK

Roberts, T (2013) An effective mediation strategy to minimize the impact of change, *Strategic HR Review*, **12** (6), pp 317–21

Schwenk, E and Kinder, A (2012) Coaching and mentoring, in Kinder, A and Hughes, R (eds) *EAP Guidelines*, UK Employee Assistance Professionals Association, Derby, UK

UK Health and Safety Executive (HSE) [online] http://www.hse.gov.uk/stress/ [accessed 2 April 2015]

Waddell, G and Burton, A (2006) *Is Work Good for Your Health and Wellbeing?* TSO, London, UK

Weinberg, A and Cooper (2012) *Stress in Turbulent Times*, Palgrave Macmillan, Basingstoke, UK

Williams, P (2008) The emergence of coaching as a new profession, in Kinder, A, Hughes, R and Cooper, C (eds) *Employee Well-being Support: A workplace resource* (2008), John Wiley & Sons, Chichester, UK

Nourishing the lotus flower:

turning towards and transforming difficulties with Mindful Compassionate Coaching

LIZ HALL

Turning towards difficulties is often the last thing we want to do – as individuals, organizations or larger systems. Yet it's often just what's needed in challenging times. Rather like the lotus we talked about in Chapter 4, which relies on mud to grow and bloom, so too can we as human beings benefit from working with all that life presents and stirs up within us, including difficult emotions. Intentionally turning *towards* the mud rather than away offers the potential for healing, for making peace with 'what is' and for transformation. This doesn't mean wallowing in pain and suffering; it means not ignoring them. As the old Sufi saying goes: 'Don't run toward pain and suffering. Just don't run away from them.'

In challenging times, we feel more vulnerable and overwhelmed. It's harder than usual to be resilient and manage stress; to be compassionate towards ourselves and others; to be comfortable with the complexity, ambiguity and not-knowing that are hallmarks of times of turbulence and transformation; and to think and act strategically, systemically and ethically, for example.

This chapter looks at how Mindful Compassionate Coaching (MCC) supports working in the aforementioned areas, helping us, and our clients, turn towards, explore, befriend, transform and transcend difficulties. It proposes that an approach drawing on awareness (mindfulness), the wisdom of the body, and compassion (ABC: Awareness, Body, Compassion) can be used to safely explore difficulty, providing a powerful crucible for transformation. It presents FELT, an evolved version of the FEEL model (Hall, 2013), and a case study illustrating the MCC approach.

Background, definitions and research

Mindfulness

There is now wide acceptance of mindfulness as a valid evidence-based intervention. Mindfulness-based Cognitive Therapy (MBCT) is recommended by the United Kingdom's National Institute for Health and Clinical Excellence (NICE) as the preferred treatment for recurrent depression, for example. And in the United Kingdom in 2015, an All-Party Parliamentary Group report *Mindful Nation* sang the praises of mindfulness, recommending further pilot projects in education, healthcare (with increased access to MBCT), the workplace and the criminal justice system. In other countries, we're also seeing mindfulness embraced in a growing number of secular settings, including in education under the umbrella of the Association for Mindfulness in Education in the United States.

Compassion

Increasingly, too, there's a focus on working with compassion. Initially developed by clinical psychologist Paul Gilbert to work with clients with high shame and self-criticism, the application of Compassion Focused Therapy (CFT) is now expanding to those with depression and those with Post-Traumatic Stress Disorder, among others. As its evidence base builds, CFT is increasingly being offered as a trans-diagnostic healthcare option in some National Health Service hospitals in the United Kingdom. And just as NICE's stamp of approval for MBCT helped to 'legitimize' mindfulness, the growing acceptance of CFT as a valid treatment option is legitimizing compassion in non-religious quarters. Already, we're seeing initiatives such as compassion in education programmes – in Saltash Community School in the United Kingdom, for example. And in organizations too, there's growing interest (eg Atkins and Parker, 2012), including in compassionate leadership such as through the Compassionate Mind Foundation. Compassion-focused

Coaching is emerging (eg Palmer, Irons and Hall in Palmer and Whybrow, forthcoming; Palmer, 2009; and as Compassionate Mind Coaching by Antiss and Gilbert in Passmore, 2014), following in the footsteps of CFT.

The body

There's also a growing body of literature and research on the contribution in coaching of explicitly attending to and working with the body (eg Strozzi-Heckler, 2014; Aquilina, 2011) and on the important role our body plays generally, including in gathering and holding information (eg Gershon, 1999; Radin and Schlitz, 2005).

So what do we mean by mindfulness, compassion, and working with the body?

Definitions

Mindfulness

At its simplest, mindfulness is about training the mind to be more aware of whatever is arising in the present moment. However, there's a particular way to do this – not only in the present moment, but intentionally, and with non-judgement, self-compassion and kindliness towards ourselves, and curiosity.

Jon Kabat-Zinn has been key in fostering the spread of mindfulness into non-religious contexts. In the 1970s he set up the first eight-week Mindfulness Based Stress Reduction (MBSR) programme, which has inspired variations all over the world in many contexts, including education. Kabat-Zinn (1994) emphasizes non-judgement and intention: 'Paying attention in a particular way: on purpose, in the present moment, and non-judgmentally.' He outlines seven attitudinal foundations for being mindful, namely, non-judging, be-ginners' mind (which we can interpret as curiosity and openness), patience, trust, non-striving, acceptance, and letting go (Kabat-Zinn, 1991).

Curiosity and openness are also core to mindfulness for Ellen Langer, a prolific researcher in the West on mindfulness, who defines it as 'a flexible, cognitive state' that's cultivated by drawing fresh distinctions about the situations that present themselves (Langer, 1989).

Cavanagh and Spence (2013) define mindfulness as 'a motivated state of decentered awareness brought about by receptive attending to present moment experience'. Arguing that it's the state of 'decentered awareness', and 'intentional attending' – the process by which this state is attained – that are most likely to deliver the purported beneficial effects of mindfulness, they distinguish between mindfulness as a philosophy (deliberate intentional practice, present moment state), and as a trait (habitual predisposition toward experience). Within my own coaching practice and for the purposes of this chapter, MCC can be seen as embracing all these, with elements such as compassion core to its philosophy.

Compassion can be seen as integral to working with mindfulness (eg Brach, 2003; Hall, 2013), hence my inclusion of it within my definition:

> Mindfulness is a particular way of being, doing, and non-doing; of paying attention in and to the present moment, with non-judgement, curiosity and compassion.
>
> (Hall, 2014)

So what is compassion?

Compassion

> I try to treat whoever I meet as an old friend. This gives me a genuine feeling of happiness. It is the practice of compassion.
>
> The Dalai Lama (accessed April 2015)

Oxford Dictionaries Online defines compassion as 'sympathetic pity and concern for the sufferings or misfortunes of others'. However, in addition to the element of empathy and 'suffering with', also core in other definitions is the motivation to act to alleviate suffering (eg Boyatzis, Smith and Beveridge, 2012; Goetz, Keltner and Simon-Thomas, 2010; Alexander and Goldstein, 2014; and Gilbert and Choden, 2013). I define compassion as:

> the motivation to empathize with another, to feel what they're feeling, to care deeply about their wellbeing, happiness and suffering, and to act accordingly... and the heartfelt emotion/s evoked within us when this motivation is activated.
>
> (Hall, 2013)

Body/somatic wisdom

The word somatic originates from the Greek *sōmatikos*, from *sōma*, 'body' and means 'relating to the body'. Some definitions of 'somatic', such as that of *Oxford Dictionaries Online* add 'especially as distinct from the mind'. In this chapter, we see the body as a place for learning and transformation, but *not* as separate from the mind, or heart, or even spirit or soul; quite the contrary.

In this chapter when we talk about body wisdom, we refer to a dual process of specifically paying attention to what's happening in the body and to what the body's telling us, as a source of information and wisdom, and where appropriate taking action to change the body shape, work with the breath and so on to promote healing and transformation.

In the next section, we look at research supporting the case for working with mindfulness, somatics/embodiment and compassion in coaching.

Delving deeper

There's plenty of research into the benefits of practising mindfulness, of actively developing compassion, and a growing body of research into working with the body too. Only a small amount explores these in relation to coaching, with mindfulness in coaching research including that by Hall (2013 and 2014), Cavanagh and Spence (2013), and Spence, Cavanagh and Grant (2008), although much of the non-coaching-related research has implications for coaching. It falls outside the scope of this chapter to go into great depth on this research, but we will explore some of it, and the following box highlights the benefits of working with mindfulness, compassion and the body, specifically in times of crisis and transition.

Benefits of working with MCC in times of crisis and transformation

Mindfulness

- Improved wellbeing, resilience levels and ability to manage stress (eg Chiesa and Serretti, 2009).

- Heightened ability to turn towards and sit with what is difficult, including overwhelm and fear when faced with perceived threat.

- Enhanced ability to operate from an approach rather than avoidance state, allowing for increased resourcefulness and courage, and creativity (eg Colzato, Ozturk and Hommel, 2012).

- Greater self-awareness and awareness in general (eg Creswell *et al*, 2007) so that more ethical and sustainable behaviour ensues (eg Amel, Manning and Scott, 2009).

- Increased ability to get in touch with and act according to values. Improvements in moral reasoning and ethical decision making, mindful attention, emotion and wellbeing (Shapiro, Jazaieri and Goldin, 2012).

- Heightened capacity within the coach to be grounded and highly present for the client, offering a safe and non-judgemental space in which to explore/challenge attitudes and behaviours, including mindless consumption and frenetic busyness.

- Increased ability to be more comfortable with ambiguity and complexity, and more able to stay with not-knowing.

- Increased awareness of the 'interconnectedness' between the individual and the wider system, with more systemic and strategic thinking and behaviour.

- Heightened compassion to self and others in clients.

- Less tendency towards polarized thinking – more flexibility, openness and curiosity about oneself and the surrounding environment.

- Greater ability to be more content with what one already has (eg Brown *et al*, 2009).

Compassion

- Leads to desired change, enhanced health and wellbeing in coaching (Boyatzis, Smith and Beverage, 2012).

- Makes people feel seen and known, and less alone (Frost *et al*, 2000; Kahn, 1993).

- In organizations, promotes healing and builds the quality of relationships among organizational members, creating relational resources such as trust and strengthening shared values of interconnectedness (Dutton, Lilius and Kanov, 2007).

- Greater creativity (Zabelina and Robinson, 2010).

- Greater presence, attunement and resonance (McCraty, 2002; McCraty *et al*, 1998)

- Predicts psychological health and wellbeing: decreased negative affect and stress responses, and increased positive affect, social connectedness, and kindness towards oneself and others (eg Fredrickson *et al*, 2008; Hutcherson, Seppala and Gross, 2008; Lutz *et al*, 2008).

- Caring social networks have also been associated with improved immunity, lower blood pressure, lower mortality rate (Boyatzis, Smith and Blaize, 2006).

- Works with more affiliative brain systems unlike self-criticism which works through the threat system (eg Longe *et al*, 2010; Weng *et al*, 2013).

- [Self-compassion] linked to psychological health and wellbeing (eg Brach, 2003; Salzberg, 1997) with lower levels of anxiety and depression (Neff, 2012), less rumination, perfectionism, and fear of failure (Neff, 2003a; Neff, Hsieh and Dejitterat, 2005), less suppression of unwanted thoughts and a greater willingness to accept negative emotions as valid and important (Leary *et al*, 2007; Neff, 2003a).

- [Self-compassion] can act as the primary antidote to the fear response within the stress cycle, and intentionally cultivating self-compassion helps people neutralize the nervous system's reactivity to the trauma response (Alexander and Goldstein, 2014).

- [Self-compassion] associated with happiness, optimism, wisdom, curiosity and exploration, personal initiative and emotional intelligence (eg Heffernan *et al*, 2010; Hollis-Walker and Colosimo, 2011).

- [Self-compassion] associated with improved ability to cope with a range of adversities, including divorce (Sbarra, Smith and Mehl, 2012) and chronic pain (Costa and Pinto-Gouveia, 2011).

- [Self-compassion] associated with improved relationship functioning (Neff and Beretvas, 2012; Yarnell and Neff, 2012), and empathetic concern for others, altruism, perspective taking and forgiveness (Neff and Pommier, 2013).

Body wisdom

- Greater presence, attunement and resonance (eg Hall, 2013; Siegel, 2010).

- Greater access to data from all over our body. Our gut, for example, gathers and holds information (Gershon, 1999; Radin and Schlitz, 2005).

Compassion

Western scientific investigations of compassion have focused on three specific orientations of compassion (eg Gilbert, 2009; Neff, 2003a, 2003b):

- having compassion for others;
- receiving compassion from others or being the object of compassion;
- compassion for oneself or self-compassion.

Self-compassion is compassion directed inward, relating to ourselves as the object of care and concern when faced with the experience of suffering (Neff, 2003a and 2003b). Researchers are increasingly paying attention to self-compassion in particular, with more than 200 papers published on the topic since Kristin Neff published her landmark papers (Neff, 2003a, 2003b). Neff highlights three main elements of self-compassion:

- kindness;
- common humanity;
- mindfulness.

She says these combine and mutually interact to create a self-compassionate frame of mind. Neff (2012) clarifies that self-compassion is *not* self-pity or self-indulgence. Nor is it self-esteem: self-compassion is not based on positive judgements or evaluations but a way of relating to ourselves (Neff, 2012, p 5). Working explicitly with self-compassion can be particularly relevant in one-to-one coaching, and in challenging times. In the workplace in general, particularly during tough times, there's a place for coaching to seek to develop compassion in all three domains.

Not easy

Self-kindness is hard. Most people report that they're kinder to others than themselves (Neff, 2003a). Whilst it's 'easier and more palatable' (Germer, 2009, p 160) than compassion for oneself, people don't always experience compassion for others. And if they do, they may not express it; they may suppress and inhibit it, and may experience fear of compassion – for others, from others and for self (Gilbert, 2010). They may fear that extending compassion towards another will threaten their self-interest or the interests of their identified group (Gerhardt, 2010).

Certain contexts make it harder not only to be self-compassionate but to extend compassion to others, as Chaskalson (2014) highlights, citing studies such as the Good Samaritan Experiment, suggesting that when people feel stressed and needing to rush, their inclination to care for others dramatically declines.

Yet, despite how difficult it is, developing self-compassion brings many benefits, as we saw in the box earlier, including supporting us to consider our inadequacies, mistakes and failures, as well as when struggling with more general life situations that cause us mental, emotional, or physical pain, according to Neff and Dahm (in press).

At work

Increasingly, employers ranging from Google (Tan, 2012), London Transport (Hall, 2013), the US Marines (Stanley *et al*, 2011) and many others, are embracing mindfulness at work, although there is at present still a lack of evidence-based case studies in the workplace.

Compassion remains a tricky concept, particularly at work. The word itself can feel alien in the corporate world and to some individuals. It may have religious associations for some which can be deemed inappropriate in the workplace, for example. Or it can feel scary.

However, although there can be a reticence to talk about compassion in organizations, this is changing, with a growing body of research highlighting benefits. And of course, we don't have to use the word compassion. Kate Pearlman-Shaw, a clinical psychologist and leadership coach who works explicitly with emotions in change management, tends to use the word empathy instead, for example.

Whatever we call it, however, acts of compassion can be found at all levels in an organization, from leaders who buffer and transform the pain of their employees, to office workers who listen and respond empathically to their colleagues' troubles (Frost, 2003). Compassion in the workplace makes people feel seen and known, and less alone (Frost *et al*, 2000 and Kahn,1993); it changes the 'felt connection' between people at work (Frost *et al*, 2000) and is linked to a range of positive attitudes, behaviours, and feelings in organizations (Dutton *et al*, 2003). Atkins and Parker (2012) cite Dutton, Lilius and Kanov (2007) who argue that compassion is transformative within organizations; it not only promotes healing but builds the quality of relationships among organizational members, creating relational resources such as trust and strengthening shared values of interconnectedness.

Atkins and Parker (2012) argue that to enhance compassion in organizations, it's critically important to focus on how organizational culture and practices build compassion (eg Kanov *et al*, 2004). However, it's vital to first understand the processes by which compassion is enhanced in individuals.

They warn that otherwise, organizations might waste resources putting practices in place when individual staff might be unable, or unready, to experience compassion. In addition, they highlight the dangers of compassion fatigue, warning that encouraging people to become more compassionate without considering the associated self-regulatory demands can lead to staff burnout or turnover, citing Boyatzis, Smith and Blaize (2006) and Goetz, Keltner and Simon-Thomas (2010).

Coaching with compassion can enhance the adaptability of the organization through creating norms and relationships of caring and development (Boyatzis, Smith and Beveridge, 2012). Adopting a compassionate coaching approach (one where the coach intentionally encourages a positive future to arouse a positive emotional state) has been linked to better coaching outcomes (Boyatzis *et al*, 2010) – clients are more likely to learn and make behavioural changes.

ABC: Awareness, Body wisdom and Compassion

In this section, we explore the value of combining working with mindfulness/awareness, the wisdom of the body and compassion, and how the body and the development of compassion can play a part in grounding awareness in the MCC approach, for example, as Figure 10.1 shows.

FIGURE 10.1 ABC

Mindful Compassionate Coaching underpinned by ABC:
Awareness (grounded in)
Body wisdom
Compassion

Two wings of a bird: mindfulness and compassion

Although the constructs of mindfulness and self-compassion are both arguably drawn from Buddhist psychology (eg Neff and Dahm, in press; Brach, 2003), there's a history of contemplation in all the major religions (eg Hall, 2013), while many secular mindfulness teachings actively encourage the cultivation of compassion to self and others. There's a compelling case made in Tibetan Buddhism, however, for attending to both compassion and wisdom/mindfulness, and for us to see these as interdependent and as balancing one another (eg Brach, 2003; Ricard, 2009; Siegel and Germer, 2012).

If we solely shine the light of mindfulness upon our difficulties, including difficult feelings, we may become more aware of what's there, yet we may continue to be harsh on ourselves. On the other hand, if we seek to be self-compassionate without the clarity of mindfulness, we may tip into self-indulgence. As Brach (2003) says, 'Instead of pushing away or judging our anger or despondency, compassion enables us to be softly and kindly present with our open wounds,' and 'If our heartfelt caring begins to bleed over into self-pity, giving rise to another story line – we tried so hard but didn't get what we so dearly wanted – mindfulness enables us to see the trap we're falling into.'

Returning to the lotus and the mud we talked about in Chapter 4, in Tibetan Buddhism, the archetype of compassion is Chenrezig, who is sometimes depicted as a being with a thousand arms and an eye on each palm which allow him to see and direct compassion to all beings. A lotus flower emerging from the mud in a beautiful lake is one of the symbols associated with Chenrezig. The mud represents our 'darker' side, emotions we might find difficult such as anger; the lake represents the depths of the psyche; and the surface of the lake the boundary between our unconscious experience and conscious lives (Gilbert and Choden, 2013). Beneath the lake, the story goes, there is a seed of our potential to transform ourselves, and to impact others. And to germinate, this seed requires the force of compassionate motivation, not just mindfulness.

Gilbert and Choden (2013) say, 'compassion is not just about focusing on the mud but nurturing the lotus flower that opens out towards the world'. They argue that we need to attend both to opening and engaging with pain but also to connecting with the positive emotional systems within us that alleviate this pain. Mindfulness alerts us when we're doing or thinking things that are not beneficial for ourselves or others, and awareness in itself can be curative. However, compassion is a powerful agent of transformation of the mind. Gilbert and Choden (2013) say, 'Both mindfulness and compassion are vital to the process of growth and transformation, but while mindfulness is the servant of the awakening heart of compassion, it is the force of compassionate motivation that reorganizes the mind and sets in motion lasting change.'

Arguably compassion doesn't have to be present when we practise mindfulness. We can also have compassion without mindfulness, such as when a mother instinctively rescues her child from their burning home. We can develop our 'muscles' of attentional control and decentred awareness without actively seeking to cultivate compassion. However, for many, increased compassion for self and others naturally develops anyway as a result of practising mindfulness, and for those seeking to develop compassion, which is indeed possible, practising mindfulness is supportive of this aim. Jazaieri *et al* (2013) found that it is possible through compassion cultivation training to improve in all three domains of compassion identified by Neff (2003a and 2003b): compassion for others, receiving compassion from others, and self-compassion. And research shows that mindfulness training increases self-compassion (eg Birnie, Speca and Carlson, 2010; Shapiro, Brown and Biegal, 2007) and compassion generally (eg Atkins and Parker, 2012; Lutz *et al*, 2008; Atkins, 2013). Neff and Dahm (in press) write: 'to give oneself compassion, one must be able to turn toward, acknowledge, and accept that one is suffering, meaning that mindfulness is a core component of self-compassion'.

The body (and breath) as crucible for transformation

As others have highlighted (eg Strozzi-Heckler, 2014), the 17th-century French philosopher René Descartes sought to alleviate the chaos of his own time, one marked by war and persecution, by developing a philosophy of rationalism, now known as Cartesian thinking. And we're still reeling from the impact of the intellectual revolution he set in motion. As Strozzi-Heckler (2014) says, 'when Descartes declared, "I think therefore I am," he removed the body from Western philosophy in one clean cut'. Descartes' solution to the crisis of 300 years ago has contributed to the crisis of our own times. Cutting ourselves off from our bodies and hence much of our ability to feel has contributed to our collective blindness in the face of the harm and havoc we're wreaking upon our collective living space – Planet Earth. Separation is behind so many of our crises (a theme picked up elsewhere in this book by Chapman, de Haan and Kasozi, and Scotton and Scott), and therefore we seek integration. The body plays a crucial role in offering ourselves, our clients and the systems in which we operate the very best chance for healing, integration and transformation. Samuel's story illustrates this below.

Samuel

One of my clients, 'Samuel', a teacher, has a long-standing meditation practice and when he went through a breakdown, found he was still able to meditate. But he realized during an eight-week MBCT programme that he'd made things harder for himself in his meditations. He wasn't paying attention to what was going on in his body – he was focusing strongly on his mind, seeking blissful states, and seeing body and mind as separate. We explored this in the coaching, and again when I contacted him while researching this book. We'd also explored in the coaching how Samuel had been drinking alcohol every day to 'self-medicate'. Had he been self-medicating through meditation too, I asked now.

> Maybe. But I think it was more that I was seeing my mind as separate. I was trying to attain certain states of mind but was cutting myself off from my body. I think that's how I managed at first to ignore all those physical symptoms I was getting like the numbness and sweating at night. And it meant I could just ignore some of my difficult feelings as well. Now, thanks to the MBCT and our coaching, I pay much more attention to what is happening in my body, which helps me spot early warning signs.

The body helps us to become both more aware and compassionate. Mindfulness teachings explicitly encourage practitioners to pay attention to what is happening in their bodies, along with whatever else arises in their fields of experience. The body and the breath are seen as anchors, as mindfulness bells to help bring us back to the present. Our bodies hold experience and emotion, not all of it pleasant, but there is a conscious/unconscious wisdom to be accessed. Gendlin, the creator of Focusing, calls this bodily felt experience a 'felt sense', which he describes as 'the holistic, implicit bodily sense of a complex situation' (Gendlin, 1996). It's not just our skull-based brain that gathers and holds information – our gut does too (Gershon, 1999; Radin and Schlitz, 2005). In fact, the enteric nervous system, labelled the 'second brain' in the gut (Gershon, 1999), contains more neurons than the spinal cord, sends messages to the brain far more often than it receives them, and can function without intervention from the skull-based brain.

In addition to helping us be more mindful, we can actively work with the body to bring about change. In doing so, we stand on the shoulders of William Reich, father of somatic psychology, who was the first to bring the body into psychoanalysis. Whether we're aware of it or not, we experience life through our bodies, and the body is key to true transformation (eg Hillman, 2011/1973; Strozzi-Heckler, 2014; Brach, 2003).

Strozzi-Heckler (2014) writes, 'If we live at a distance from the life of our body we're unable to feel ourselves, and if we are unable to feel it's difficult to learn, change, and transform ourselves.' Hillman (2011/1973) writes, 'Transformation, to be genuine and thorough, always affects the body.' And Brach points out that in both Buddhist psychology and Western experiential therapy, 'this process of experiencing and accepting the changing stream of sensations is central to the alchemy of transformation. Emotions, a combination of physical sensations and the stories we tell ourselves, continue to cause suffering until we experience them where they live in our body' (2003). This process is core to MCC too.

Many of us have a long-standing mindfulness practice grounded in compassion, and use the body as a vehicle for developing insight and compassion. However, even amongst those of us for whom this is the case, in tough times, compassion for self and others can fly out of the window, and we can get too caught up in what's happening in our heads. And becoming aware of what's happening in our body may only go so far. It's often helpful to do something with that information – hence the element of somatic coaching we weave into MCC when appropriate.

So how can we pull this all together within a MCC approach, grounded in ABC, to turn towards, sit with and where appropriate transform the difficult? We look at this in the next section.

Turning towards difficulty: using MCC

> The cure for the pain is in the pain
>
> Rumi

There is a Vietnamese expression which asks, 'Why do we always come back to swim in the same old pond, even though it's mucky, just because it's "ours"?' (Hanh, 2011). We get used to our own mucky pond and it can be tough to break away. Mindfulness is about shining the light of awareness on whatever is in the pond, muck and all, and compassion helps us not to stay paralysed by ego games, fear or anger. Little by little, we may or may not find that there is less 'muck', but at the very least we might find we're not carried away by the 'muck'. And we may even find we've moved outside the pond to a clear blue sea.

Mindfulness advocates turning towards everything, including difficulties. When things seem really hard, this can feel pretty counter-intuitive. Why would we want to face the pain, those 'negative' thoughts and emotions that make us feel uncomfortable or desperate even? According to Brach (2003), 'pain is the messenger we try to kill, not something we allow and embrace'.

Our ability to recognize pain helps keep us safe but we don't like pain so we naturally seek to suppress it through a number of ways, including excessive consumption, keeping very busy, or self-medicating through alcohol and drugs. Yet we can end up deadened, living a zombie-like existence. At some level we may realize this, which, according to Professor Ernesto Spinelli, explains the fascination many have with literature and films portraying zombies. Interestingly, people can sometimes be resistant to practising mindfulness because they fear turning into someone who doesn't care about anything. In fact, practising mindfulness enables us to be better able to cope with everything – so in that sense, we *do* mind less. But we are not mindless – mindfulness helps us be much more present, to notice so much more. We feel more alive and mind more about things that matter. When we talk about acceptance in mindfulness, we're not talking about resignation or self-indulgence, and we are most definitely not saying action cannot be taken. The hope is that any action that is taken is informed by clarity and deep-rooted authentic values.

Mirror, mirror

In addition to actively encouraging turning towards difficulty, another important element in MCC is to act as a mirror, reflecting back to the client what we see and confirming what's happening, so they feel heard. This can be highly transformative in itself. Hillman (2011) writes, '[an analyst's] desire is to give recognition to the states of the soul which the person concerned is undergoing, so that they may become realized in the personality and be lived consciously. The analyst is there to confirm what's going on – *whatever is going on.*' This is the same in coaching, and as in therapy, we need to make sure we don't get so close to the client that we can no longer reflect, and 'become too much like the other' and 'unconscious together in the same place' (Hillman, 2011). He suggests having 'one foot in and one foot out'.

Feeling our way through crisis and transformation: the FEEL/FELT model

One way of working explicitly with ABC is to use a model I have developed, FEEL (Hall, 2013), which I've now evolved into FELT and which I present below. FEEL involves Focusing (setting our intention and what we seek to explore); Exploring (mindfully, non-judgementally and compassionately); Embracing (not grasping nor rejecting, just sitting with and gently embracing); and Letting go.

Since I first presented the FEEL model, I've used it with many more clients and shared it widely with numerous coaches. Many coaches absolutely love it, finding it offers the potential to go deep quickly whilst offering a compassionate space in which the client feels held and able to explore safely what may be uncomfortable terrain. Some coaches report that they particularly like the 'letting go' element of the framework; other coaches (usually internal coaches, interestingly), however, report that they struggled with this element. Some wanted a 'next steps' element. There is also resistance sometimes to the possibility of 'stirring up difficult emotions', again, with internal coaches primarily, which we explore further on.

FELT now offers more choice at the 'L' step, namely letting be and letting in, in addition to letting go. And it offers the option at the 'T' step to identify and take a transformative next step and/or identify and embody a transformative insight, new belief, new behaviour and so on.

Figure 10.2 shows the model. It can be used in a linear fashion but doesn't have to be. It can be used to guide self-coaching or for coaching individuals and teams. It's particularly helpful when exploring something which might be difficult.

Before we explore using the model, let's first look at letting go.

Letting go

The practice of letting go has much to bring to the process and experience of crisis and transformation and is a key component in mindfulness meditation, in which we're encouraged to observe and experience whatever arises, then to let it go. Frequently suggested metaphors include watching clouds pass in the sky, with the clouds representing our thoughts, feelings and sensations. We tend to find letting go difficult, particularly of possessions or pleasant feelings and even of painful memories and emotions. However, being able to let go – into the present moment, and of 'stuff' that no longer serves us – can be very valuable for clients (and ourselves as we process what

FIGURE 10.2   The FELT model (Hall, 2015)
for Mindful Compassionate Coaching

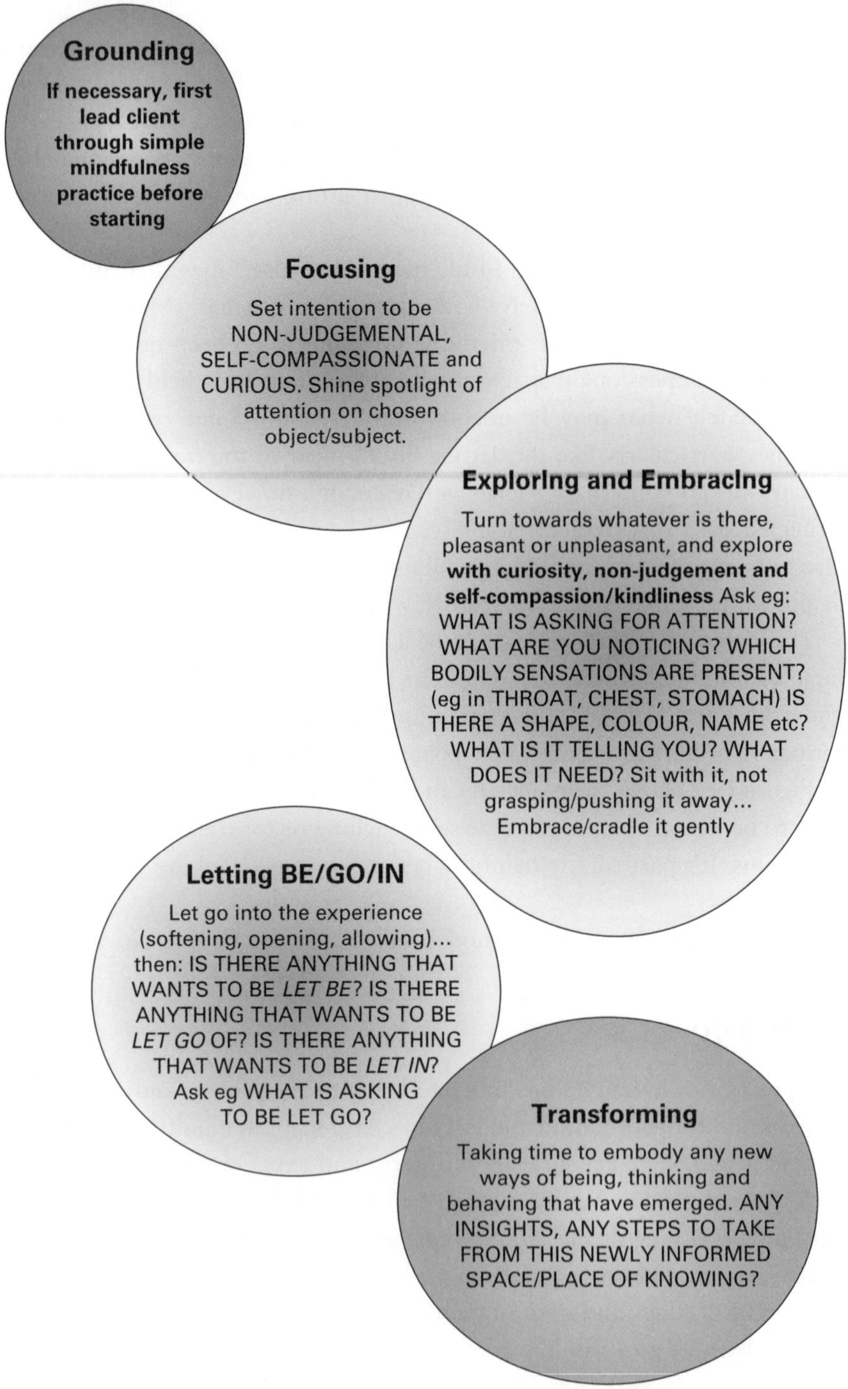

Grounding

If necessary, first lead client through simple mindfulness practice before starting

Focusing

Set intention to be NON-JUDGEMENTAL, SELF-COMPASSIONATE and CURIOUS. Shine spotlight of attention on chosen object/subject.

Exploring and Embracing

Turn towards whatever is there, pleasant or unpleasant, and explore **with curiosity, non-judgement and self-compassion/kindliness** Ask eg: WHAT IS ASKING FOR ATTENTION? WHAT ARE YOU NOTICING? WHICH BODILY SENSATIONS ARE PRESENT? (eg in THROAT, CHEST, STOMACH) IS THERE A SHAPE, COLOUR, NAME etc? WHAT IS IT TELLING YOU? WHAT DOES IT NEED? Sit with it, not grasping/pushing it away... Embrace/cradle it gently

Letting BE/GO/IN

Let go into the experience (softening, opening, allowing)... then: IS THERE ANYTHING THAT WANTS TO BE *LET BE*? IS THERE ANYTHING THAT WANTS TO BE *LET GO* OF? IS THERE ANYTHING THAT WANTS TO BE *LET IN*? Ask eg WHAT IS ASKING TO BE LET GO?

Transforming

Taking time to embody any new ways of being, thinking and behaving that have emerged. ANY INSIGHTS, ANY STEPS TO TAKE FROM THIS NEWLY INFORMED SPACE/PLACE OF KNOWING?

the client is experiencing) going through crisis and transition. As coaches, we can let go too of our attachment to outcome; this is not to say that we no longer desire positive outcomes for our clients, but we can loosen our grip, and thus become more open to the 'plane of possibility' (Siegel, 2010) to which Brown and Leeder Barker refer in Chapter 6. We explored in Chapter 3 other models including the Transition Curve and Kübler-Ross's Five Stages of Grief – both of these emphasize the importance of letting go.

In FEEL/FELT, the letting go element is invitational only – there may be nothing to let go of or it may not serve the client to do so, or they may not be ready. Sometimes, it is more a case of letting be. And I now explicitly include the element of 'letting in'.

Using the model

First, unless you feel the client is already calm and centred, lead the client through a brief mindfulness practice, encouraging them to sit/stand 'tall', relaxing and paying attention to their breath for a few 'rounds', for example. Then work through the following steps.

Focusing

Setting the intention. Choosing the focus of the mindful compassionate enquiry you're about to embark upon, and setting the intention to be curious, self-compassionate and non-judgemental. For clients who struggle to be self-compassionate, you may like to separately do some compassion-building practices or even do one before going into FELT, as I did with 'Fred' (see case study).

Exploring and embracing

Here, I've now merged the Exploring and Embracing steps from FEEL but the idea is to do both, encouraging the client to explore in a self-compassionate/ kindly, curious, non-judgemental way just being open to whatever arises. Invite the client to close their eyes, and offer the options of sharing as they go along, or remaining in silence if they prefer (this can be powerful if a little disconcerting for the coach!), debriefing afterwards.

Prompt them if you feel comfortable doing so with questions such as those below (you may have your own).

Without seeking to change anything, and with curiosity and openness, self-compassion and non-judgement, turning inwards:

- What is asking to be noticed/what are you noticing?
- Where are you feeling this in your body?

 – Does whatever it is have a name?

 – Does it have a colour?

 – Does it have a shape?

 – What is it asking for?

 – Is there any wisdom from your body that is making itself known?

Whatever comes up, you can suggest they sit with it, not grasping after it, not turning away from it... cradling it, embracing it gently perhaps – whatever it is.

If the client finds this exploration 'too much', guide them gently to pay attention to their breath. And of course if they want to stop at any time, that is fine. Remind them to be self-compassionate and non-judgemental as best they can.

Letting be, letting go, letting in

Invite the client to just let whatever it is be (let them sit with this option)... and then ask if there's anything that wants to be let go of (again, let them sit with this), and then ask if there is anything they want to let in... and sit with this. As coach we can be led by what has come up.

Transforming

Invite the client to sit with all that has arisen, noticing what is going on in their body – again any wisdom making itself known – and ask them if anything needs to transform. This might involve actively changing something, a behaviour or mindset, or even a value, but all coming from a place of wisdom, of compassion, of 'knowing'. This step can be about really taking time to embody a shift that has arisen from the exploration, and there may be somatic practices such as centring which can support this step.

Pandora's box: working with difficult emotions

I sometimes meet concerns among coaches that developing mindfulness and/or compassion in general, or specifically working with the FELT model, can 'open a Pandora's box', stirring up 'negative' emotions, perhaps traumatic memories, best left untouched. In particular, internal coaches – and organizations generally – can be reluctant to work explicitly with emotions, although this is changing. Kate Pearlman-Shaw has been working explicitly with emotions in her coaching and change management consulting work for many years. She agrees there's still widespread resistance to addressing emotions but is noticing a sea change, with more organizations becoming willing to take on board the important contribution being more emotionally literate can make in times of change, transition and crisis. She says if we work with emotions at work, we can have more credible and effective conversations: 'Emotions are at the basis of everything. Emotions affect behaviour. If we're overt about attending to emotions, we can cut to the chase rather than spend time going round in circles.' She says, 'People are becoming more receptive and recognizing there is a real danger in *not* attending to emotions.'

Some coaches may not feel comfortable working in this arena, or feel ill-equipped to do so. And in some organizational settings, the delineation of the role of coach is such that the coach is expected to work more at the skills and performance-related end, rather than the transformational, developmental end of the spectrum (see Kinder and Buon, Chapter 9). For me, personally, however, working with emotions makes complete sense – it feels wrong to compartmentalize parts of the client, to reject certain aspects of them as inappropriate to look at in our coaching. Coaching at its best is about helping the client to integrate all their different aspects. And whilst we can choose which parts of ourselves to cultivate, we can't just throw away bits we don't like. We can't ignore difficult emotions as they will just come back in a different form, or create blocks to change. Gilbert and Choden (2013) point out that 'the key thing with emotions is understanding and transforming them, not trying to cleanse or eradicate them, partly because these emotions are hardwired in our brain – we are designed to experience them – and so we cannot simply "get rid of" them'. When a client walks through the door, in the workplace or anywhere else, they walk in with all their multiple personalities or inner archetypes, all their thoughts and emotions and behaviours. They present 'warts and all'.

For those coaches who are comfortable and willing to turn towards potentially tricky emotions, of course it's vital that we respect boundaries, adhere to a clear ethical code, get regular supervision and coaching and/or therapy, and have a clear sense of when to refer on (see Chapter 9). Respecting boundaries includes not overstepping the role we've been contracted to fulfil, being explicit about how we coach and so on, and of course, only accompanying the client to where they want to go. And it's important to find approaches that help us enable the client to go deeper safely. MCC, working with ABC (the combination of awareness/mindfulness, the body's wisdom, and compassion we've been talking about) offers such an approach, for the many reasons we've explored. These include the focus on being non-judgemental and open. We know that MBSR and MBCT, and CFT, are being applied widely with highly vulnerable individuals, that exploring difficult emotions is part of the process, and that there's a wide evidence base highlighting the value of this process.

Trance

Mindfulness in general, and the FELT model, offer the potential for inducing a trance-like state in which difficult memories and associated emotions can be re-experienced without pain. When using this model with clients, I've noticed that at times they can go into a trance-like state, as have others using the model. I am not necessarily suggesting that coaches actively seek to bring this state about in their clients, but to be aware that it can happen, with positive outcomes. Alexander and Goldstein (2014) suggest using mindfulness-based practices within a session may induce a quality of trance similar to that induced by hypnotherapy. They explain that the person's consciousness can shift from the normal waking state into a very deep state of relaxation characterized by theta waves. They say that healing and transformation can then occur as a result of state-dependent learning, which they define (p 668) as 'learning that occurs when the unconscious mind is directly engaged via altered states of consciousness, such as hypnotic trance or a state of reaction and awareness achieved through mindfulness meditation'. Guided by the helping professional, 'the client is able to feel emotions typically associated with trauma, such as fear or sadness, without becoming panicked or dis-associating' (pp 649–50). At the same time, they continue:

> The client is able to perceive space between the self and what is being experienced, accessing what is called the observing or witnessing self. Awakening the observing self helps the (client) to remain present when experiencing uncomfortable emotions rather than avoiding them or becoming engulfed by them. The [client] feels a sense of control over the experience, no longer perceiving it as overwhelming. In this state, the [client] begins to develop the ability to choose new responses to feelings and memories.

I've found, again, as have others using FEEL/FELT, that within this relaxed, centred state, it is much more possible to explore difficult emotions, and often to reach peace with them or to have an insight about what to do next.

This all said, it is true that encouraging our clients and ourselves to engage more fully with potentially painful emotional material, be that through MCC or any other approach, is not going to be an easy ride. There can be overwhelm. Some long-term meditators report experiencing the equivalent of the dark night of the soul referred to in mystic Christianity. Willoughby Britton is spearheading a research project aiming to create a taxonomy of the full range of experiences which arise from contemplative practice, including difficult ones (see **http://cheetahhouse.org/**).

Other useful models, practices and exercises in MCC

In addition to FELT, there are a number of other tools and techniques that can be fruitful to work with in challenging times within the MCC approach. The following box shows some of these.

Useful practices and activities

- All the practices from the MBSR/MBCT programmes including the Body Scan (eg Hall, 2013, pp 51–52).

- Compassion-focused imagery (eg Gilbert and Choden (pp 237–304, 2013; Palmer, 2009).

- Compassion meditations including The Loving Kindness Meditation (a Buddhist practice, included in many MBSR programmes, known as Befriending Meditation in MBCT) and others (eg Gilbert and Choden, 2013, pp 237–304).

- Exploring the Three Affect Regulation Systems (Gilbert, 2009) framework which is particularly important in CFT. In CFT, the three systems are allocated a colour to help clients remember them. The Threat and Protection system is red; the Achievement and Pleasure system blue, and the Contentment, Soothing and Connection system green. Talking these through and bringing them to life for clients can help them see more clearly their thinking and behaviour patterns, helping them be more mindful, more self-compassionate, and to get in touch with what really matters to them, using the body as a vehicle for this. Obviously it is all about balance – we need all three systems.

- Centring (eg Hall, 2013, pp 46–47 adapted from Strozzi-Heckler, 2007).

- Future Self (adapted from Kimsey-House, Kinsey-House and Sandahl, 2011).

- Mindful enquiry with no fixed goal in mind.

The following case study illustrates how these practices, and the MCC approach in general, can be used with a client.

CASE STUDY   It's a jungle out there

An unwanted relationship breakdown and a controlling boss were contributing to a debilitating crisis of confidence for Fred, triggering memories of highly critical parents telling him he would never achieve anything worthwhile. He frequently felt criticized by others and their words would ring in his ears for days, and he was finding it even harder than usual to trust others.

Drawing on her own mindfulness and compassion-focused practice helped the coach build rapport and trust with Fred in the first session, and to be fully present so he felt genuinely heard and un-judged as he shared his tale of perceived woes. A Future Self exercise in the second session helped him fast-forward to a time in the future in which he was invited to describe what he was seeing and feeling and reported feeling 'tall, powerful and spacious', and that he had 'little to lose' in the big scheme of things. He smiled as he described what he saw and felt, and was encouraged by the coach to really embody these higher emotions and state. In another session, having been invited to shine awareness onto whatever was arising in his field of experience (informally and using FELT), he became aware of a host of challenging thoughts, bodily sensations and emotions including anxiety and a tightness in the chest, sadness at the loss of his partner, and the heat of shame as he contemplated how poorly he was performing at work.

Noticing whatever arises in our field of experience can of course be transformative in itself. Journalling regularly and practising mindfulness in coaching sessions and at home helped Fred notice just how often he felt criticized, giving him an inkling that it might not all be 'real'. He noticed more how this 'criticism' impacted him. He felt demotivated, ashamed, and rejected.

In the subsequent session, the coach guided Fred through two meditations designed to help him be more self-compassionate. In the first, Developing a Compassionate Image/Symbol (eg Gilbert and Chodon, 2013), he imagined a vast pink heart as his 'compassionate image'. In the second, Loving Kindness Meditation, he found extending loving kindness to himself and to certain people very challenging. Having established some grounding in compassionate feelings, the coach then guided him through FELT to explore his feelings of rejection. He shared how he'd turned towards a recurring image of being in a jungle, with thick tangled undergrowth dragging him down.

He felt the undergrowth represented his 'negative' thoughts and feelings. Eventually, he shared that he seemed to be looking down at the undergrowth from higher up. After exploring this further, the coach invited him to move physically to a spot representing the 'future self' he'd tapped into in a previous session, and to re-inhabit that space, describing again all that arose for him. Again, he said he felt powerful and spacious, and then said the undergrowth had shrunk and seemed even further away. The coach asked if the undergrowth needed anything from him, and he said, 'it just wanted to know I hadn't forgotten about it'. The coach asked him if there was a phrase or insight that was coming up for him, and after remaining silent for some time, he said, 'That it's all OK.'

Working explicitly with how Fred was holding some of the identified emotions in his body added a further dimension, helping to embed healing and transformation more deeply. He became aware that he often sought to make his body small, hunching his shoulders and contracting his abdomen, which was taking its toll on his digestive system. Becoming more aware of these patterns, but also consciously taking action to redress them made a big difference. He found he was able to consciously stand taller and with more dignity. And that when he held himself like this, and paid attention to his breathing and/or conjured up his compassionate image, he could see the 'criticism' from others as something outside himself. He still felt rejected at times, but it didn't last as long. He felt more confident and got accepted onto a training programme which he hoped would help him leapfrog into another role away from his boss.

Having looked at some of the practices and exercises which might be used in MCC – for the coach as well as the client – and explored some of the underlying qualities such as compassion, we look at principles, behaviours and aspirations for an MCC approach before concluding.

Mindful Compassionate Coaching: Principles, behaviours and aspirations for coaching mindfully, compassionately and somatically

- Be prepared to sit with and in silence.
- Don't be overly attached to outcomes.
- Be non-judgemental.

- Be present.

- Be curious, open and enquiring.

- Be comfortable with ambiguity and not-knowing.

- Be empathic and compassionate to self and others.

- Practise mindfulness (including mindful movement such as yoga or tai chi) and compassion development regularly.

- Prepare mindfully for each session.

- Reflect mindfully after each session.

- Get regular coaching supervision, including sometimes with a supervisor grounded in mindfulness or similar (eg Gestalt; somatics).

- Think systemically.

- Attend to what arises in the present (not solely) in coaching sessions.

- Pay attention to, listen to and where appropriate act upon the wisdom of the body, as well as the heart and mind (whilst holding a sense of these being a whole and not separate).

Conclusion

Mindful Compassionate Coaching, an approach drawing on mindfulness/ Awareness, Compassion and Body wisdom (ABC), offers a safe, gentle, yet powerful way to coach in challenging times, be they internally or 'externally' driven. It promotes mental and physical wellbeing, and enhances emotional intelligence, creativity, cognitive functioning, compassion for self and others, and wisdom, amongst others – all of which are particularly relevant in crisis and transition. It enables integration – of body, mind and heart/soul, for example – and fosters an appreciation of interconnectedness – of all beings, for example – rather than separation. And in so doing, it can support individuals, teams, organizations and society as a whole, to turn toward and transform difficulties, including overarching crises for humanity such as excessive consumption and unethical behaviour.

References

Alexander, R A and Goldstein, E (2014) Mindfulness, trauma, and trance: a mindfulness-based psychotherapeutic approach, in (eds) Le, A, Ngnoumen, C T, and Langer, E J, *The Wiley Blackwell Handbook of Mindfulness* (1st edn), John Wiley & Sons, Chichester, UK

Amel, E L, Manning, C M and Scott, B A (2009) Mindfulness and sustainable behavior: pondering attention and awareness as means for increasing green behavior, *Ecopsychology*, **1** (1), pp 14–25

Antiss, T and Gilbert, P (2014) Compassionate mind coaching, in Passmore, J (ed) *Mastery in Coaching*, Kogan Page, London, pp 225–52

Aquilina, E (2011) Tuned In, *Coaching at Work*, **6** (2)

Atkins, P W B and Parker, S K (2012) Understanding individual compassion in organizations: the role of appraisals and psychological flexibility, *Academy of Management Review*, **37** (4), pp 524–46

Birnie, K, Speca, M and Carlson, L E (2010) Exploring self-compassion and empathy in the context of mindfulness-based stress reduction (MBSR), *Stress and Health*, **26** (5), pp 359–71

Boyatzis, R E, Smith, M L and Beveridge, A J (2012) Coaching with compassion: inspiring health, well-being, and development in organizations, *The Journal of Applied Behavioral Science*, 0021886312462236

Boyatzis, R E, Smith, M L and Blaize, N (2006) Developing sustainable leaders through coaching and compassion, *Academy of Management Learning & Education*, **5** (1), pp 8–24

Boyatzis, R *et al* (2010) Coaching with compassion: An fMRI study of coaching to the positive or negative emotional attractor, presented at the Academy of Management annual conference, Montreal

Brach, T (2003) *Radical Acceptance: Awakening the love that heals fear and shame within us*, Random House, London

Brown, K W *et al* (2009) When what one has is enough: mindfulness, financial desire discrepancy, and subjective well-being, *Journal of Research in Personality*, **43** (5), pp 727–36

Cavanagh, M J and Spence, G B (2013) Mindfulness in coaching: philosophy, psychology, or just a useful skill? *The Psychology of Coaching and Mentoring*, pp 112–34

Chaskalson, M (2014) Mindful managers care more readily, *Huffington Post* [online] http://www.huffingtonpost.co.uk/michael-chaskalson/mindful-managers-care-mor_b_5554226.html

Chiesa, A and Serretti, A (2009) Mindfulness-based stress reduction for stress management in healthy people: a review and meta-analysis, *The Journal of Alternative and Complementary Medicine*, **15** (5), pp 593–600

Colzato, L S, Ozturk, A and Hommel, B (2012) Meditate to create: the impact of focused-attention and open-monitoring training on convergent and divergent thinking, *Frontiers in Psychology*, 3 (116)

Costa, J and Pinto-Gouveia, J (2011) Acceptance of pain, self-compassion and psychopathology: using the chronic pain acceptance questionnaire to identify patients' subgroups, *Clinical Psychology & Psychotherapy*, 18 (4), pp 292–302

Creswell, J D *et al* (2007) Neural correlates of dispositional mindfulness during affect labeling, *Psychosomatic Medicine*, pp 560–65

Dalai Lama, official website of His Holiness the 14th Dalai Lama [online] http://www.dalailama.com/messages/compassion [accessed April 2015]

Dutton, J E *et al* (2003) The organizing of compassion, manuscript submitted for publication, University of Michigan

Dutton, J E, Lilius, J M and Kanov, J (2007) The transformative potential of compassion at work, in S K Piderit, D L Cooperrider and R E Fry (eds), *Handbook of Transformative Cooperation: New designs and dynamics*, Stanford University Press, Palo Alto, CA (pp 107–26)

Fredrickson, B L *et al* (2008) Open hearts build lives: positive emotions, induced through loving-kindness meditation, build consequential personal resources, *Journal of Personality and Social Psychology*, 95 (5), p 1045

Frost, P J (2003) *Toxic Emotions at Work: How compassionate managers handle pain and conflict*, HBS Press, Boston

Frost, P J (2004) Handling toxic emotions: new challenges for leaders and their organizations, *Organizational Dynamics*, 33 (2), pp 111–29

Frost, P J *et al* (2000) Narratives of compassion in organizations, in S Fineman (ed), *Emotion in Organizations*, pp 25–45, Sage Publications, Thousand Oaks, CA

Gendlin, E (1996) *Focusing-oriented Psychotherapy: A manual of the experiential method*, Guilford Press, New York

Gerhardt, S (2010) *The Selfish Society*, Simon and Schuster, New York

Germer, C K (2009) *The Mindful Path to Self-compassion*, Guilford, New York

Gershon, M (1999) *The Second Brain: A groundbreaking new understanding of nervous disorders of the stomach and intestine*, HarperCollins, London

Gilbert, P (2009) *The Compassionate Mind*, Constable, London

Gilbert, P (2010) *Compassion-Focused Therapy*, Routledge, Hove

Gilbert, P and Choden (2013) *Mindful Compassion: Using the power of mindfulness and compassion to transform our lives*, Hachette UK, London

Goetz, J L, Keltner, D and Simon-Thomas, E (2010) Compassion: an evolutionary analysis and empirical review, *Psychological Bulletin*, 136 (3), pp 351–74

Hall, L (2013) *Mindful Coaching: How mindfulness can transform coaching practice*, Kogan Page, London

Hall, L (2014) Mindful coaching, in Passmore, J (ed), *Mastery in Coaching: A complete psychological toolkit for advanced coaching*, Kogan Page, London, p 197

Hanh, T N (2011) *Peace is Every Breath: A practice for our busy lives*, Random House, London

Heffernan, M, Quinn Griffin, M T, McNulty, S R and Fitzpatrick, J J (2010) Self-compassion and emotional intelligence in nurses, *International Journal of Nursing Practice*, **16** (4), pp 366–73

Hillman, J (2011) *Suicide and the Soul* (2nd edn), Spring Publications (original Harper Colophon, 1973) pp 48–49

Hollis-Walker, L and Colosimo, K (2011) Mindfulness, self-compassion, and happiness in non-meditators: a theoretical and empirical examination, *Personality and Individual Differences*, **50** (2), pp 222–27

Hutcherson, C A, Seppala, E M and Gross, J J (2008) Loving-kindness meditation increases social connectedness, *Emotion*, **8** (5), p 720

Jazaieri, H *et al* (2013) Enhancing compassion: a randomized controlled trial of a compassion cultivation training program, *Journal of Happiness Studies*, **14** (4), pp 1113–26

Kabat-Zinn (1994) *Wherever You Go, There You Are: Mindfulness meditation for everyday life*, Piatkus, London

Kabat-Zinn (1991) *Wherever You Go, There You Are: Mindfulness Meditation for everyday life*, Piatkus, London

Kahn, W A (1993) Caring for the caregivers: patterns of organizational caregiving, *Administrative Science Quarterly*, **38** (4), pp 539–63

Kanov, J M *et al* (2004) Compassion in organizational life, *American Behavioral Scientist*, **47** (6), pp 808–27

Kimsey-House, H, Kimsey-House, K and Sandahl, P (2011) *Co-Active Coaching: Changing business, transforming lives*, Nicolas Brealey, Boston

Langer, E (1989) *Mindfulness*, Addison-Wesley, Reading, MA

Leary, M R *et al* (2007) Self-compassion and reactions to unpleasant self-relevant events: the implications of treating oneself kindly, *Journal of personality and social psychology*, **92** (5), p 887

Longe, O *et al* (2010) Having a word with yourself: neural correlates of self-criticism and self-reassurance, *NeuroImage*, **49** (2), pp 1849–856

Lutz, A *et al* (2008) Regulation of the neural circuitry of emotion by compassion meditation: effects of meditative expertise, *PLoS ONEW*, **3** (3): e1897

McCraty, R (2002) *The Energetic Heart: Bioelectromagnetic interactions within and between people*, Publication 02-035, Heartmath Research Center, Institute of Heartmath, Boulder Creek

McCraty, R *et al* (1998) The electricity of touch: detection and measurement of cardiac energy exchange between people, in Pribram, K H (ed), *Brain and Values: Is a biological science of values possible?*, Lawrence Erlbaum, New Jersey, pp 359–79

Neff, K D (2003a) Development and validation of a scale to measure self-compassion, *Self and Identity*, **2**, pp 223–50

Neff, K D (2003b) Self-compassion: An alternative conceptualization of a healthy attitude toward oneself, *Self and Identity*, **2**, pp 85–102

Neff, K D (2012) The science of self-compassion, in C Germer and R Siegel (eds) *Compassion and Wisdom in Psychotherapy*, Guilford Press, New York, pp 79–92

Neff, K D and Beretvas, S N (2013) The role of self-compassion in romantic relationships, *Self and Identity*, **12** (1), pp 78–98

Neff, K D and Dahm, KA (in press) Self-compassion: what it is, what it does, and how it relates to mindfulness, in Robinson, M, Meier, B and Ostafin, B (eds), *Handbook of Mindfulness and Self-Regulation*, Springer, New York

Neff, K D, Hsieh, Y and Dejitterat, K (2005) Self-compassion, achievement goals, and coping with academic failure, *Self and Identity*, **4**, pp 263–87

Neff, K D, and Pommier, E (2013) The relationship between self-compassion and other-focused concern among college undergraduates, community adults, and practicing meditators, *Self and Identity*, **12** (2), pp 160–76

Neff, K D, Rude, S S and Kirkpatrick, K (2007) An examination of self-compassion in relation to positive psychological functioning and personality traits, *Journal of Research in Personality*, **41**, pp 908–16

Palmer, S (2009) Compassion-focused imagery for use within compassion focused coaching, *Coaching Psychology International*, **2** (2)

Palmer, S, Irons, C and Hall, L (in press) Compassion-focused Coaching, in Palmer, S and Whybrow, A (eds) *Handbook of Coaching Psychology* (2nd edn), Routledge, Hove

Palmer, S and Whybrow, A (in press) *Handbook of Coaching Psychology* (2nd edn), Routledge, Hove

Radin, D I and Schlitz, M J (2005) Gut feelings, intuition, and emotions: An exploratory study, *Journal of Alternative & Complementary Medicine*, **11** (1), pp 85–91

Ricard, M (2009) From consciousness to ethics, in Luisi, P L, *Mind and Life: Discussions with the Dalai Lama on the nature of reality* (ed Houshmand, Z), Columbia University Press, New York

Ruedy, N E and Schweitzer, M E (2010) In the moment: the effect of mindfulness on ethical decision making, *Journal of Business Ethics*, **95** (1), pp 73–87

Salzberg, S (1997) *Lovingkindness: The revolutionary art of happiness*, Shambhala, Boston

Sbarra, D A, Smith, H L and Mehl, M R (2012) When leaving your ex, love yourself: observational ratings of self-compassion predict the course of emotional recovery following marital separation, *Psychological Science*, **23** (3), pp 261–69

Shapiro, S L, Brown, K W and Biegel, G M (2007) Teaching self-care to caregivers: effects of mindfulness-based stress reduction on the mental health of therapists in training, *Training and Education in Professional Psychology*, **1** (2), p 105

Shapiro, S L, Jazaieri, H and Goldin, P R (2012) Mindfulness-based stress reduction effects on moral reasoning and decision making, *The Journal of Positive Psychology*, 7 (6), pp 504–15

Sheth, J N, Sethia, N K and Srinivas, S (2011) Mindful consumption: a customer-centric approach to sustainability, *Journal of the Academy of Marketing Science*, 39 (1), pp 21–39

Siegel, D J (2010) *The Mindful Therapist: A clinician's guide to mindsight and neural integration*, WW Norton & Company, New York

Siegel, R D and Germer, C K (2012) Wisdom and compassion: two wings of a Bird, in Germer, C K and Siegel, R D (eds) *Wisdom and Compassion in Psychotherapy: Deepening mindfulness in clinical practice*, Guilford Press, New York

Spence, G B, Cavanagh, M J and Grant, A M (2008) The integration of mindfulness training and health coaching: an exploratory study, *Coaching: An International Journal of Theory, Research and Practice*, 1 (2), pp 1–19

Stanley, E A *et al* (2011) Mindfulness-based mind fitness training: a case study of a high-stress predeployment military cohort, *Cognitive and Behavioral Practice*, 18 (4), pp 566–76

Strozzi-Heckler, R (2007) *The Leadership Dojo: Build your foundation as an exemplary leader*, Frog Books, CA

Strozzi-Heckler, R (2014) *The Art of Somatic Coaching: Embodying skillful action, wisdom, and compassion*, North Atlantic Books, Berkeley, CA

Tan, C M (2012) *Search Inside Yourself*, HarperOne Press, New York

Van Der Kolk, B (1994) The body keeps the score: memory and the evolving psychobiology of posttraumatic stress, *Harvard Review of Psychiatry*, 1 (5), pp 253–65

Weng, H Y *et al* (2013) Compassion training alters altruism and neural responses to suffering, *Psychological Science*, 24 (7), pp 1171–80

Yarnell, L M and Neff, K D (2013) Self-compassion, interpersonal conflict resolutions, and well-being, *Self and Identity*, 12 (2), pp 146–59

Zabelina, D L and Robinson, M D (2010) Creativity as flexible cognitive control, *Psychology of Aesthetics, Creativity, and the Arts*, 4 (3), p 136

Self-coaching

11

RACHEL ELLISON

> *Coaching is my tool... it's more useful to me than any previous training, even my MBA*
>
> **PRIME BROKER, GOLDMAN SACHS**

> *The coaching we did three years ago is giving me the resilience I need now to think clearly through this economic crisis*
>
> **GLOBAL RISK ANALYST, HSBC BANK**

One of my clients, a sales and innovation executive at large UK-based drinks company Diageo, reported that as he sat on the train on his way to our coaching session, he was thinking up a range of questions he felt sure I would ask him. And then some more he hoped I *wouldn't* ask. To me, this suggested an exciting junction in this leader's self-development and capacity for reflective practice and his ability to self-lead, enabled by coaching. And with it, the potential for this leader's self-development to be sustained beyond the end of his coaching programme. It also resonated for me around the ethics of best practice in coaching, including encouraging independence from, rather than developing dependency on, a coach.

You might call it self-talk or a conversation with yourself; a conscious inner dialogue, self-empowerment or the capacity to self-manage thoughts and feelings. I choose the term *self-coaching*, which I define as the conscious decision and ability of a leader (or other clients) to reflect and ask themselves coaching questions – including questions they would rather not be asked – in order to rise to a leadership challenge or think through a vision. Being able to self-coach in times of transition or in a crisis, and to carry on self-coaching through continuously challenging times can be highly valuable, as we will explore.

Whilst there are examples in other contexts including social work and teaching which have talked about self-coaching, the concept in business leaders has been under-researched. The chapter seeks to start to redress this, exploring, for example, how and when self-coaching occurs, how it helps or hinders in times of crisis, and what coaches can do or not do to build another's capacity to self-coach. It draws partly on my research for my MA in Executive Leadership Coaching, examining self-coaching from an individual perspective. This research was carried out in 2008, which saw the beginning of a double dip global economic crisis, and involved 16 in-depth interviews with individual clients from sectors including banking, sport, diplomacy, retail, broadcasting and humanitarian aid. Further research has been carried out for this chapter, including nine interviews with coaching buyers and coaches.

Findings from the first phase of research suggest that self-coaching has the potential to impact the wider system both inside and outside the work environment, and in some cases is already doing so. Teams, peers, colleagues, organizations and even a person's family, stand to benefit in an enduring way. The research also suggests that self-coaching becomes particularly pertinent in times of crisis or uncertainty, when, almost inevitably, leaders and their teams feel vulnerable, fear change and find it difficult to be creative and hold steady amidst the swirling emotions and shifting practicalities linked to ambiguity, uncertainty and modern, globalized working life. One client I interviewed, for example, reports that self-coaching helped them 'be more innovative in a crisis', while another that they are 'more consciously self-coaching because my environment at work is so tense, I can't talk to colleagues safely'.

In addition to considering the leader's perspective, this chapter considers the perspectives of their team, organization, industry sector, those in their home, and perspectives of coaches, coaching buyers and the coaching industry. It examines questions including the following: How might a self-coaching leader embrace and accelerate change *because of* the uncertainty around them? And how might this influence a whole organization's ability to bend, adapt and innovate in response to fierce economic, climatic, social or other existential threat?

Not a replacement

Before we begin our exploration, let's be clear that self-coaching is *not* intended as a replacement for coaching. Nor as a defence against having executive coaching, by leaders who are resistant to self-development interventions. Self-coaching as an outcome of coaching should not deter organizations or coaching clients from seeking future coaching. On the contrary – self-coaching leaders may be able to develop themselves, starting at a higher level of self-awareness, and thus achieve a higher level of business success as a result of subsequent coaching programmes or ad hoc top-up coaching during crisis. I believe self-coaching is a skill that can live beyond a coaching programme, as one of several outcomes or sustainable ROIs for the client, their organization and for buyers of coaching within companies. And that the capacity to self-coach occurs because of, and/or can be strengthened as a result of, the professionalism and in-depth skill of excellent executive leadership coaching.

As we will explore, developing the capacity through coaching of leaders' ability to self-coach can help them not only become more innovative and generate more creativity in themselves and others, but also become better decision makers, and more resilient to burnout. Self-coaching stimulates the ability to generate new thinking, connections and viewpoints, resulting in fresh ideas, solutions, decisions or actions. There is also the potential of self-coaching leaders transferring self-coaching skills to colleagues, role-modelling different ways of being and acting in a VUCA (volatile, uncertain, complex and ambiguous) environment. We explore benefits and potential negatives in more depth further on. But first, let's start by defining self-coaching.

Definitions

So what does self-coaching mean? Here's my personal, evolving definition:

> A coaching conversation with oneself to produce a thinking or behavioural outcome that has the potential to benefit the individual, their team or peers at work, their organization or even their family life outside work. Self-coaching is a conversation that occurs consciously or is deliberately evoked, in the face of a challenge or desired vision. It's mindful, conscious thinking about thinking, about self, about solutions, about choice of attitude and resultant action. Self-coaching can happen inside a coaching session with the coach present. Or it can happen between coaching sessions, including just before or just after a coaching session, or a weeks and months later. Self-coaching can also happen after a coaching programme has ended. It can occur in different environments, eg in the office, in the car, whilst walking the dog, on holiday or at home.

Let's see how some of my **coaching clients** defined self-coaching:

> Taking yourself out of yourself, in the moment, to analyse what to do next. It's making yourself think.
>
> Global Risk Analyst, HSBC

> I'd be amazed if someone self-coaching did not hear the voice of their coach in their head; the client is recalling questions, tone of voice, the moment that helped them.
>
> Buyer of coaching, Samsung

> The ability of someone to be able to provide guidance for themselves, to deal with a situation in their personal life or at work… Self-coaching is the ability to articulate the challenges and have appropriate strategies to address those problems. It's a tool kit. You're doing what a coach would do but to yourself. You are talking to your ego.

> Time away from yourself at work… it's a presence of mind that makes me stop and think before a meeting or teleconference… it's a little 'you' [meaning the client imagines/conjures up their coach] on the shoulder… what question would Rachel ask me…? Self-coaching is continuing the coaching work you did with me, further.

> The difference between chance and active behaviour.

> Applying what happened in a coaching session but without the coach being there. It's probing questions, asking why, how, doing things differently or looking at something from different angles. Self-coaching is taking it outside the coaching session and asking myself the same questions in the car… what are my or others' reflections, thinking, feeling, motivations… with difficult challenges. I wouldn't call it self-coaching. I would say 'application'. It's the self-application of what worked for me in coaching, but I'm using it on myself.

> I can be driving the car, thinking. It's like having a little 'you' [meaning his coach] sitting on my shoulder. The conversation goes back and forth between what I say, and what I think you'd say.

> I would say self-coaching is being able to reflect and make changes from your own perspective immediately. It's a huge change in me to be open enough and vulnerable in the moment; to take challenge from yourself, then use it to add to what you then *do*.

Now let's see how **coaches** might define self-coaching.

Former Head of Executive, Leadership and Management Coaching at the BBC, Liz Macann, defines it as:

> Asking yourself the questions you wouldn't normally ask yourself, in order to make you think beyond the obvious and automatic. It's also listening to your tummy.

For chartered psychologist and coach Dr Alison Whybrow, it's:

> where a client starts to implement the things that you have done together *in* their coaching sessions, to inform them *outside* the coaching sessions. It's where the client asks themselves, in the moment of challenge: 'What's the smallest step I can take to move forward from here? What do I want to do/think/feel right now?'

Dr Carole Pemberton, who specializes in resilience coaching, offers this:

> Self-coaching is the ability to insert a glimmer of space between oneself and one's thoughts, feelings and actions so that new connections can be made. I think clients often don't see it as self-coaching, but as carrying the voice of the coach into their thoughts, which acts as an interruption to their practised thoughts... Self-coaching is the ability to observe oneself in action, and to be able to stand outside of the situation, to reflect on the appropriateness of one's behaviour, thoughts and feelings. It is the ability to both take a mindful approach, ie, I notice that I am doing that 'beat myself up thing again'. But also to be able to take a position that allows one to ask oneself questions that allow honest recognition of one's responses. And to allow in the question one does not ask, in the heat of the moment, opening up new choices from which action follows.

Coaching buyers

Buyers of coaching are in a fascinating position. In commercial and insight terms, they are the client. But in pure coaching terms, they're not. The buyer of coaching is invested in helping the individual grow as a leader. They're also wanting to deliver for the boss and ultimately, for the business. What might the impact, sustainability and potential value in crisis of self-coaching be, as a result of offering a coaching programme to a member of staff, from their perspective?

Anthony Ryland, former coaching buyer at Samsung Electronics UK, wanted to introduce a leadership and a learning culture to the organization's high-performance culture. When interviewing prospective coaches for the executive team, he watched for coaches who challenged themselves in the moment:

> If you see evidence that the coach is self-coaching, it's likely that they'll help build the capacity of the client to self-coach. Another thing – great coaches just can't turn it off... they pick up on everything; there are tangents in the conversation, they're absorbing the whole room... they're inquisitive, they build, they are riveted yet detached listeners. When I meet a coach who even challenges

the buyer of coaching, I have a gut reaction that this is a coach that's going to help the leaders of my business. And that includes in crisis and through change.

Here's how he views self-coaching:

> It's like a switch going on in your head when you're receiving coaching; you realize that what you think isn't your best thought unless you ask yourself the amazing and insightful questions your coach asked you. You start from *not* challenging yourself, to consciously challenging yourself, to internalizing that self-challenge as a natural habit. I believe true emotional intelligence lies in understanding your need to do things differently, which is how many people end up having coaching in the first place. The client picks up on the role-modelling the coach is doing – visual, audio, kinaesthetic cues. I believe self-coaching is seeing the value of coaching.

UK Sport (which is funded by the UK Treasury and the National Lottery Fund), invests £100 million each year in high-performance sports. It's selected some of Britain's most successful sports coaches to join an elite leadership programme, which includes one-to-one coaching with an executive leadership coach. Whilst some businesses want to make more money or gain market sector dominance, UK Sport wants to achieve more points and more medals in national and international competitions. Its coaching buyer David Bunyan, who is also a men's hockey coach, defines self-coaching as:

> taking appropriate action or not, whilst taking into account experience, learning and models; self-coaching leaders will reflect on events that happened in their past, on relationships, on business situations.

The impact of self-coaching

> You can't afford not to self-coach.
>
> Global banking client

I asked clients, coaches and buyers of coaching about the potential impact of self-coaching, including when travelling through an organizational or existential crisis. Self-coaching certainly seems to encourage the deeper levels of reflection, analysis and new thinking needed to solve increasingly complex, globally interconnected commercial and social challenges. It appears to offer a range of benefits for the individual, the team, the organization and potentially society as a whole. For example, clients say that as leaders they are doing more thinking, challenging and learning, and bring greater perspective. They feel less afraid of making mistakes and, as a result of self-coaching, become more influential.

In this section, we will look at potential impact on the individual, then broaden out to take multiple perspectives from the potential of a self-coaching leader on their team, the organization, and even at home.

Individuals

> Self-coaching is even more essential in times of crisis, when old thinking clearly isn't enough or hasn't worked. You need to generate new solutions, and do so under internal and existential pressure.
>
> Global retail client

This quote suggests to me that leaders need to develop self-coaching as a critical skill to maximize their potential and effectiveness under pressure. It's about staying mindful and grounded, when there's barely any time to think. Executives are leading live in the moment. They have to think, solve, decide and act fast.

Clients say they feel more trusted and respected. They report more inner confidence and deeper insight, especially with decision making on tough issues. One says:

> I've come out of self-doubt... telling myself that it's OK to learn from a mistake and move on... consistently building my confidence, instructing myself to have another crack at it.

Clients report experiencing greater energy and excitement, together with being able to think through more angles rather than coming up with just one solution and then stopping. They say they consciously take multiple perspectives into account, compared to before coaching and before subsequent self-coaching.

> The last three months have felt like five years. It's the intensity; I'd have gone crazy by now if I hadn't made self-coaching a habit. In the banking sector, you're dealing with board directors, regulators, complexity, intensity.... you can see people who've physically and emotionally deteriorated because of the economic crisis. Self-awareness gained from coaching and self-coaching off the back of that have helped me come through it all.

This banking client says self-coaching has helped him cope with the intensity of these VUCA times and the speed of change expected of individuals and the organizations they're leading. He says self-coaching has helped him develop resilience, and to read what counts now, which is not the same as what counted before the economic crisis, for example. All of this influences whether a decision is a good one or a bad one. As a result of self-coaching, my client says he now prepares and rehearses before meetings, for example: 'I'm making myself think. I can see the impact of my behaviour and choices of how to lead. It's immediate.'

Another coaching client was about to be interviewed for a very senior job in the World Bank. He was anxious to land the job because he was being made redundant. He had worked with his coach on how he needed to be, and the story he needed to take into that interview, so as not to undermine himself. Sitting in the anteroom, the client saw himself being caught by his story of failure. He reminded himself of what we had done the previous week, then coached himself back into the place of the affirming story.

For another client, self-coaching in the moment enabled her to think beyond her normal stopping point. She was able to challenge her own assumptions, look at her issues from different perspectives and demonstrate respect for the 'other's points of view'.

The team

There are potential benefits of self-coaching for team members and the team as a whole, including improving individual and collective decision making, as junior staff follow the role-modelling of their senior leaders. One client says:

> I'm a better role model, compared to before I had coaching. Self-coaching helps me generate six solutions instead of being grateful I'd thought of one. As a leader, I'm raising the bar for junior staff coming up the ranks... The team is in great shape – and it's self-perpetuating... self-coaching is really working for me as a leader. My team have a more confident leader who can try things, adjust and bounce back if they don't always work.

Leaders report better results with their teams, who seem to have greater purpose, motivation, passion and commitment to deliver. One client's team members now tell him they feel more empowered, appreciated and trusted by him, and the team is better at choosing the most productive focus and priority tasks.

A client who is coach to an Olympic squad of athletes says that, through her newfound ability to self-coach during a crisis, there is more openness, vulnerability and sharing within the team; she sees more collaboration, cooperation and contentment in the team, despite the challenge of some difficult funding news. The *perception* of negative news has become more positive. There are fewer barriers between team members, because their leader is more effectively managing herself. This leader also credits her ability to conjure up her coach in her head, and talk herself through a potential scenario and her choice of approach, with another shift in behaviour. Instead of being directive with her team of sportswomen, she now offers them a deeper understanding of how what she is asking them to do benefits them and fits into a longer-term view:

> I was like a mother feeding the little robins in the nest... there they all were, with their heads turned up towards me and their beaks open. Now we talk things through, rather than me just expecting them to do it.

This leader puts that shift down to coaching and subsequently, her ability to conjure up her coach in her head and talk herself through a potential situation.

The organization and the wider system

> Without that 'self-process' and increased self-confidence, I would have ducked below the bar.

> I could see myself about to fight my corner, when a voice in my head said: 'Are you doing this for yourself or for the good of the whole?' I stopped, took a breath, resisted the urge to beat myself up in my head, and asked how my division could help.
>
> Board Director, transport and infrastructure

> When I presented to the board, I went in on the back foot. And because of how I had self-coached beforehand, I saw I was changing people's minds.
>
> Team GB Olympic Coach

Leaders tell me that they believe self-coaching has positive outcomes for their organizations. It can result in better personal relationships, cross-functional influence, cross-functional contribution and increased efficiency. Ideas travel from one part of the company to another, for example improving connections between finance and sales, bringing increased efficiency which can suffer in challenging times.

Leaders say through their own self-coaching they feel more at ease sharing their feelings openly if they think the company is wasting time on the wrong priorities. Self-coaching can produce leaders who are more insightful, reflective and challenging. It also has the potential to 'raise the bar' across the department or beyond, as leaders role-model self-challenging thinking, self-accountability and the habit of constantly reviewing the performance of themselves and the organization.

> I realized the red mist had come down again and if I didn't quickly stop myself, I was in danger of messing up my new role, that I had worked so hard to land. I was about to fight to win and prove my point, rather than act in way that would actually achieve a much better result.
>
> Group CEO, financial services

Self-coaching is enabling my sport to become more self-aware. It is able to adapt, change and take action in a different way from before. The team dynamics are noticeably improving. My athletes' physical, technical and even artistic performance has gone up.

Team GB Olympic Coach

Organizations with self-coaching leaders have leaders who can keep learning. They can fix themselves. And therefore they can fix or recreate the organization. They can execute with an urgency and an intensity. They can manage change. And manage the friction around change.

Global Risk Team Leader who commissions coaches for his team, HSBC

Self-coaching is a transferable skill. If a leader can make better decisions through self-coaching, athletes in their teams will also become better decision makers.

Coaching buyer, UK Sport

A self-coaching leader is a more confident role model, asks better questions, brings more flexibility to their leadership style and promotes more knowledge sharing across the organization, which leads to higher profits. Having said that, there's a risk that leaders who self-coach procrastinate or don't take action at all, because they're still searching for the utopian solution.

Coaching buyer, Samsung Electronics UK

Samsung's coaching buyer spots similar benefits and/or potential downsides to self-coaching as some of the leaders I spoke to. He also shares his analysis around the potential of self-coaching to impact on the quality of leadership, linking that to increased profits. He says leaders who self-coach:

- are more confident;
- are 'more asking, less telling';
- make faster decisions;
- seek out opinions from a higher level of thinking, because the leader has self-coached themselves through a few questions first;
- ask better questions of their reports;
- are more flexible, showing variety in style according to which employee or part of the business they are trying to lead;
- add coaching and supporting to their skill sets of delegating and directing;
- encourage knowledge-sharing across the business, leading to more information, leading to better decisions, leading to higher profits;

- break the status quo because what works today may not work tomorrow;
- ask: Is this the right way? Is this the best way?
- create a culture of change and innovation which ultimately helps the organization survive challenge, crisis and change by adapting faster and accelerating change, as the global picture changes;
- are more aware of their ego, and thus hopefully more willing to create more collaborative organizations – less of the 'me', and more of the 'we', maintaining this stance during times of crisis.

He adds, 'You don't need to change the culture of an organization to cope with VUCA, you need to create a culture *of* change.' Perhaps self-coaching is about the client holding themselves *in* the situation longer, instead of running for the first solution or 'exit' from a situation that they generate as an option. Buyers of coaching say coaches who promote self-coaching help the client generate many more options – and evaluate them – before jumping into action. In promoting the capacity to self-coach, the hope is that after their coaching programme has ended, the client will re-enact some of that holding, dwelling, generative thinking and conscious resistance of the temptation to power forward out of discomfort in order not to be seduced into thinking that *doing something* in a crisis, is the *right something*, just because it offers temporary relief to act, rather than to think.

In the view of the Global Risk Team Leader at HSBC, post-2008, society faces a very different battle to the one after the Great Depression of the 1920s, when Europe descended into World War II not long after the end of World War I. Now it's a case of 'fighting it out with the regulators, through the courts, with the EU', a battle he sees as signifying progress in societal terms, one about changing and adding perspectives, developing and retaining personal, team and organizational flexibility and resilience, with ambiguity threaded through it. But crisis is taking its toll, he says:

> The cost to companies in time, energy, money and organizational effectiveness is immense if people are resigning because they are burning out or just can't cope with the change thrown up by crisis. The impact of poor decision making is immeasurable and immense. Coaching and the self-coaching that resulted helped me develop the ability to handle ambiguity and vulnerability. I need that more than my technical skills, which increasingly look irrelevant.

And he agrees self-coaching can help in times of crisis, producing leaders who make better decisions, amongst the other benefits, cited on page 231 – leaders who keep on learning, who can manage change, and the friction it causes.

This leader argues that self-coaching causes you to wait. He believes that in a fast world and under stress, those seconds, minutes, days or weeks can result in greater effectiveness: 'In terms of the quality of your decision making under huge time pressure, ironically, it can pay to take a tiny pause.'

David Bunyan of UK Sport, agrees that self-coaching allows a pause which can be very helpful. He says:

> The impact of self-coaching is to stop an over-emotive responsive to a certain stimulus; your self-coaching tells you to go through a procedure to deal with it, instead of being emotive/having a gut response. Your gut response might be right, that's true... but I believe self-coaching can help you become a better judge of your initial response to a situation, before deciding whether to go with it or not.

Although Bunyan says he doesn't know at what point in a coaching programme a client starts to be able to self-coach, he is certain, 'you can see when self-coaching has started to happen'.

Like my client in the finance department at Diageo, Bunyan also believes self-coaching goes beyond merely impacting the individual: 'Self-coaching is a transferable skill. If a leader can make better decisions through self-coaching, athletes in their teams will also become better decision makers.'

I think this point about self-coaching being a potentially transferable skill, which cascades through an organization, lends further support to the efficiency and value for money of developing self-coaching leaders. Making this a *conscious* endeavour of coaches and the leaders they work with could give new shape to the way companies behave and the business and leadership outcomes they achieve.

I believe self-coaching can form part of a sustainability strategy for the client and their organization, giving greater value for money and return for the investment of time and money in a coaching programme. There's also food for thought for those developing new internal or external coaches, for buyers of coaching who are selecting and assessing coaches, and for supervisors tasked with stretching the practice of executive leadership coaches. I would recommend more widespread, explicit development and testing of coaches, coach training and coach supervision, to build the capacity of clients to self-coach.

Impact at home

> You asked me about the impact at work, but you didn't ask me about the impact of self-coaching at home.
>
> FCO, international retail

I jumped for joy inside, when during our interview for my research, my client – a rather emotionally self-contained CFO of an international retail organization – spontaneously offered to share how the self-coaching he now does, as a result of having leadership coaching, was causing positive change at home with his wife and children. I have long been pretty convinced that self-development of any kind and learning from virtually any source the potential to benefit other areas of one's life, including the potential of therapy done outside work to benefit one's leadership capacity. Equally, coaching done in a work context can benefit at home. One could argue, after all, that's it's all about self-awareness, conscious reflection, mindful presence and examination of the impact of one's choice of attitude or behaviour.

Leaders tell me that they are more honest with themselves about their shortcomings as a partner or parent. They're more honest in how they communicate with their partner and/or children. They bring more awareness to managing their relationships for success and fulfilment for everybody, rather than achieving a personal win at the expense of the home 'system'. They're more articulate and communicative, including 'setting expectations within our marriage better'.

Here's what others say:

> Before self-coaching, I was grumpy and I switched off when I got home from work.

> There's less dancing on eggshells in our marriage... it's more honest, there's more communication, it's more mature...

> I consciously praise and reward the children more... I'm a more authentic father; I give my children real eye contact now, I make time to really listen to what they're saying – I make more time for them.

> The most powerful part of self-coaching has been to think how what I do lands for the various people in my family.

Clients evidence multiple perspective-taking in a home context, including being more aware of their own deficiencies, being more honest with their partner and building better, more frequent communication in their relationships. Some clients report they are listening more actively and are more engaged with their partner and children, and feel they are a more authentic parent. In some cases there are fewer arguments, partners say they feel less frustrated and that there is more harmony in the home. Self-coaching enriches family life and generates a feeling that there is potential to achieve more as a family.

We've looked at potential benefits at a range of levels; these are set out in following box.

Potential positive outcomes of self-coaching

For the individual leader:

- more confident;
- more insightful;
- better at making tough decisions;
- more self-challenging;
- better able to generate ideas and choice of solutions;
- more focused on team priorities;
- better able to empower and boost productivity of teams;
- better able to influence the board;
- improved physical, technical and artistic performance;
- raises the bar for self;
- increased harmony and less frustration in home life;
- enjoys better relationships with partner and children – more active listening, more authentic and more present;
- more honest with oneself.

For organizations:

- Enhanced leadership capacity, with leaders who: are better at thinking; are more challenging; are more resilient; have wider perspective; are better able to learn; raise the bar for others in their role-modelling; are more flexible, less afraid of making mistakes; can fix themselves and therefore the organization.
- More connectedness and cross-fertilization, with individual leaders across the business making more contributions.

- Wider ability among employees to constantly question performance.

- Increased thinking about the interests of the whole, the collective.

- Saved time, energy and funds due to lowered costs of poor productivity, absenteeism, resignation and poor decisión making.

At home:

- individual more aware of own deficiencies;

- more honest in relationship with partner;

- more active listening and engagement with partner and children;

- more frequent communication and better relationship building;

- fewer arguments, partners less frustrated, more harmony;

- enriched family life;

- potential to achieve more as a family;

- multiple perspective taking;

- more authentic parenting.

Beyond

In addition to the impacts described above, I wonder at the potential for self-coaching's impact beyond today's client leader. The leader who parents differently, who role-models their own thinking and self-manages better at work and at home. What potential might this have societally for the quality of relationships and leadership developed within organizations, and beyond? What might the potential of those organizations now be, as a result? And what is the potential positive or indeed negative impact as these leaders develop the next wave of employees at work or, outside work, find themselves becoming parents to a future generation of leaders?

Potential downsides

Self-coaching doesn't always have positive outcomes, at least not in the short term. Self-coaching can become destructive rather than constructive if clients become hyper self-critical and/or reach 'analysis paralysis'. We explore how to tackle potential problems, among other steps, in the following practical section.

Developing self-coaching

I believe it's important that coaches be transparent about enabling the client to self-coach as part of making coaching sustainable, promoting ongoing learning and successful self-management beyond the coaching programme, and contract at the outset to do so. I believe coaches should be supported on professional coach education programmes or as part of coach supervision, for example, to become more able to be *explicit* about how they coach, in the moment, in order to facilitate the client's ability to self-coach. Aside from being more explicit in contracting, what else can the coach do to encourage self-coaching in the client?

The ideas offered are based on my personal observations around what clients told me their coach did that helped or hindered most. There are suggestions for what to do and what to avoid. Buyers of coaching might reflect on how to better select coaches and how to support clients in making the right choice of coach to work with them. Below is a collection of behaviours and questions that clients say helped them self-coach. They also comment on when self-coaching is *not* a constructive process, ie when under extreme pressure, some of them ended up in the 'analysis paralysis' mentioned above.

Firstly, my own observations

I believe self-coaching can occur with or without a coach being present. It may occur on the way to a coaching session, prompted by the mere thought of what the coach might ask, as in the example of my Diageo client quoted at the beginning of this chapter. Or it might take the form of the client 'conjuring up' their coach whilst thinking about a work issue, as clients of mine have also reported happening. Self-coaching might happen spontaneously, far away from the official place of 'work'.

If self-coaching occurs whilst the coach is in the room, the coach may not need to do or say anything. They may just need to hold the space in order to allow and support the client to generate their own thinking – *new thinking*, in the moment. Self-coaching may happen naturally, or be a leadership capacity that coaches can intentionally help develop in their clients. Or it could be both; if the coach sees this might be happening, I suggest they highlight this to the client, to increase their consciousness of their out-loud thinking process, and how, going forward, they could do more of this to help themselves work through a challenging work issue. My own supervisor pointed out the importance of self-coaching not being a defence against having coaching in the first place, but as an *outcome* of executive leadership coaching.

The following box shows some of the issues clients say they have self-coached around.

Issues for self-coaching

- emergencies;
- market crises;
- funding cuts;
- leadership challenges eg environmental crises, bombings, disease outbreak, logistics emergencies;
- times of vulnerability;
- new thinking – working out what counts now;
- dealing with the intensity of the global economic crisis;
- enhancing resilience to cope with the speed and intensity of change;
- developing the capacity to hold ambiguity;
- survival in the credit crunch – not being fired;
- competitive colleagues;
- board preparation – presentations;
- potential conflict or difficult conversations;
- improving communication with their team;
- thinking about the different mindsets and motivations of others;
- assumptions;
- prioritizing;
- 'bad news' announcements;
- differentiating oneself in the workplace and being recognized;
- how to show one's value to the organization;
- pay.

Self-coaching questions

I asked leader clients and former clients working in international banking, retail (fast-moving consumer goods), diplomacy, sport, and development aid, if they remembered any particular questions their coach had asked them that they felt built their capacity to self-coach and whether they had generated any useful questions themselves. The following box sets out their responses.

Self-coaching questions

From the coach:

- If I weren't here, what question would you ask yourself?

- What question are you hoping I won't ask you?

- That's a great question... why don't you have a go at answering that yourself?

- In our coaching sessions you catch my *exact* word – then ask me what I meant by it. Now I do that for myself when I'm preparing to present to the board.

- What am I noticing in myself?

- Where is my energy?

- What do I know about myself?

- What are my values and how can I live them in this situation?

- What is my role here? Am I confusing my roles?

- What are you wanting to do right now? If you do that, how will that help you?

- What are you not wanting to face?

- What would you tell someone else in your situation?

- What do you know helps you when you are thinking, feeling like this?

- What is the story you are telling yourself right now? What is missing from that story?

- Write down your story, and then read it out aloud – how do you want to change this story?

- What is the shift that is needed?

- What have I learnt? What am I learning? So what do I need to learn?

- What do you want xxx to know, to feel and to do?

- What's the smallest step you can take to move forward here?

From themselves:

- What would [name of my coach] ask me if s/he were here?

- Given I am an able person, why am I allowing this to happen to me?

- What would xxx do in this situation?

- How does that move me towards what I want?

- What do I not want to take into the room with me?

- How am I going to cope with the current ambiguity?

Clients reflect that in a fast-moving, high-pressure situation such as a market share price tumble, they feel unable to act or think clearly. Their thinking loops round and round, disabling rather than enabling them to make good decisions. One prime broker at Goldman Sachs tells me:

> Too much self-coaching could lead to executives reaching hypercritical over-analysis. That becomes destructive instead of constructive. In my view this depends on the quality of self-coaching. Mine is variable and inconsistent; it depends on the quality of the coach, what mood I'm in and whether I feel I can trust my self-coaching.

He also voices how in the banking sector, especially during crisis, the atmosphere becomes less collegiate and more about personal career survival. So reaching out to colleagues is not an option he perceives himself to have. In times of crisis, he says he needs to be able to call HR and re-engage his coach for a couple of top-up sessions. This suggests that for some individuals, self-coaching can become a negative process which does not support the leader during particularly high-challenge events.

Individuals and organizations might need to be actively aware and self-reflexive so they are ready to bring in the external coach again where necessary, accessing the safe, confidential, non-competitive containment they offer. The experience and self-analysis of this banking client might also suggest the need to temporarily resource extra coaching capacity in high-stress situations. This might mean fewer sessions than normally constitute a full coaching programme, but with funding and sign-off already in place. Nevertheless, this experience makes the case for contracting for bringing in the external coach again, albeit temporarily, where necessary. During the initial coaching programme, the coach can help the client identify not just when they are self-coaching and when they need to but also when they need to stop themselves self-coaching and ask for support from their line manager or HR. Coaches can encourage greater awareness in the client so they can monitor the quality and the efficacy of their self-coaching. They can help the client identify when their self-reflexive thinking is enabling them to act and when it's stopping them. And buyers, line managers and sponsors of coaching can anticipate and budget for additional coaching need, as and when crisis strikes and spikes.

Another client shares how 'Self-coaching is like a box of tools that become less sharp over time,' which adds to the argument for some kind of future maintenance coaching interventions.

In addition, coaches can help to pre-empt paralysis by encouraging clients to learn breathing techniques which can be practised in the coaching session then replicated in a real moment of crisis, 'to give the client some space' and to bring a sense of calm, suggests Dr Alison Whybrow, for example.

Below, we look at some other steps coaches can take to hinder or help self-coaching.

What can coaches do?

> It's too much of a coincidence that self-coaching started after the coaching sessions with you, to say it wasn't you…!

To my surprise, clients seem to be highly sensitive, both on a conscious and subconscious level, to their coach's behaviours. They know intuitively what behaviours or questions enabled self-coaching. They also seem to find that the more challenging the coach – this challenge being built on a foundation of deep rapport and positive regard for the client – the more learning and retained learning they gain.

Below clients share some of what they have found effective in promoting their ability to self-coach:

- 'You gave me the confidence to know what I was doing wasn't rubbish… it took away my self-doubt – it's the difference between chance and active behaviour.'

- 'Going emotionally deeper on the issue helped me find the solution there on my own.'
- 'You enabled me to verbalize the conversation I was having in my head.'
- 'Asking me tough questions, using language that made all this accessible... and using that language again and again, so I could repeat it for myself later.'
- 'Your rigour. Not letting me off the hook.'
- 'Pushing me to go deeper.'

Other comments were around the coach listening for a long time, being impartial, asking questions which prompt deep thinking and emotional exploration, and being confident.

What hinders self-coaching, both on the part of the coach or the client? Here are some client responses:

- Coach's ego.
- Client's ego.
- Time (lapsed) since coaching programme end.
- Lack of self-discipline: it felt like 'being on a diet and giving in', says one client. He felt daunted by the lack of 'independent emotions', finding himself in a muddle and overwhelmed by his own feelings, whereas with his coach, he could manage these feelings. The important thing for him was that the coach not be caught up in the internal organizational environment.
- Collusion from the coach: colluding coaches were perceived as 'nice' but 'not sufficiently challenging'. Therefore ultimately the colluding coach offers the client less independence of thinking in the longer term.
- Failure of the coach to challenge sufficiently.
- Lack of deep relationship with the coach, in order to 'have a go'.
- Tools/techniques which don't resonate with the client fractured rapport temporarily and 'stopped/hindered' the self-coaching development process.

What about trust and the relationship between client and coach? Is trust a predictor of self-coaching as an outcome of a coaching programme? Some think it reinforces self-coaching, while others think it is not so much about trusting the coach but about trusting their process:

> No. What sparked self-coaching was great, fruitful sessions. It wasn't about trusting or liking you. But I did trust your questions and your process.

Another client says:

> I don't need to trust or like my coach, because I respect the process and that's giving me results. But if I respect the coach I am more likely to *apply* it.

Building the capacity to self-coach is related to the results obtained. Impressed by those, clients become more likely to want to adopt self-coaching:

> I got so much that's positive out of coaching, it made me think you'd be mad not to take this on yourself! If coaching with you as my coach hadn't worked, I'd never have done more of it on my own afterwards.

My research was only small scale and raises many further questions. Before we conclude, I will set out some ideas for further studies.

Future research

Whilst conducting this research, I was genuinely amazed by the clarity of analysis clients offered. My exploration suggests a number of implications for coaches in their conscious practice and outcome endeavours. I also suggest that those training, accrediting and supervising coaches improve the calibre of coaches – and thereby the industry standards and reputation – by supporting them to build self-coaching skills in their clients, and scrutinizing coaches on this capacity. And I suggest that organizations use these findings to help them be discerning and more knowledgeable about the potential or desirable outcomes of coaching, with self-coaching being one of them.

There are also areas including home life or broader society, even future generations, for further exploration, as to the potential impact of developing a client's capacity to self-coach.

I would like to see comparison studies, including longitudinal ones, so we can learn more about self-coaching from gender, culture, East–West, ethnic and national, and industry sector perspectives.

Questions to explore include: How does the length of a coaching programme and the length of time since it started or ended influence a client's capacity to self-coach in a crisis – both at the time and months or years later? At what point does self-coaching start to occur? How might such data inform the design and timing of coaching programmes? What sustains self-coaching, and what can coaches do differently to foster self-coaching not only as an outcome of a coaching programme, but to create durability and sustainability of this very outcome itself? What do coaches do or not do which helps or hinders clients' self-coaching capacity? Does it matter if a coach is explicit or not when building the client's capacity to self-coach? Should coach training courses, examination processes, accreditation, CPD opportunities and coach supervision be altered to help coaches develop *their* own ability to self-coach and enable this in others? If so, how? And what can organizations do to be more demanding and discerning when selecting and buying coaching?

For clients, what motivates them to want to self-coach or develop their self-coaching muscle? Is it the challenge their coach offers? Is it the empathic rapport and trust? The fun?

With all the potential positives from self-coaching, future research must also explore the negative side of self-coaching from an individual, team, organizational, societal and home perspective. Speaking of which, it would be fascinating to interview partners, children, parents, team members, personal assistants, work canteen staff or company drivers, to find out whether and how the self-coaching leader has changed, and how the impact of this spreads wider than the obvious work context.

Conclusion

This chapter has examined definitions of self-coaching from the client, coach and buyer of coaching perspectives. It has reported positive impacts of leaders self-coaching on themselves, their teams, their organizations and even those they share their homes with. It has also offered pointers for how to build the capacity in clients to self-coach, and begun to explore what might hinder its development. We've heard from leaders, coaches and coaching buyers from a range of backgrounds, and clients have commented on the effectiveness of self-coaching in times of difficulty and existential crisis – when their capacity to lead, think anew and self-manage is really tested. This revealed instances when self-coaching may even sabotage their ability to think clearly and make good decisions.

The chapter argued the case for extra ad hoc coaching support at certain times, for some types of client (especially in certain industries such as banking) to help leaders cope in highly challenging times, suggesting coaches learn how to develop self-coaching and how they might do this, and that they make this element explicit in their coaching offers.

As well as calling for further research into self-coaching, the chapter also proposed that more coach trainers, supervisors and accrediting bodies explicitly test for this criterion in recognition of its potential to raise the bar in leadership and other contexts.

Thanks for contributions and client examples

Liz Macann, Dr Carole Pemberton, Dr Alison Whybrow, Dr Anton Obholzer, Dr Caroline Horner, Anthony Ryland, David Bunyan, and unnamed clients who have kindly contributed to my research for this chapter.

Legacy Thinking: 12
an approach for
a better now,
and a better future

NEIL SCOTTON and ALISTER SCOTT

Possibly the most interesting aspect of some of the current 'crises' is that in some ways nothing has actually happened. Most countries are relatively stable. Trade largely continues. Whilst there is much conflict, there has not been a 'world war' for 70 years. As we write this chapter, despite the best efforts of bird flu and Ebola there has been no worldwide epidemic. Despite anticipated 'peak oil' and energy shortages, oil prices are currently low. Life expectancy generally is up, as are literacy and access to education. Despite the rise of 'terror' and some nightmarish conflict zones, in most parts of the world where coaching is popular, things are creaking perhaps, but still very functional.

So why do so many feel lost, disengaged, numbed, exhausted? How come so many images of the future involve deserts, charred and desolated cities, and dysfunctional societies? Why, despite the huge collective knowledge in this expert world, do we paradoxically seem to face more not-knowing and uncertainty than ever before? What's going on?

In our work bringing people together to address highly complex challenges, one thing is becoming increasingly clear: while the crises are real, the root causes are rarely out there in the world. They're within us. They exist in our habits of thinking. Where systems we've designed are failing it's because the thinking behind them is flawed. Where social systems are failing there's almost always a lack of understanding, ambition and compassion. Natural systems are collapsing because our beliefs about our relationship with nature are ignorant. Familiar narratives that define success, happiness and self-worth are often short-sighted, narrow and ultimately unfulfilling.

In the thick fog of these challenging times, people want a compass that helps them find 'better', ideally bringing with it a sense of meaning and purpose. And that's exactly where Legacy Thinking comes in: an approach we have developed from our research, coaching and consultancy practice and inspiration from others.

This chapter explores how Legacy Thinking can positively intervene at a range of scales: with the individual experiencing crisis as they struggle with the complexities of work and life; with teams wanting to work coherently and effectively together towards an inspiring shared purpose; with organizations whose products, services and business models need to change dramatically; and with organizations collaborating to address the biggest global challenges.

Fundamentally, Legacy Thinking is an antidote to the mindsets that create the systems and behaviours that lead to the crises and overwhelm that many experience. It helps address the root of problems, not simply find a temporary fix or a cure that rescues one but leaves others to sink.

This chapter will guide you to help your clients to create their legacy but also, importantly, guide you to create your own. Without a sense of your own legacy, Legacy Thinking is potentially a reckless use of a powerful tool.

Exploring Legacy Thinking

To get a flavour, try the following. Thinking of yourself, or your work with clients...

What if... before making the next big business decision, time is given to consider what impact the decision will have on all stakeholders, including those who are often easily forgotten; the societies you work in, the natural world you draw resources from and give back to, and children in the future?

What if... As a member of a sports team, before you step onto the pitch together, the aim foremost in your mind is not simply 'to win', but 'to unite and inspire the nation'? This is part of an extensive canon of philosophies and practices that have made the New Zealand All Blacks the highest-performing team in any sport ever (Kerr, 2013).

What if... When facing a challenging situation, before you respond, you stop to consider: 'How do I wish to be remembered?'

Questions like these affect decisions, courage, will and commitment. They fire up the sense of purpose and shared endeavour. They inspire and engage the support of others.

Legacy Thinking is not just useful to our clients. As coaches we affect conversations. That's why we are invited to be there. And those conversations result in actions. So what we do as coaches inevitably has consequences out in the world. Legacy Thinking will help you, and your clients, recognize the ripples that your coaching conversations create. And to mindfully, skilfully and professionally create the ones for which you wish to be remembered.

In concept, Legacy Thinking simply involves stepping outside ourselves and paying attention to how our actions will be felt, seen and experienced by others. It's about looking beyond, to another moment in time, possibly beyond our own life, and imagining what the ripple out of our actions has been. It's about ensuring that what we do today is building the story we want others to tell of us in the future, and indeed what we want to be telling ourselves when we look back. It's about doing the right thing now, so that we can sleep knowing that we have done our best to contribute to a better world. It includes being deeply respectful of what is passed on to us from those that have gone before.

At its heart, Legacy Thinking is about recognizing that independence is an illusion. Many philosophies talk of individuals and whole civilizations evolving from dependence to independence to interdependence. When we interviewed Professor Peter Hawkins, a leading systemic thinker, for *Coaching at Work* magazine, he referred to author Gregory Bateson and the concept that the unit of success and flourishing is not the individual, or the team or indeed the organization or nation; the health of each of those depends on the health of those around them. 'If the niche you are in is not flourishing, you cannot flourish,' Peter explains.

Legacy Thinking is a powerful tool for ourselves and our clients that has a much greater tendency towards health and flourishing than familiar 'What do we want?' goal setting. Its wisdom is ancient yet fresh. Patently obvious and deeply challenging, it forces us to reconsider business practices and life assumptions. It tells us that sustainable success for our organizations and fulfilment for ourselves cannot come from purely acting in self-interest. It demands humility, awareness and often a deep and challenging personal 'inner journey' for leaders. It poses challenging questions for us as professionals, and as a profession (we explore the latter further on).

In these challenging and uncertain times we find this approach provides answers for organizations and individuals seeking direction, clarity, courage; ways to engage staff and supporters and create inspiring places to work; and ways to deliver long-term success.

CASE STUDY   Southern Railway – on track to a sustainable future

In my role I faced a genuine challenge. I had joined the company as someone keen to deliver real change to make the business more sustainable. Early on I noticed something that really concerned me – as this was a franchise I could only write a strategy for the remaining three years. At that time I also faced the problem of everything hinging on me.

In my heart I knew this was the real issue. How could I ensure that any actions taken would be lasting, enough to go beyond the end of the franchise? This was a particular worry because I also knew that on the handover of a franchise all roles would be reviewed, so I might not make the cut, threatening continuity of our actions.

It was around that time that I started to explore my role as a leader, through my studies on the One Planet MBA with Exeter University, but also through broader reading. It was pure chance that I met Neil and Alister at a local event and read through the One Leadership Project blog. I came across the word Legacy.

In this context, for me, legacy is not about my personal reputation, it's about what is left behind by the work that I do as a representative of the company.

I wish I could say it was an epiphany moment and all the answers came to me in a flash, but it took months of development followed by months of implementation to define the idea, shape it and enable it.

The answer was in the people.

I had a team of volunteers working as Area Champions for the Environment (ACEs) focused on environmental initiatives. I needed to aim for a future where every individual in the company was an ACE purely by the decisions they made, the actions they took and the example they set. That would provide the longevity I needed, with the commitment to the environment embedded in the collective hearts and minds of the business.

My plan was twofold.

First of all, I set about creating a development pyramid which set a series of levels for the ACEs to aim for, with the pinnacle enabling formal qualifications and the opportunity to take on more responsibility. Not only did they rise to the challenge, some developed their skills in presenting their own ideas and, with support, learnt to implement them. One has even been promoted into a full-time environment role while others are developing their potential to achieve this.

Second, I developed learning opportunities for the senior leaders, helping them to build business cases for larger projects and engaging them to provide opportunities for ACEs to work with them too.

The results are about to be tested. We are now in the transition phase of the franchise but with recognition for this approach through awards – our 14001 Environmental Management System audits and also Investors in People – I'm confident that the legacy will be positive.

Lao Tzu said leaders should aim for people to think they did it themselves. My legacy is that many of my ACEs actually have done it themselves!

Sandra Norval is Head of Environment at Southern Railway

In Table 12.1 we set out some of the key benefits of Legacy Thinking, while below we offer some more examples of Legacy Thinking in challenging situations.

For a team – A board had agreed to tackle a range of difficult topics at its away day. It could easily have become mired in detailed and complex arguments. After discussions, the greater purpose of the organization was printed and displayed prominently on each wall. We often find the overarching purpose is all too easily forgotten. In addition, throughout the day there was regular reference to different stakeholder groups; staff, trustees, members, communities. The combination of constant reminders of what the organization was ultimately there to do, and how the issues under discussion would affect those beyond the room, contributed greatly to big decisions on previously 'stuck' issues, completion of the agenda, greater coherence and growing sense of 'team': 'That was the most useful, well-run board event that I have attended – ever – anywhere,' commented one director.

For an individual – An HR director managing a series of redundancies realized the distress this would cause to those affected, and personally felt the pressure to the point he was becoming 'locked up'. Our conversation explored the situation from the perspective of those affected, including families, long into the future. How did the director want people to look back on their experience and the process they had gone through? Seen from that place, how had they then moved forward? How did he personally want to look back on this, and what qualities did he want to see demonstrated through his actions? This exploration transformed the task to a committed demonstration of humanity, integrity, professional skills and compassion under difficult circumstances. The director now looks back and recognizes the pain that was avoided, the professional competency demonstrated and the opportunities provided.

TABLE 12.1   The benefits of Legacy Thinking

For individuals	For teams and organizations	'Beyond'
Clarity	Unity around shared endeavour	Improving the quality of life and opportunities for many
Sense of meaning, purpose, direction	Greater motivation, higher quality teamwork	Improving opportunities and prospects for those who come after
Motivation	Clarity on priorities	Role-modelling inspires others well beyond the person/team/ organization
Courage (many speak of it being easier to stand for others than to promote themselves)	Easier to attract support, contribution and resources when the work is 'beyond self'	Positive legacies enable more positive legacies to be created by others
Greater sense of connection to work	Improved reputation	A sense of shared inspiration and hope in the face of the doom-and-gloom news and predictions
Greater achievement of 'what matters'	Higher performance in the long term, and often in the short term too	
Closer bonding with colleagues	A solid foundation for partnerships with other organizations, and a reason to forge such partnerships	
Recognition by others		
Enhanced self-worth, fulfilment and satisfaction		

For a profession – Sport is clearly about winning. Or is it? Focusing totally on winning can lead to behaviours that individuals, a club or the whole sport may not in the end be proud of. So we brought a question to a group of top rugby coaches: 'Beyond winning, what does it really mean to be an elite coach?' The essence was to reach the deeper values and connection they had with the game, the players they work with, and the ripple-out impact it has. We won't kid you, we were a tad nervous going into this – they were hardened coaches and included ex-international players – and we had no idea how they would react. A powerful part of the work was a visualization exercise where the coaches let their imagination connect, one step at a time, with their team, club, community, nation, world, and 'beyond' (see Stepping Out exercise further on in this chapter), stepping beyond time into the sense of 'making history' and seeing the whole world from a distance. The impact on the coaches was profound. Feedback included:

> We must make ourselves available to all nations... Give people the opportunity to fulfil their dreams and be what they can be... Make the values transcend all levels in society... Support small nations in delivery and finance... It's been like coming out of the cocoon... Reassured and optimistic we share the cherished values... If I have self-doubt I will go back to my values as they will carry me through... Remember and continually reconnect with my reason why (for being and doing)... Pay less attention to the details and go back to 'why?'... Concentrate time on what really matters...

Notice the absence of words like 'winning' and 'performance'. It's recognized implicitly that when you play with purpose the results will follow, and that there is much more to leading as a coach than the results. The ripple-out of this, and legacies it has set in motion, continues.

Inspirations and lessons

History is full of examples of Legacy Thinking. In many cases, it is the Legacy Thinking that transforms the people and their actions from everyday into notable history. For example:

> In 1989 Tim Berners-Lee envisioned HTTP (the software protocol that enables computer programmes to talk to each other), domain names and the World Wide Web. By making his ideas available freely, with no patent and no royalties due, he immediately created a legacy that led to a complete revolution in business, technology and everyday living that has undoubtedly transformed your life. It is hard to imagine the technology revolution of recent years if his ideas had been patented.
>
> In reaction to the devastation of two world wars and the part played and price paid by ordinary men and women in them, Aneurin Bevan brought his dream of universal healthcare to life with the birth of the National Health Service in the UK. A legacy that, whilst having struggles of its own in current times, continues to save and improve thousands of lives daily.
>
> Martin Luther King stood up for civil rights, using all his capabilities as a preacher in his power and eloquence to take a dangerous stand and share a dream that inspired transformation far outlasting his cut-short life.
>
> Jonas Salk developed the first polio vaccine. He was insistent that it be patent-free, and therefore became quickly and widely available. He has a quote that embodies Legacy Thinking – 'Be a good ancestor.'

But it's important to remember that you do not have to be thinking of 'changing the world' or run a global organization to leave a valuable legacy.

A friend and colleague told us of his aunt's funeral. Hundreds of people turned out. Why? Because throughout her life she held to a simple motto; 'Be useful.' She had been. It touched others. And they came out to share their respects and gratitude.

Similarly, Charles Handy (Handy, 1999), best-selling leadership writer and inspiring thinker, recounts the story of attending his father's funeral. Driving to the church he was reflecting on the 'unchanging rhythm of Sundays' and how he thought his father, a Protestant vicar in rural Catholic Ireland, was always in 'boring meetings'. Then he noticed that they had picked up a police escort. And that the route to the country church was getting congested. Then, at the church, that choir singers had assembled from all corners of Ireland. And that the Archbishop who was supposed to be in hospital was there. Handy describes 'I saw tears in the eyes of the hundreds of people who had come from everywhere to say goodbye to this "quiet" man". A man who, in the words of the Archbishop, was "remembered forever by so many whose lives he had touched".'

So it is not always the big things that make a difference. Sometimes it is the small, mundane, even boring things – because they are done with love and care.

From all these stories, our experiences and research, a number of lessons become clear, which we set out in the box on the following page.

1   Knowingly or not, we are all contributing to our own legacy all the time.

2   We can begin to create a new legacy at any time, regardless of what has gone before or who we are.

3   You don't have to wait until you die to begin to witness the legacy you will leave.

4   Positive legacies are always founded in generosity.

5   Legacy is usually less about one big act, and more about the accumulation of thousands of smaller ones.

6   Not all legacies are pre-planned or consciously pursued, but are often a living expression of what people care about. As Gandhi said, 'My life is my message.'

7   Inspiration for our legacy can surprise us, and come 'by accident'.

8   Legacy is not about simply noticing something. Or being first. It is about being able to do something with your awareness that benefits others. And then holding true to the generous, positive intent even when one encounters life's inevitable hurdles and distractions.

9   Legacies are rarely the work of one person. An individual may be the catalyst, but full realization requires the contribution and generosity of many, often with the help of simultaneous events in science, technology, politics, society, economic markets and more.

10   Legacies are made easier by the legacies of those before. By building our legacy, and helping clients build theirs, we in turn enable others to build theirs. The more we build, the more becomes possible.

11   Doing the 'right' thing can appear 'wrong' to the current paradigm. You may stand in a lonely place. There will be temptations to conform organizationally or socially, turn a blind eye or 'just follow orders'. So how can you know? Here's the simple acid test: If it is for the good of all, it is very likely to be the 'right' thing.

12   Allow yourself to dream big. It might just happen. But don't allow the dream to overwhelm you. One step at a time. Each step is one step closer.

13   The biggest legacies are often created quietly; the right question asked of the right person at the right time in the right way; simple acts of kindness; naming a truth about what is going on – which in turn inspire a ripple-out of other acts.

14   With systemic problems, no one has 'the answer'; many will have a piece of it. So no one can, or should attempt to, do it all. It's about each person playing their part. Convening a group of people to create dialogue on an issue can therefore be a powerful legacy act in itself.

15   Our current reality is the sum total of all the legacies – good, bad or however we wish to label them – so far. In what we choose to do now the reality of the future emerges.

Where to begin

In this section we outline five methods for getting at the Legacy you or your clients want to create:

1 Look inside;

2 Think beyond self;

3 Serve your stakeholders;

4 Play with time;

5 Bring it all together.

We believe it's important to do your own Legacy Thinking first, so you can act with integrity and bring the best understanding and experience to your clients. So we invite you to try the exercises yourself first. In a later section we explore the challenges of working as a professional coach with clients on Legacy.

Some of what follows may be familiar to you. Legacy Thinking may be a new term, but the principles are very old, and many coaching tools and techniques draw upon those principles.

If you are working with a team you will notice there is an iterative, almost spiral nature to applying these techniques. It often begins in the centre with looking into self, then spirals out as you look beyond. And then as you co-create with others, coming around to the same questions and exercises again and exploring them together. This can mean working with a CEO, then top team, then board of trustees, staff, revisiting the same sorts of questions each time, building and co-creating as you go. For personal work, it can mean deep personal thought, then reflecting with colleagues, friends and loved ones.

1. Look inside

We have learnt that there is always an Inner Journey that matches the Outer Journey. Here are some questions you might want to play with. Adapt them to suit your situation and preferences. It is not a definitive list. Remember – as with coaching work with clients, often it's not always about finding an answer in the moment. It can be about launching a thought, question or curiosity that takes you on a longer journey of exploration.

Consider your strong feelings; what makes your heart sing? When do you feel angry? What do these tell you about what matters to you?

When have you experienced a sense of deep insight, or a powerful sense of connection, and that touched you to the core? What is that telling you?

As the poet David Whyte asked at the ICF conference in Paris in 2010, 'What are the questions that won't go away?'

What is the work that will bring *all* of you to your work with others?

Have you ever had an experience of 'not of me but through me'? When have you been speaking or acting with clarity, conviction and passion but not sure where it was coming from? What does that tell you about what you are here for?

Do you have a quiet inner voice? What is it saying to you about what's wise and truly important, and perhaps what you may be here to do?

2. Think beyond self: Stepping Out, or The Six Circles of Wisdom

Activity

Your legacy will be defined by others. You will create it – but they will describe it based on their experiences and impressions of you and what you have done. The previous challenge of 'looking inside' helps you connect with what is meaningful for you. Now you need to connect to the needs and wishes of others. You can do this by yourself. Or often more powerfully with a friend or colleague familiar with visualization work.

In a standing position, relax and allow yourself to connect with yourself – simply noticing your breathing and feeling your weight on the floor. When connected, ask, 'What is important to me? What do I deeply care about? What is the work I want to do for me?' Give this time.

Then, maintaining the mindful connection, take a step, beyond self to the next circle out – this can be family or colleagues. Ask, 'What do these people need? How can I best serve them?'

Again, having taken a good and relaxed amount of time, allow yourself to know what you have experienced here, and when ready take a step forward to the next circle. This could be your organization, your community (professional, spiritual, shared interest or geographic) or wider family. What is happening for these people? What do they need? What might they be calling forth from you?

When ready, take another step out – allow yourself now to look at your nation. Allow your imagination to travel through towns and cities, landscapes and wild places. What is going on here? What are you noticing? What connects with you? Where do you feel called? What are you noticing that matters to you? Where are your gifts, abilities, connections needed?

Then, when ready, step one step further out into the world, again in your imagination and with connection to self, travelling through towns, landscapes and wild places around the world. Notice what calls you, where you feel drawn to.

Then, when you are ready, step further – to 'beyond'. This is where the world can be seen at a distance, as a whole planet, beyond the human. A place where time can fast-forward or rewind, where if you have a spiritual nature you have some sense of connection with whatever greater spirit is real for you. What are you noticing from this place? What is calling you?

When you are ready, begin the journey back. Knowing the experience you have had is safely with you, step back and notice what you see or feel as you revisit the places you went before. At the level of world, nation, organization, community, family. Take time at each level – things may well be different on the way back.

And finally back to self. Take time to just be with whatever you are experiencing. This is about listening and noticing. Rationalization can come later. Note: this exercise can be deeply moving.

Now allow yourself some quiet time to make notes.

If doing this with others, maybe in a group, sharing experiences can be very powerful. Put a ground rule firmly in place – this is about listening to each other. No commenting, critiquing, coaching, fixing, improving, praising. Ensure people know they only need to share whatever they feel comfortable sharing; a listening round can create an extraordinary richness of views, bonding of people, and alignment of teams.

3. Serve your stakeholders – The Seven Key Groups

For Professor Peter Hawkins, 'stakeholders' means leaders (and their coaches) meeting the needs of six groups:

1 investors and regulators;

2 customers;

3 employees;

4 suppliers and partners;

5 communities in which the organization operates;

6 the natural environment – the more than human world.

He describes how as chairman of a couple of companies, he ensures that the annual reports cover these stakeholders, and in each case asks: 'What have we received from them? And what have we contributed to them?'

In conversation with Peter we suggested a seventh stakeholder – 'the generations to come', and that landed well. Peter spoke of how working with the City of Cape Town on their development of a coaching culture, he had people listen to the strategy representing all the different stakeholders including two people representing 'the collective grandchildren of the region, who will inherit what we plan today'.

So as an individual, team, business or organization, thinking through these seven groups, who are the stakeholders? Are they specific people or a more generalized 'sense'? What do they need? And what do they need from you? What is the impact you wish to have on them? How do you wish to be remembered?

Note: you can adapt the Stepping Out exercise to explore your work, connection, contribution and potential legacy with each of the seven stakeholder groups in turn.

4. Play with time

Here we share five ways to use different perspectives to help you find and deliver the legacy you wish to create. The basic principle is the same within them all; imagine someone else in the past, present or future who is looking at you, and what you are doing and have done. And see things from their perspective.

Start with the end in mind – Stephen Covey

Covey (1992) offers this visualization:

> Witness four speakers at your funeral: a family member, a friend, someone from work, and someone from your community, church or organization you have served. Once you have decided on the speakers (add others if you wish), settle into your visualization in whatever way works best for you. Hear each speaker clearly. What are they saying and how are they saying it? Is it what you want to hear? Then reflect on what you want to do or be now that will affect what is said.

Win an award

Some people find the visualization of a funeral unhelpful. Instead you could consider somebody reading your or your team's achievement at an award ceremony (feel free to choose the award and awarding body to suit what's important for you and the team). What is the award? Which category? What is being cited as the reason for you receiving the award? The important part here is to hear what the speaker says about the impact you or your work has had *on others*. The secret is to avoid an ego-fest. Again, this is powerful in a team exercise.

Quiet thanks

For some, an award can feel selfish or too heroic, perhaps creating a separation between themselves and the people they want to feel connected to or positively impact upon. In this case the visualization can be adjusted away from a ceremony, to a quiet conversation, perhaps a look in the eye, or a thank you letter, from someone who matters deeply to them.

Write an article from the future

Another alternative is to imagine someone, real or imaginary, writing an article in the future about you, your team, your organization, your project. When are they writing – a day later, a year, a decade, further? Who or what are they writing for? What are they saying? What really touches and matters to you as you think about reading it? Again, this works well with teams. You can flip this around and imagine yourself to be at a time in the future; write it now, as, say, a blog.

Build on your inheritance

We all have an inheritance – language, culture, values and stories passed on through the generations. Who and what from the past can you draw inspiration from? Who and what do you wish to emulate? What are the wisdoms and truths that can help guide you through today's uncertainties? After all, every day in the past was itself once facing an uncertain future, so the things that have endured have done so for a reason. Note however that you do not have to be defined by your past. So two thoughts: first, in our interconnected world we can choose to see ourselves as part of a much wider 'humankind' than previous generations, who were more restricted in defining who 'they' were by birth, geography, religion, gender etc. One of their gifts to us in most of the world today is that we have more choice and freedoms in joining our dots with the past and writing our stories. We can choose our 'tribe'.

Second, there is always a time to hold on, and a time to let go. Sometimes what has served well in the past has lived its course, and the legacy you are creating is about drawing a chapter to a close and starting a new one.

Before moving on, take a moment to reflect – what has been your experience with these exercises? What do you need to bear in mind when using these with clients? When you act from integrity it has to come from your own wisdom too.

5. *Bring it all together*

Having gone through the looking inside, outside and then thinking through time and inviting the perspectives of others, now is a time to revisit the big questions (examples below) and bring it together. For each question, take stock of your experiences so far, including these exercises. Write it down. Or draw it in some way. Ask: Does it excite you? Challenge you? Seem truly important to you? Capture an essence of you? Are they your words or ones you have inherited or taken on from somebody else? Sometimes the question can morph. For example, in one client organization it became, 'What are we really all about?'

It can be important to 'suspend disbelief' at this stage. Few big aspirations in life come with clarity on how you will achieve them. It begins with 'What?' and 'Why?' The 'How?' follows later. The 'Who?' obviously includes you, but almost inevitably involves others, many of whom may not yet be known to you. Yet we have seen many times that even when people cannot see how they will achieve something, if they are clear, inspiring, persistent – and take action and connect with others – sooner or later things start to shape up.

Finally, allow your answer for each question to inform the other answers. In our experience this is organic. There is no simple formula or 'A to B to C'. It is systemic; just as each part of the system affects each other part, each of your answers will affect the others.

Question 1

This is simple, central, and so powerful in imagining your legacy – well worth spending time on: 'What do you want to be remembered for?'

Question 2

Buckminster Fuller, the pioneering futurist, asked: 'What is my job on the planet? What is it that needs doing, that I know something about, that probably won't happen unless I take responsibility for it?' (quoted in Kabat-Zinn, 1994) What would your response be?

Question 3

You are a leader in your own life, and an active part in creating what others around you experience. Ask yourself: As a coach, what am I coaching *for*? As a leader, what am I leading *for*? Leadership is sometimes defined as creating a future different from the past. So consider here what changes ripple out from your work – who or what is it helping, serving, enabling?

Question 4

What's the story? Imagine key events in the past, now and the future; these may be experiences in your life, or events before, outside, or after your life that somehow matter to you. Draw or write them down. Perhaps use blank paper card with a different key event on each one. How do these arrange, cluster and link up? What story are you writing when you join them up this way? It's interesting that we call it re-membering; putting the bits of the body back together again. And re-collecting; gathering up the pieces and bringing them together. Sometimes events can be seen as pieces of Lego – there's more than one way to connect them with other pieces, and the way you connect them can depend upon the thing you wish to build from them. If you want, try rearranging the pieces. Which feels nearer the truth for you? Note: when working with clients, timelines (either on paper or physicalized) can help, as can including an axis at right angles, of good times and tough times.

Question 5

As Kerr (2013) recounts, the All Blacks rugby team members are asked, 'Will you be leaving the shirt in a better place?' For an All Black the shirt is a powerful talisman, representing all those who have worn it before. Each player knows their time will come to pass it on again. Has the reputation been built whilst they have been wearing it? Is the position stronger? We can apply this metaphor to our own work and helping clients think about theirs.

Now we've showcased Legacy Thinking and set out some practical ways to prompt it, let's explore practical questions you may still be holding as coaches.

Practicalities

We have found that people have a range of questions and concerns when starting to use a Legacy approach in their client work – 'how does it vary from traditional approaches?', 'isn't this imposing on my agenda?', 'how can

I legitimately bring this to client conversations?' and 'are there obstacles or even dangers for clients and myself?'.

How does Legacy Thinking vary from traditional approaches? A systemic and holistic focus

Everyone is familiar with goal setting, and mission and vision. However, traditionally the frames of reference are, 'What do I/we want? What are we setting out to do?' From this starting point, any goals, missions, values may potentially create a positive legacy but also tend to be self-focused, possibly even self-centred and self-serving, and often ignore the bigger system and wider, long-term considerations.

By starting with others in mind (or at least including them in the thinking), Legacy Thinking builds a connection between us and others, and between the past, present and future. It inherently invites us to create healthier systems in which many flourish, not just individuals or individual organizations or indeed individual sectors. If you start with others in the future in mind, you are less likely to create a path that creates emotional or physical damage.

We also notice that traditional goals and mission can be driven by linear thinking, data and analysis – the 'head'. Legacy Thinking includes this, but also 'heart' and 'soul' because of its inherent consideration of others. Many organizations have a 'head' office, but where is the soul to be found? Where is the heart nurtured and cherished? Legacy Thinking brings the heart into the boardroom. And potentially every team meeting, and every decision.

Isn't this imposing my agenda?

This is a common question for coaches, and one we have explored with many pioneers in the field. And the answer is... 'probably not, at least when working with true leaders'. The future of the organization is the leader's agenda. So is the reputation of the organization, and the wellbeing of employees. The needs of their stakeholders are their agenda, and for the more enlightened, so is the efficacy with which the organization serves and delights. Their own sense of direction, and fulfilment, is their agenda. Simply, their legacy is their agenda. It's certainly not the only thing on their mind, but it is not disconnected.

Ryuzaburo Kaku (Kaku, 1997), Honorary Chair of the Board of Canon, recognized this:

> Many companies around the world believe that they have a moral duty to respond to global problems such as Third World poverty, the deterioration

of the natural environment, and endless tribal battles. But few have actually realized that their survival actually depends upon their response... To put it simply, global companies have no future if the earth has no future... My point is this: if corporations run their businesses with the sole aim of gaining more market share or earning more profits, they may well lead the world into economic, environmental, and social ruin.

It is interesting that as a coaching profession we seem comfortable to use tools like the Wheel of Life. We introduce these without the client necessarily talking initially to us about health, relationships or finances, for example. Why? Is that not also imposing ideas and an agenda? Maybe. But there is a reason. The Wheel invites them to see the bigger picture, the fuller system – in this case of their life. It invites them to see the connections and interaction. It creates new awareness and wiser actions.

Culturally, as a profession, we seem challenged to do the same thing by inviting leaders responsible for an organization to consider its longer and wider impact. Perhaps that is something for us to get over. Or evolve into.

How can I legitimately bring this to client conversations?

We have found a number of simple core principles and practices that help to ensure that a coach can legitimately and effectively bring Legacy Thinking into conversations with clients.

Make people aware that you care about this

If there is an area where you want your coaching to make a difference, try the following to make it easy to talk about with clients:

- Build it into the name of your organization, product or service.
- Write about it – in blogs and mailings. Invite your clients' thoughts and responses.
- Mention it in your initial contracting. Tell them what matters to you.
- Connect with people and groups who share the interest – sounds obvious but it's interesting to see how often a coach cares deeply for something then does business building somewhere else.

In a global conversation we curated on LinkedIn, Nick McBain shared: 'If you don't run a coaching business based on your core values, what exactly are you running it on?'

Good question.

In our research among other coaches a wisdom emerged: 'There are clients we work with and clients we fly with.' Know the types of conversations where you serve the client best, and make it clear to them – it's good for them and for you.

The principle of informed consent

This is essential. Informed consent is the simple yet vital act of ensuring you don't do something with someone without their permission and full understanding of what is being offered and the consequences of their saying yes or no. If your experience, sense of ethics, contracting and interpretation of 'serving the client' tells you that raising Legacy Thinking is the right thing to do, put it on the table. But do it as an offer and invitation and an informed choice.

Don't forget the simple questions

Speaking with coach and writer John Blakey, he shared the value of asking, 'How do you think this would appear in the newspapers?' Simple questions are often the most powerful.

Are there obstacles or even dangers for clients, and myself?

Heroism and delusion

Yes. There are traps. John Heron usefully talks about 'illusion, delusion and collusion' – three linked but different traps. 'How will I be remembered?' for example, can lead to heroism and delusion. Heroic leadership is increasingly recognized by subtle thinkers as a dangerous thing. There are many examples of heroic leaders who, in order to fulfil their sense of identity (hero), require a battle, challenge or extreme situation (villain). Often unknowingly, they define events around them as threats and draw conflict and potential disaster towards them and their organization in order to prove their heroism. As coaches, raising awareness is a core competence – we can challenge the client on this. We can also struggle to overcome our own cultural mores that love empire building and stand-out heroes (we need to be careful about what inviting clients to 'fulfil their potential' means in practice). The antidote? The more perspectives we invite the client to consider, and the further out in time they look, the more this danger is reduced.

Diminishing self

There is another danger – that the client has an aspiration, but feels 'It's all too big, and I/we are too small.' Many experience this. We have known people who led organizations of thousands, who felt they could do nothing. And others who have caused life-changing positive effects, yet do not see them because they have different 'measures of success'. Their work so far may not have created the global organization they wanted, transformed the system, or won the top award – so they label themselves as failing. That's where awareness raising comes in. Helping people to realize the way their life and work touches others, just in the everyday, is vital. How we simply listen to people and respond can have a massive impact and set off extraordinary ripples. And knowing that we often will not see the shores on which those ripples land requires us to trust that by doing 'the right thing', other good things will flow for others.

Lack of clarity

At a 'Coach as Catalyst' training event we hosted, we were surprised at how many coaches knew they wanted their coaching to bring good, but beyond a happy client at the end of the session they struggled to know what they ultimately wanted to support. The greatest wisdom here came from an interview with Tom Rippin, who started On Purpose, an organization dedicated to helping develop leaders for social enterprise. When approached by people struggling to decide which enterprise they want to work with, he advises, 'just begin'. By taking one step we learn a little more about the journey. As we take more steps the journey and path unfolds and we become more able to see the direction of travel and if it is right.

Overemphasis on positivity

In our research on people up to good things we spoke with Phil, a gifted film and media professional. Inspired to create a project with teams around the world capturing and sharing 'good news' and inspiring stories, all went well until the financial crash of 2008. But people kept telling him it was a great idea, and he recounts how his ego sang at hearing that. His coach also supported him, by helping him see the positives, be resilient and plough on to overcome the difficulties. What actually happened? It financially exhausted him and he lost everything. That raises profound questions for us. For example, if a client says, 'I feel like giving up' do we immediately go to 'Sure, how can I help?' Unlikely. There is an almost unquestionable assumption in our profession – 'Be positive'. Does it always serve? Phil's journey took him through a dark period involving deep soul searching, then emerging. He now recounts how the experience of the dark times has helped him be stronger, clearer, wiser, with a greater insight into what matters and a much healthier understanding of himself.

Burnout

Leading for something we care about can be exciting, inspiring, passionate work, and also exhausting, overwhelming and frustrating. Clients often face rejection, abuse and betrayal when the legacy they are looking to create involves changing systems and habits. Many systems contain people and organizations with an interest in the status quo. Change can be perceived as a threat and those inspiring change looked upon unkindly. People leading systemic change can face powerful forces, and this can take its toll. Realism is required. At times like this it is vital to remind clients of the importance of 'breathing in as well as breathing out' and not to confuse self-care with selfishness; that by looking after themselves they are better enabled to look after all they care about. In working in partnership with inspiring organization Frameworks for Change and leaders in the healthcare sector, self-care and self-compassion emerged as the most important starting point for leaders wanting their staff and clients to experience compassion.

Is it worth it?

Legacy Thinking often leads to stepping away from the norm. There are times where you stand naked and vulnerable. The criticism and rejection hurt, and there is much that confuses and frustrates. But when you have a sense of what you really want to do, the energy and resilience come. And we and clients consistently find it is easier to be courageous when you are working for the good of people and things you care about. The challenge is to step ever more fully into what really matters and not be compromised by fears and desires. Easier said than done. But isn't this the very sort of people and work that coaching is being called into the world to support?

Does this raise questions for us as a profession?

Certainly. Take a moment to consider our legacy as a profession. When people look back on these times, what will we be remembered for?

Peter Hawkins asked after the financial crash, 'What were the coaches doing while the banks were burning?' It's a great question. Some were no doubt doing highly professional work. But did it fully serve the client, their organization, or society more widely? Clearly not all. So what systemically should we learn?

What frame do we set for our conversations? We typically start our coaching conversations with something like, 'What would *you* like from this time together?' and 'What would *you* like to take from this session?' What about the other stakeholders, the wider system? The individual is a vital part, but they are not the whole. There's a balance of individual, team, organization, and all the stakeholders beyond. How do we get all of that into the conversation? Are we too 'individual' centred? As Peter Hawkins advocates, what would the difference in a session be if we shifted from 'What would you like from today?' to 'What would your *stakeholders* like from today?'

Who are we serving, as coaches, and as a profession? The client in front of us? The person paying the bill (if different)? The organization? The investors in the organization? The clients of the organization? The wider world? Future generations? Where in that list did you jump off?

If we suspect the ripple-out from a coaching conversation will cause hurt or pain, what are our ethical responsibilities? Is 'the client is expert and guide' sufficient defence if a conversation leads to harm in the world? Yet how do we avoid becoming high priests and 'holier than thou'?

Thoughts from the professional coaching bodies

What do the leaders of the professional bodies think? In our research over the years we asked them about the role of coaches in addressing the big social, economic and environmental issues of our time – basically inviting Legacy Thinking. Here are some of their thoughts:

Deborah Price, past President, UK ICF:

> We have a moral obligation to embody authenticity and bring all of ourselves to the coaching table... How would a coach feel if they failed to address key issues affecting our global society – what would it take to suppress that part of a coach who is a parent, child, brother, sister, colleague, neighbour... and is living through, and with, generations of 'turning a blind eye', 'not rocking the boat', 'waiting to be asked'? Knowing what we now know, can we really afford not to dive in with devil's (and angel's) advocate questions?

Lise Lewis, President (International), European Mentoring and Coaching Council:

> There is a social movement towards a better world. Coaching and mentoring enable people to be more engaged with each other... We need to tell our stories more – with members and between organizations. We need more community conversations. Go across the world. Tell us what you are doing that's making a difference... We need to collectively ask, what can we do for the benefit of mankind? What is our social responsibility in making a difference?

Darren Robson, Director of Strategy, Innovation and Partnerships (International), Association for Coaching:

We can change the world. We have a responsibility to influence, impact, reach out and get people to question how they can live their lives better. It's not about be the change, or lead the change – it's about lead the charge... We need to be challenging mindsets. We have a responsibility to push agendas... Addressing the social, economic and environmental issues of our time is a core principle. It should be a foundation for coaches and the coaching bodies.

What now?

Legacy Thinking is not 'the whole deal' – it's simply one component amongst many competencies and practices we bring as coaches. It's an example of what we call 'salt on the chips'; a little brings full flavour, and too much makes things unpalatable. How much to bring to each assignment and conversation can be unique. One question offered, in one conversation, in a long series of sessions, can be enough to raise a whole new area of awareness for the client.

Helping clients do more legacy thinking will no doubt inform and strengthen their organization and bring benefits to their people and all their stakeholders, because it has them all in mind. And the giver receives. The paradox is that by thinking of others first we ourselves achieve greater fulfilment and our organizations gain a better reputation, increased loyalty and perhaps a brighter future. It's easier to flourish if our sector, society and world are flourishing. Through millions of Legacy Thinking conversations, we may untangle and resolve the massive challenges we face. Maybe. We haven't heard of a better idea.

Whatever it is you decide to take and do from here, may those who come after you speak of you the way you wish.

References

Covey, S R (1992, 1999) *The 7 Habits of Highly Effective People*, Simon and Schuster, UK

Covey, S R (2014) *The 7 Habits of Highly Effective Families*, St Martin's Press, New York City

Handy, C (1999) *Thoughts for the Day*, Arrow Books, Random House

Kabat-Zinn, J (1994) *Wherever You Go There You Are*, Hachette UK, London

Kaku, R (1997) The Path of Kyosei, *Harvard Business Review*, July [online] https://hbr.org/1997/07/the-path-of-kyosei

Kerr, J (2013) *Legacy*, Hachette UK, London

INDEX